THE GRILLING ENCYCLOPEDIA

Written and Illustrated
by
A. Cort Sinnes

THE
GRILLING
ENCYCLOPEDIA

*An A-to -Z
Compendium of How to
Grill Almost Anything*

Atlantic Monthly Press
New York

Published simultaneously in Canada
Printed in the United States of America

This book was designed and produced by
Hearth & Garden Productions
A. Cort Sinnes, Design and Illustrations
Christine Beyer, Production Manager
Ruth Lively, Editor
Pete Ruhl, Artist-in-Residence
Mary Harrison and Katie Lazar, Copy Editors
Alison Courtney, Proofreader
Network Graphics, Kansas City, Missouri, Lithography

Library of Congress Cataloging-in-Publication Data

Sinnes, A. Cort
The grilling encyclopedia: an A-to-Z compendium of how to grill almost anything / written and illustrated by A. Cort Sinnes

Includes index.
ISBN 0-87113-563-9 (pbk.)

Atlantic Monthly Press
841 Broadway
New York, NY 10003

99 00 01 02   10 9 8 7 6 5

For KTB,
and the KCKCKC, where this
and a lot of other good things were
cooked up — ILU-ACS

ACKNOWLEDGEMENTS

A project like this requires support from every corner. I am especially indebted to Katie for her understanding and acceptance, not to mention the willingness to switch hats, roll up her sleeves and enter the fray when the heat was on. To Brooke and her friend Margaret for sampling so many weird foods and giving their insightful and immediate reactions. To my parents, for introducing me to the pleasures of outdoor cooking at such an early age. And a huge thank-you to Christine for her technical expertise, dogged determination and good-natured encouragement, day after day after day. Last, but hardly least, profound thanks to The Very Bright Right Reverend Dr. John Puscheck of the Charlotte Street Remission, whose motto is: "Ask me. I know. I'm an artist." I asked him. He *knows*.

Special thanks to:

John Barstow and Peter Knapp for their enthusiasm and support, early on, when it was sorely needed and much appreciated.

Kay Caughren of Household Words, not only for offering a wonderful selection of rare and out-of-print cookbooks, but for her ability to answer even the most esoteric of questions.

Charles Eisendrath of the Grillworks for fielding yet another call from the curious.

Gary Embrey, not only for simply being Gary Embrey, but for his skillful help in putting a cover on this book and getting it out the door.

Morgan Entrekin for accepting the torch when it was passed to him.

Howard Griffin of Hasty Bake for providing one of their luxury grills for use during the writing of this book.

Betty Hughes of Weber-Stephen for graciously answering so many questions.

John Kelly of J & G Market, our corner store, for his good-natured ribbing, his excellent ribs and ready supply of other comestibles.

Barbara Knecht, for that last go-around when she was supposed to be relaxing and for having friends in high places at the French embassy.

Mike Landis (who has grilled more things over more grills than anyone I know) for his long-distance advice and willingness to share it — not to mention his photographic expertise, as witnessed by the cover of this book.

The Lobel Brothers for being so free with their considerable knowledge.

Mike McGonigle of McGonigle's Market (which ranks as one of this country's best meat markets) for keeping the information in this book within the bounds of reality.

Helen Pratt for shepherding this project in the right direction.

William Roenigk of The Broiler Council, Peggy Babler of the National Live Stock and Meat Board, and Robin D. Ganse of the American Lamb Council.

Chuck Rubin and Frank Barker for their continued, good-natured support.

Dr. Susan for providing a second home for my child when the pressure was on.

Baron von Ruhlhaussen, for his willingness to turn a pastime into a profession.

Cara Windsor and David Babcock at Network Graphics, for their professional expertise in a field where technology brings a surprise everyday. Thanks for smoothing the way.

Tim Wolfe, for his weekly telephone calls, letting me know that there were, in fact, people out there simply enjoying themselves around the grill.

I'd also like to thank the following authors and publishers for kindly allowing me to use selections of their works:

The Alice B. Toklas Cook Book, by Alice B. Toklas. Published by Harper & Brothers, New York, NY, 1954.

The Cattleman's Steak Book, by Carol Traux and S. Omar Baker. Published by Grosset & Dunlap, New York, NY, 1967.

The Complete Book of Outdoor Cookery, by James A. Beard and Helen Evans Brown. Published by Perennial Library, Harper & Row, New York, NY, 1989.

Cook it Outdoors, by James A. Beard. Published by M. Barrows & Co., New York, NY, 1941.

Cooking Under Pressure, by Lorna J. Sass. Published by William Morrow and Company, Inc., New York, NY, 1989.

Gardening and Cooking on Terrace and Patio, by Dorothy Childs Hogner. Copyright © 1964 by Dorothy Childs Hogner. Used by

CONTENTS

ENCYCLOPEDIA CONTENTS

PREFACE

I was rattling around the kitchen the other day, trying, without much success, to find a particular cookbook. For some reason, a very battered copy of *Jennie June's American Cookery Book* caught my eye. In all honesty, I probably hadn't looked at the book since buying it. The book, which was published in 1866, contains a very frank and opinionated overview of housekeeping and cooking, "dedicated to the young housekeepers of America."

What made me sit down and finally read the book was Jennie June's endearingly forthright introduction, which began: "Why another cookbook, when there are already so many?" It was probably a legitimate question in 1866; it's certainly even more legitimate today. Old Jennie June would probably jump out of her grave if she knew how many cookbooks have been published since!

So how does a self-respecting cookbook author answer Jennie June's question? For her part, Jennie said she was simply filling the need for "a good, practical cook-book...arranged in a clear, available form, unencumbered with unnecessary and wordy details." I'd have to follow in her wake, saying that beyond anything else, *The Grilling Encyclopedia* is meant as a practical manual, intended for the home cook using the most readily available equipment, supplies and ingredients — a book that anyone can pick up and follow, to successfully prepare a grilled meal.

There were personal reasons for writing this book, as well. Not long after the 1985 publication of *The Grilling Book,* which I co-authored with Jay Harlow, I started receiving long-distance telephone calls on a regular basis, all of which contained the sharp edge of panic: "How many coals do you use?" "How hot should they be?" "Do I leave the lid on or off?" "How can I tell when it's done?" Feeling more than a little responsible for the long-distance bills and unwarranted confusion, I felt a clear need for a cookbook that went behind fashion to the fundamentals of grilling. *The Grilling Encyclopedia* is meant to answer those and hundreds of other questions. And, like Jennie, I hope you will find the information arranged in a "clear and available form."

– A.C.S.

EQUIPMENT

O ther than the few tools you personally find useful, successful grilling relies on procuring the best quality food you can find and adopting a relaxed willingness to mess about with the ingredients and procedures outlined in this book. Remember what Water Rat said to Mole in *The Wind in the Willows:* "Believe me, my young friend, there is *nothing* — absolutely nothing — half so much worth doing as simply messing about in boats." What boats were to Water Rat, grilling is to me. The reward comes not only in being able to enjoy the results of the grill, but in the process itself.

There's something satisfying about an activity that requires very little equipment. Happily, grilling falls into this category and I, for one, am all for keeping it that way. The only true essentials are a grill, some fuel and whatever it is that you're going to cook. Items beyond this very short list are not only what I call "not necessarily necessities," but highly subjective, as well. Where one person might not be able to do without a pair of long-handled, spring-loaded tongs, I wouldn't give up my two-foot-long piece of scrap 1 x 2 — but more on that later.

Common sense implies that if you're reading this book, you probably already own a grill, one that works just fine and that you intend to keep. For this reason I have purposefully kept the discussion of grills short, starting on page 22. I've taken the liberty of discussing some of the deluxe models that are currently available, but not in a wanton attempt to produce lust in your heart. After all, it is fun to dream, isn't it?

"There's something satisfying about an activity that requires very little equipment. Happily, grilling falls into this category..."

Not Necessarily Necessities

Most grillers get by with surprisingly few gadgets and gewgaws, although such items make great gifts for those otherwise "hard-to-buy-for" types. For years, my own pared-down *batterie de cuisine* has consisted of a long-handled fork, a set of good metal skewers with flat shanks, plenty of inexpensive bamboo skewers, a meat thermometer and my trusty 1 x 2, about 30 inches long, used for everything from moving coals around on the fire grate to lifting off a hot cooking grill.

This piece of scrap lumber, which requires occasional replacement as it burns down to a nub, is truly a multi-use tool. In addition to its practical uses, it can also be used as a striker on those special occasions when you're compelled to use the top of the kettle grill as a gong. And, on a less benign note, it's quite effective if raised in a threatening manner when that oft-repeated line, "Is it done, *yet?*" is repeated once too often.

If you don't already own a meat thermometer, buy one. There are two types: the type you put in the meat prior to cooking (which can withstand the heat of the grill), and the newer "instant-reading" type, which reports the internal temperature in a second or two. Instructions in this book favor the old-fashioned thermometer, only because it is so easy to forget to test with an instant-reading type before it's too late. While on the subject of thermometers, beware of those that purport to tell you the various degrees of doneness of everything from beef to veal. This information seems to vary from thermometer to thermometer; better to consult an up-to-date chart, such as the one found on page 39.

When it comes to skewers, look for those with flat shanks, which keep skewered food from spinning around as you try to turn it over. Bamboo skewers will accomplish the same trick if you use them in pairs, running them parallel through the food. For more information, see *Skewer Cooking,* page 56.

To this subjective and short list of equipment, I admit to occasionally purloining an old basting brush and a metal spatula from the kitchen. Any professional grill chef will advise you to purchase a professional-quality offset spatula for turning delicate flat foods, such as fish filets, but I lost mine some time ago and I haven't missed it yet. The same holds true for basting brushes: larger-sized, long-handled

"This piece of scrap lumber, which requires occasional replacement as it burns down to a nub, is truly a multi-use tool. In addition to its practical uses, it can also be used as a striker on those special occasions when you're compelled to use the top of the kettle grill as a gong."

basting brushes made just for grilling are nice, but a regular kitchen basting brush will do just fine, as will a brand-new, small paint brush from the hardware store.

If you don't use the twig and paper method for starting fires (as outlined on page 31), a metal flue starter should be added to the list of essential equipment. Using one of these units is probably the easiest and most reliable way for igniting charcoal. Flues are inexpensive, widely available at hardware and cookware stores, last for many seasons and consistently work — even for those people who have trouble lighting fires.

If this all sounds simple so far, then we're on the right track.

The Importance of Place

Before proceeding any further in the practical vein, a few words should be said about *where* you grill. A pragmatic person might be quick to ask, "What does place have to do with preparing food?" But we're not just talking about food here, we're talking about a process that should be as enjoyable as possible. A relaxed, happy chef is far more likely to turn out tasty food than an uptight, cranky food technician.

Over the years, I've lived in a lot of different places, but each had room for a grill. I've stuck grills out on 6- x 12-foot, enclosed balconies in urban settings, built custom models into lush garden settings and perched kettle grills on landings where there was barely room for the two of us — me and the grill. One thing is certain, though: I can remember, with pleasure, the view from each of those locations as clearly as if I were standing in any of them this moment.

Early evening is a splendid time to slow down, sit down and enjoy yourself. Going outdoors to your own cooking spot should not only result in a delicious meal, but a delicious frame of mind as well. Although totally subjective, here's my list of criteria with regard to place:

1) view
2) stool
3) light
4) table
5) protection from rain
6) easy access to kitchen

"A relaxed, happy chef will be far more likely to turn out tasty food than an uptight, cranky food technician."

The first requirement — view — will help immeasurably in producing a beneficial frame of mind. By all means, don't place your grill where the only thing you see is the neighbor's untidy yard, a couple of air-conditioning units or a storage shed. Before rolling your grill into position, walk around a bit until you find a spot that appeals to your sensibilities: some leafy trees that catch the setting sun in an agreeable way, a stretch of lawn where long shadows and small children run, or maybe, if you're particularly fortunate, a view of the mountains, across a valley below or even the ocean!

Once you find your spot, outfit it with something to sit on, such as a stool or a bench; a small, sturdy table for landing platters full of food; and some kind of light, so you can see what the food looks like when it's pitch black outside (if worse comes to worst, equip yourself with a big flashlight).

Now you're set!

The Grill Itself

There are a lot of grills in the marketplace, but they all fall into one of two categories: open or covered. There's no point in describing each one because certain cooking traits remain constant with every type. For purposes of discussion only, I have chosen a couple of examples in both categories, from the simplest to the very sophisticated.

Open Grills

In infinite variation, open grills are the type used around the world. From Spain to Thailand to Turkey to Africa to the Caribbean, when you say "grill," an open grill is what you're talking about. In most instances, even today, this consists of nothing more than an adjustable grate somehow suspended over live coals. Open grills not only represent the crudest and oldest method of cooking, they are also the type favored by the most sophisticated grill cooks, professional and otherwise.

The cook who uses an open grill has a much harder time cooking large cuts of meat, such as roasts, controlling flare-ups from fatty foods, such as chicken, and would never tackle something like a whole turkey, unless it were on a rotisserie, which very few of today's open grills feature. Professional chefs will argue that some foods, such as steaks, chops and certain types of fish, are best cooked on

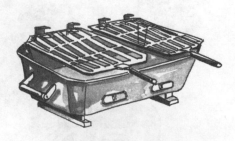

Hibachis are definitely a mass-produced item of only moderate quality, but when the very low price is considered, the hibachi represents a good value.

an open grill with an adjustable fire grate, preferably with the coals up close to the cooking surface. This may be so, but most home cooks find the expertise and precise timing this cooking method requires to be overly demanding, especially for an activity that's supposed to be relaxing. For tips on cooking with an open grill, see page 40.

The Hibachi. The simplest open grill commercially available in this country is the little hibachi, commonly sold in variety stores, hardware outlets, import stores and, during the high season, even supermarkets. They are definitely a mass-produced item of only moderate quality, but when the very low price is considered, the hibachi represents a good value. And it works like a champ for as long as it lasts.

I try to keep a hibachi around at all times. It's just the thing for grilling a few skewered hors d'oeuvres, or for a couple of steaks or chops when only two of you are dining. The modest hibachi is also excellent for putting in the trunk of your car and taking along on a trip. For mountain cabin use during the winter, it can be positioned in an indoor fireplace (with the flue wide open) for a rustic, satisfying cooking experience. To tote a hibachi from one place to another, I have yet to go as far as one meticulous friend, who sewed a custom canvas duffle for his, complete with a drawstring top.

The "Grillery." At the opposite end of the open grill spectrum is the "Grillery." It was invented by Charles Eisendrath, who, when he isn't inventing grills, runs a journalism fellowship program at the University of Michigan. After spending considerable time in Buenos Aires, France and the Middle East, Eisendrath returned home with the desire to recreate some of the cooking he experienced abroad. "Appalled" by the domestic grills he was confronted with, he decided to design an open grill unlike any other available in this country. The result was the "Grillery."

Handmade of stainless steel, the Grillery has a crank that precisely raises or lowers the cooking surface (or the twin rotisseries that come with the unit) a full 16 inches. Once the cooking height is selected, the grill automatically locks into place. The cooking surface is constructed of one-inch-wide, stainless steel, V-shaped bars, set one inch apart. The V-shaped bars channel the cooking juices away

'Handmade of stainless steel, the Grillery has a crank that precisely raises or lowers the cooking surface (or the twin rotisseries that come with the unit) a full 16 inches."

"I've been using one for nearly ten years, and for my money, the Weber is the most versatile and easy-to-use grill on the market."

from the fire, into a collecting pan where they can be embellished with any type of flavoring and used for basting the food.

The other unique feature of the Grillery is that it is made to be fueled with wood rather than charcoal — although charcoal can easily be substituted. Because of the extent to which the Grillery's cooking surface can be adjusted, it's possible to start cooking over a fire that is still in a flaming stage (rather than ash-covered coals) by simply moving the cooking surface farther away from the flames. As the flames die down, the cooking surface can be adjusted closer to the heat.

No less an authority than the late James Beard called the Grillery "a magnificent new grill...brilliantly thought out and well-constructed." More information on the Grillery can be obtained by writing: Grillworks, Inc., 1211 Ferdon Road, Ann Arbor, Michigan 48104 (Telephone: (313) 995-2164).

Covered Grills

Covered grills run the gamut from rectangular hooded models with adjustable grills to elaborate charcoal-fired ovens. They range in price from well under $100 to well over $1,000.

The Covered Kettle Grill. When it comes to covered grills, the overwhelming favorite with most backyard cooks is the covered kettle grill, as popularized by the Weber-Stephens Product Company, based in Palatine, Illinois. Since its invention by George A. Stephen in 1951, an estimated 15 million "Webers" have been sold, making it the world's most popular grill.

Interestingly, the 1952 version of this famous grill, then called the Custom Bar-B-Q Kettle Model BK 710, sold for $46.95 — an astronomical figure, roughly five times as expensive as other grills of the period. Today's 22-inch "One-Touch Kettle Model 71001" (which doesn't look much different from its 1952 predecessor) has a suggested retail price of under $90.00, making it look like quite a bargain.

In fact, it *is* quite a bargain. I've been using one for nearly ten years, and for my money, the Weber is the most versatile and easy-to-use grill on the market. There are two unique aspects to the Weber grill: one is the fact that neither the charcoal grill (the grate on which the coals are placed) nor the cooking grill is adjustable. Secondly, the unit was designed to be used with the lid in place at all times. Grilling with the cover on speeds up cooking time by rotating the heat around the food and, just as importantly, eliminates flare-ups, one of the chief causes of burned food.

If yours is a covered kettle grill, I urge you to try grilling using the indirect method (see page 42). By initially positioning the food away from the fire, you greatly increase your chances of producing perfectly grilled fare, no matter what it is. You'll love the control it gives you, and you (and everyone else sitting expectantly around the table) will enjoy the tasty results.

The Hasty-Bake Story. Hasty-Bake Gourmet Charcoal Ovens have been manufactured in Tulsa, Oklahoma, since 1948. The original model was designed by the company's founder, Mr. Hastings, using his garage as a manufacturing facility. Company lore indicates that it was Mr. Hastings who introduced the first portable, covered "barbecue," and was the originator of a new method of charcoal cookery, which he termed "indirect cooking."

Be that as it may, the Hasty-Bake Gourmet Charcoal Oven is unique in the marketplace: it is the only unit I know of that is truly a combination of a charcoal oven (like the covered kettle grill) and a professional open grill with an adjustable firebox. In addition, an optional rotisserie unit can be purchased — a much appreciated but rare feature on grills these days (see *Spit Cooking,* page 46).

It should be pointed out that the versatility of a Hasty-Bake doesn't come cheap; in fact, these units are extremely expensive. Owners of Hasty-Bakes are a fiercely loyal and passionate lot, in much the same way as are the owners of Bentley motorcars.

Hasty-Bakes are constructed by hand, of either stainless steel or cold-rolled, black powder-coated steel. The ventless, hinged hood allows heat and smoke to rotate around the food for even distribution and penetration. This design, as the Hasty-Bake brochure says, "turns the heat instead of the meat." Adjustable draft vents are located on either side of the adjustable firebox. A heat deflector can be put into place over the coals to create even heat across the grill, or removed completely in instances where the

"Owners of Hasty-Bakes are a fiercely loyal and passionate lot, in much the same way as are the owners of Bentley motorcars."

Hasty-Bake is used as an open grill rather than an oven.

As with The Grillery, the Hasty Bake's cooking grill is made up of V-shaped bars that channel grease to a disposable foil pan, eliminating flare-ups. Most convenient of all is the fact that the full-width firedoor can be opened and the firebox pulled out for refueling *during* the cooking process, without opening the hood. This is a real plus when preparing foods that demand a long cooking time.

I was fortunate to have a Hasty-Bake for use during the writing of this book (in addition to four other grills). No doubt about it, they are wonderful units. If your enthusiasm for charcoal cooking is matched by the size of your bank account, by all means consider one. The Hasty-Bake folks can be reached at 1-800-4AN-OVEN (1-800-426-6836), or by writing Hasty-Bake, P.O. Box 471285, Tulsa, Oklahoma 74147-1285.

A Somewhat Extravagant Solution

The argument between open versus covered grills can be easily solved by buying a covered unit with an adjustable cooking grill. There are many brands to choose from, including several that are far less expensive than the Hasty-Bake just described.

In looking for a solution to this controversy in my own backyard, I found myself hemmed in on both sides: After having used the Weber charcoal grill for so many years, I was reluctant to give it up for one of the covered, adjustable grills. On the other hand, I admit to fantasies about being able to cook a whole rack of lamb the way I saw it done once, a long time ago, over an open grill at Vanessi's restaurant in San Francisco (now long since gone, after burning down due to a fire started at the grill). Allow me to relate the scene.

It was a typical cold, foggy night, but the counter was snug-full with a rich collection of characters, the type San Francisco seems to specialize in. There was always plenty of action to watch at the three cooking stations behind the counter and this night was no exception. I happened to be seated directly across from the old-fashioned, brick-lined grill, the fire crackling merrily while the chef expertly wielded his knife, partially cutting the bones away from a rack of lamb, sticking in a few sprigs of rosemary, a little garlic, a few grinds of pepper, before tying the whole thing back together again.

"I happened to be seated directly across from the old-fashioned, brick-lined grill, the fire crackling merrily while the chef expertly wielded his knife, partially cutting the bones away from a rack of lamb, sticking in a few sprigs of rosemary, a little garlic, a few grinds of pepper, before tying the whole thing back together again."

Orchestrating with his long-handled tongs, the chef alternately kept up a steady banter with the prostitutes who came in to pick up their to-go meals, joked with the patrons at the counter, argued with the other chefs, and through this three-ring culinary circus somehow managed to keep his eye on that rack of lamb. He finally pulled it off the fire, and placed it on a platter right in front of me. The aroma made the diamonded dowager seated down the counter swoon; it made me change my order. The cook peeked inside the meat and took a whiff. Smiling at his skill, he called to a waiter to pick up the order. Every head at the counter turned and watched that meal make its way to one of the booths in the back.

Admittedly, coveting an open grill just because of something I witnessed in a restaurant years ago is a fairly weak reason to add yet another piece of equipment to an already bulging back porch, but it became something of an obsession for me.

When it came time to remodel the back porch, I made gifts of all the grills I owned, save for one 22½-inch Weber. Throwing caution to the wind, I ordered a 36-inch open grill (including a heavy-duty rotisserie unit) and had both the Weber and the open grill installed, side-by-side, in an outdoor cabinet.

This is a somewhat extravagant solution, but it's worked out great and has finally brought at least one fantasy to reality. In case you're wondering whether or not I ever cooked a rack of lamb on the open grill, I did — once. Quite frankly, they are a lot easier to cook on the covered grill. Isn't that just the way it is with fantasies made real?

Gas Grills

Given their ease of lighting, and the fact that they don't require charcoal, gas grills have become quite popular. I have tried to warm up to these units, but I miss not having a fire to light and charcoal to tend. For me, these are important steps in a pleasant, time-consuming ceremony, of which cooking food is only one of the elements.

Most gas grills have dial settings for high, medium and low heat levels. These generally correspond to the temperature recommendations of very hot, hot and moderate that are provided throughout this book.

"When it came time to remodel the back porch, I made gifts of all the grills I owned, save for one 22-inch Weber. Throwing caution to the wind, I ordered a 36-inch open grill (including a heavy-duty rotisserie unit) and had both the Weber and the open grill installed, side-by-side, in an outdoor cabinet."

STARTING THE FIRE

Many people don't grill simply because they don't really know how to make a fire. I firmly believe this is the sole reason for the popularity of gas grills. Luckily, there are three widely available products that should give everyone the ability to start a fire like an old pro — the metal flue or chimney, the old reliable electric coil starter and a relatively new product, wax-coated wood chips.

Although there are many other ways to start a fire, I have chosen these three as sure bets. If you employ another method and it consistently works, more power to you. The following advice is for those who have yet to find a way of starting a fire that suits them comfortably.

Note: After years of causing whole neighborhoods to smell like an oil refinery, charcoal lighter fluid seems to be on the way out, having already been banned in a number of localities.

The Metal Flue

The metal flue or chimney has gained considerable popularity in the past few years. No doubt about it, using one of these units is a simple and effective way to start charcoal.

Begin by removing your grill's cooking grate. Clean out any remaining ashes from previous fires. Set the flue in the middle of the fire grate with the bottom draft holes of the grill completely open. Crumple one double sheet of *dry* newspaper (avoid magazine or "slick" paper stock) and place it in the bottom chamber of the flue. Fill the top part of the flue with charcoal and light the newspaper. That's all there is to it. You should get red-hot charcoal, ready for dumping onto the fire grate, in about 10 to 15 minutes. (Even the wood-handled chimneys can become very hot at this point, so you might want to reach for a mitt before pouring them out.)

Don't interfere with the simplicity of this method by pouring the coals out too early; wait until the top layer of charcoal has caught fire before pouring them out. After the charcoal has been dumped on the fire grate, push the coals together and let them burn a few minutes longer until they are covered with a fine gray ash. That's when the fire's ready for cooking.

More than one person has fired up the metal flue, gone into the kitchen to prepare the food and returned only to find cold black lumps instead of glowing coals. This is not only dispiriting, but it can throw the timing off for the rest of the meal as well. If you're using a chimney to start your cooking coals, stick around for a couple of minutes to make sure that the coals actually catch fire. Although I've seen these things fail on the first try, I've never seen them fail after a second or third attempt. If the charcoal doesn't catch the first time, simply stick another sheet of crumpled newspaper underneath and relight it.

"Virtually fool-proof, the electric charcoal starter demands only a grounded, three-prong outlet that's close to the grill, usually within five feet or so."

To make the flue even more fail-safe, one manufacturer (Christen, Inc., in St. Louis, Missouri) makes charcoal lighter blocks to place under the chimney. These small, compressed blocks are impregnated with a flammable substance and make successful lighting of the briquets a "first time, every time" endeavor.

Sold under a variety of trade names, these chimneys and flues are more or less standard in size, holding about 65 charcoal briquets or approximately two pounds of lump charcoal (a little more if you mound the charcoal over the top), enough for most of the procedures outlined in this book. If you need more coals than the flue holds, use one of the following methods for starting a fire.

The Electric Starter

Virtually fool-proof, the electric charcoal starter demands only a grounded, three-prong outlet that's close to the grill, usually within five feet or so. To use, remove the cooking grill and place the electric starter on the fire grate. Mound almost any amount of charcoal on top of the looped electric element and plug 'er in. The element will become red-hot, igniting the charcoal closest to it. Once the bottom layer of charcoal has caught fire, unplug the starter and remove it. The coals that are already burning will ignite the others in the pile.

If you leave the starter in the coals too long, you'll shorten the life of the element considerably. Find a safe place to stow the electric starter while it cools down, out of the way of both people (particularly kids) and flammable objects.

Wax-Coated Wood Chips

When I first saw this product on the grocery store shelf, I was suspicious. The information on the box said that the product "replaces lighter fluid," which sounded like a good idea. "But with what?" I thought to myself. I was expecting a smelly alternative of questionable efficacy. I was pleasantly surprised on both counts.

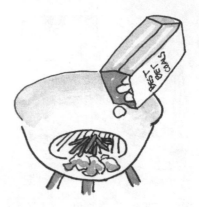

"It seems right, somehow, to start the fire from twigs and branches found in my own backyard, or gathered on walks around the neighborhood."

The brand I brought home was "Fire Flakes." The instructions said to place two handfuls in the bottom of the grill (*under* the fire grate), first making sure that the ash pan is in place. I then mounded the charcoal in a pile on the fire grate, right above the Fire Flakes. The instructions advised me to drop a lighted match onto the wax-coated wood chips. You may find it easier to light them with one of those long-handled fireplace matches, or by holding a match under one of the bottom draft holes. However you manage to do it, once they're lit, they really take off!

Much to their credit, the Fire Flakes burned brightly for at least ten minutes, more than enough time to ignite the charcoal. I have used this product many times since, in some fairly rigorous conditions (extreme cold and wind) and have been pleased every time. The burning chips smell like wax for the first few minutes, but then the odor completely dissipates. You can light any amount of charcoal you need with just two handfuls of chips. I consider the development of this product a real advance in charcoal fire-starting, especially suited for those who worry about their ability to start a fire.

The Scout Method

For years now, I have ignited charcoal using the "scout method." Use this method only if you find it appealing and can lay your hands on a ready supply of pencil-diameter twigs or small kindling. Start by crumpling two or three sheets of dry newspaper in the bottom of your grill, *under* the fire grate. The draft holes in the bottom of the grill should be completely open. Put the fire grate into position and lay a couple of handfuls of twigs in the middle of the grate. Mound up whatever amount of charcoal you need on top of the twigs, and light the newspaper. The coals should be ready for cooking in about 15 minutes.

The process of gathering the twigs, building the fire and watching it as it takes hold has evolved into something of a ritual, taking me back to childhood scout outings in the foothills of California. It seems right, somehow, to start the fire from twigs and branches found in my own backyard, or gathered on walks around the neighborhood.

I happen to like the smell of the burning wood, although I have occasionally alarmed the neighbors with the odor of what they're convinced is a house fire. Once, when I was starting a fire on a second-floor balcony, a passerby notified the fire department that our building was on fire. The arrival of the fire department thoroughly broke my scout reverie for that evening, but it didn't deter me from continuing in this merit badge mentality.

Like I said, use this method only if you find it appealing and can stand the excitement of occasionally terrifying your family and neighbors.

Charcoal

I don't mean to give it short shrift, but too much can be made of what kind of charcoal is best to use. In a nutshell, here's the story: your choice is between charcoal briquets and lump charcoal.

Charcoal briquets are manufactured from ground charcoal, a little coal dust and some type of starch to bind the mixture together. They are formed into their familiar, uniform, pillow shapes and packaged in 5-, 10-, 20- and 50-pound bags. A few companies add a substance such as sodium nitrite to increase the ease of lighting the briquets.

Lump charcoal, on the other hand, is a hardwood, such as oak, mesquite or fruitwood, which has been burned in the absence of oxygen to create charcoal. Nothing is added to lump charcoal. The resulting charcoal is non-uniform in size and shape.

About the only thing that can be said with certainty regarding the differences between briquets and lump

"About the only thing that can be said with certainty regarding the differences between briquets and lump charcoal is that lump charcoal burns hotter than briquets..."

charcoal is that lump charcoal burns hotter than briquets: an even layer of briquets will produce a temperature of approximately 300 to 350 degrees F. at the level of the cooking grill; lump charcoal may produce temperatures of more than 600 degrees F. Professional chefs are keen on lump charcoal's higher burning temperature for its ability to quickly sear certain cuts of meat and fish. This may or may not be important to the home griller.

Much has also been made of the lingering odor and off-taste resulting from the additives in charcoal briquets. Quite frankly, it would take a palate of astounding sensitivity to detect such flavors or aromas. Once charcoal is at the red-hot stage, any additives will have long since burned away.

I have used both types of charcoal extensively. Lump charcoal takes a little getting used to: its lack of uniformity calls for a little more care when creating an even bed of coals and the high heat it produces demands respect and close attention once the food goes on the grill. Charcoal briquets produce the same fire from one day to the next. If you use briquets, my single bit of advice would be to stick with a premium brand; budget briquets may not be as dense as better brands, causing them to burn out quickly at a comparatively low temperature.

Wood

There are some outdoor cooks who shun packaged charcoal altogether in favor of building a cooking fire from wood. In fact, wood is the most popular fuel for grills the world over. I have one friend, who lives in a wooded area, who has never used anything except wood in his covered kettle grill. By his estimates, has burned an astounding 10 cords of wood without burning a hole in the bottom of his grill.

Some types of wood are more favored for grilling than others. The U.S.D.A. has even gone so far as to grade different wood with regard to its evenness in burning, amount of smoke produced and whether or not it tends to throw sparks. By their standards, the following types of wood come out on top: hard maple, hickory, red oak, white oak, pecan, dogwood, beech, birch and ash.

Wood for your grill should always be smaller than the wood you use in your fireplace; my wood-burning friend favors sticks about 12 inches long and four inches in

"Wood for your grill should always be smaller than the wood you use in your fireplace; my wood-burning friend favors sticks about 12 inches long and four inches in diameter..."

diameter, which he starts with dry newspaper.

When cooking with wood, give yourself a little extra time for the wood to burn down to a nice layer of ash-covered coals. In general, wood fires are considerably hotter than a briquet fire. Use the method described under *How Hot Is Hot* on page 39 to determine when the fire is ready for cooking.

Smoking Chips

A variety of packaged chipped or shredded wood is widely available, even found in some grocery stores. Common types include mesquite, hickory, apple and, sometimes, alder. These wood chips are meant to be soaked in water prior to being thrown on hot coals for their aromatic, flavor-enhancing properties. What some would call gilding the lily, others consider standard operating procedure; the choice is up to you. Personally, I limit their use to hickory or mesquite for traditional barbecue foods, such as beef brisket and pork spareribs, and, occasionally, alder or apple wood for salmon.

The only precaution is not to add too many dampened chips at one time, for fear that you'll put the fire completely out. For best results, the amount of chips you add at any one time should not exceed one-quarter of the total number of coals in the grill.

Keeping the Fire Going

When a long cooking time (more than 1 hour) is required, you will probably need to add additional coals to the existing fire to keep the temperature steady. There are two ways of going about doing this: the first is simply to add unlit coals (about one-quarter of the amount of existing coals) directly on top of the fire; the other method is to have a separate supply of hot coals to add in any amount, whenever necessary.

The trick to the first method is not to let the coals burn down so far that they won't readily ignite the fresh coals. In general, wait no longer than 30 minutes between the times you add additional coals.

The secret to the second method is in having either a second grill in which to start the charcoal, or improvising a fireproof container, such as a clay flower pot or a coffee can (with holes pierced in the bottom using a pointed can opener). If you're starting the coals in a container, place it

"...wood chips are meant to be soaked in water prior to being thrown on hot coals for their aromatic, flavor-enhancing properties."

on a large, clay saucer and, for safety's sake, keep a close eye on the coals.

Safety

Any time you deal with a live fire, certain precautions are called for. Your two goals should be to keep the fire under control and to keep people from accidentally hurting themselves.

As a course of grilling habit, it's a good idea never to leave the fire unattended, especially while the fire is just starting and the grill is uncovered. Make sure there's a garden hose nearby — one that's hooked up to the spigot. If there's a 5-pound, ABC, all-purpose fire extinguisher within reach, so much the better. A pair of fireproof fireplace gloves are good to have on hand as well. If you own a covered grill, controlling a worrisome fire is a simple matter of putting the lid on, or down, and closing the vent holes, effectively smothering the fire.

Under normal conditions, charcoal briquets rarely emit sparks, but hardwood (lump) charcoal is another story. While the fire is starting, it will occasionally send up impressive showers of sparks; this is particularly true of mesquite charcoal. Keep the grill well away from walls, overhanging eaves, wood fences and any foliage or dry grass that might catch fire. The sparks can carry for quite a way, so be doubly careful if there's a breeze blowing. Many locales prohibit grilling during windy, dry conditions. Never add charcoal lighter fluid (assuming that it's still available where you live) to coals that are already lit and *never* use gasoline to start any fire.

If there are kids in the household, make sure they know not to play around or with the grill when it's lit. That said, there's something about a live fire that draws kids like a magnet, so be aware that even the sternest of warnings may go unheeded. The best insurance is to simply keep your eye on the action at all times. As with lots of activities, the smart course is to use common sense. If you are going to err, err on the side of caution.

"Make sure there's a garden hose nearby — one that's hooked up to the spigot. If there's a 5-pound, ABC, all-purpose fire extinguisher within reach, so much the better."

GENERAL GUIDELINES

The information found on the following twenty-four pages is meant as a "ready reference guide." It includes tips for using both covered and uncovered grills, temperature charts and specific instructions for spit and skewer cooking. It is important imformation, presented in pared-down form, in the hope that it will be read.

The blank pages, from 58 to 61, are, perhaps, the most important in this chapter. For most people, the idea of writing in a book takes a little getting used to, a holdover, no doubt, from elementary school days. If you can bring yourself to do it, however, customizing this book with the specifics of your own grilling experiences will make it an invaluable reference.

The reason this chapter is called "General Guidelines" is because all of the information contained herein is exactly that, *general.* Grilling is a notoriously inexact process, a fact that confounds some, and pleases others. As the late, great James Beard wrote in his book *Cook It Outdoors,* "experience is the only teacher," which may be the most important reason of all for keeping a record of your own.

When you go about grilling, make yourself comfortable, take your time and feel free to experiment. It cannot be stated any more emphatically than the following no-nonsense directive (found in an old piece of product literature): *"Remember this always: Outdoor or barbecue cooking must be a pleasure. If it is a chore — stop it — use your oven."* How's that for being to the point?

BEFORE YOU GET STARTED

• Always start with the best possible ingredients, whether it's fresh corn-on-the-cob or a standing rib roast. Nothing that transpires on the grill will transform mediocre ingredients into a first-class meal.

• Allow food to come to room temperature before grilling. Generally speaking, this means removing it from the refrigerator approximately 30 minutes prior to cooking.

• Clean out the bottom of the grill so air can circulate through the draft holes.

• Plan on 30 to 40 minutes from lighting the fire to having charcoal that's ready for grilling — when the fire has burned down and the coals are covered with a fine, gray ash.

• Amounts of charcoal vary according to what is being grilled. Specific information is given for each individual entry in the encyclopedia.

• Always use the best quality charcoal available. Budget brands cause more problems than the cost savings can justify.

• Always put the grill in place over the hot coals for a few minutes before putting the food on. As an extra precaution against foods sticking to the grill, brush it with vegetable oil or, it you are cooking a piece of beef, cut off a small piece of its fat, stick it on a fork and rub the hot grill.

• As a rule, do not partially cook vegetables before grilling. Parboiling, steaming or microwaving prior to grilling will change the texture of the finished product for the worse.

• If you have a covered kettle grill, please read *Covered Grill Techniques* on page 42 and *Charcoal Roasting* on page 44. The information found these pages may be the most important in the book.

• Serving grilled food at room temperature, or cold, not only eliminates some of the tension associated with cooking, but is often the preferred method of serving. Give it a try. Exceptions to this are venison and nearly all types of fish, which are best served hot off the grill.

HOW HOT IS HOT?

Three temperature designations are given throughout the encyclopedia section of this book: very hot, hot and moderate. Here's how to determine the temperature of your fire:

Very Hot: At the very hot stage, it will be impossible to hold your hand an inch or so above the cooking grill. Flames will still be licking around the coals.

Hot: At this point it will be possible to hold your hand an inch or so above the cooking grill for 2 or 3 seconds, or as long as it takes to spell MISSISSIPPI moderately fast. The coals will be covered with a fine gray ash and the flames will have died down.

Moderate: When the fire has reached the moderate stage, you will be able to hold your hand an inch or so above the cooking grill for five seconds.

TEMPERATURE CHART

Food	Rare	Medium	Well Done
Beef	140 F.	160 F.	170-180 F.
Lamb	140 F.	160 F.	170 F.
Pork	*	160 F.	170 F.
Poultry	All domestic poultry should be cooked to 185 F.		

* The U.S.D.A. now considers 137 degrees F. as the temperature at which the parasites that cause trichinosis are destroyed.

UNCOVERED GRILL TECHNIQUES

The way the coals are arranged in an uncovered grill can significantly increase its versatility. For most people there's a tendency to arrange the coals in an even layer across the entire bottom of the grill. This is a little like a gas or electric stove with all of the burners turned to the same setting — which, in the case of charcoal grills, is likely to be "high." This situation not only leads to a stressful cooking situation, but greatly increases the chances for a culinary disaster.

When you arrange the live coals under an open grill, mound some of the coals in a double layer, arrange some of them in a single layer with their sides touching, some in a single layer with space inbetween each piece of charcoal, and finally, leave part of the fire grate completely free of charcoal. Arranging the coals in this manner effectively gives you a cooking surface with four temperature settings — high, medium, low and off, if you will. If something starts to burn or cook too quickly, you can simply move it to a cooler part of the grill. Conversely, if something is cooking slowly but not browning, move it to a hotter spot.

The only time this arrangement doesn't work is when you're cooking a whole fish or a large piece of meat. In these situations it's best to arrange the coals in an even layer slightly larger in area than whatever it is that you're cooking. Even so, give yourself some flexibility by leaving part of the grate free of coals so you can move the food closer to or farther away from the heat source as the conditions dictate.

If you are using a rotisserie attachment on an open grill, never position the coals directly under whatever you might have on the spit. Fat will drip down onto the coals, causing flames to erupt and produce an unholy amount of smoke. In most instances it's best to bank all of the coals on the back side of the spit. When higher temperatures are called for, arrange the coals in a U-shape around the back and sides of the drip pan. Leave the area in front of the drip free of coals to make it easier to baste the food. For more information, see *Spit Cooking,* page 46.

Using an Uncovered Grill

One of the best aspects of an uncovered grill is the fact that either the cooking grill or the fire grate is adjustable. This means that it's very easy to get the food closer to or further away from the fire as needed.

Here's a tip from professional grill chefs who spend a lot of time over an open grill: Instead of laying a solid bed of hot coals across the entire fire grate, divide the grate into make-believe quarters. In one of the quarters, make a double layer of coals; in the next, a single layer of coals with sides just touching; in the third quarter, leave a little space between each piece of charcoal; and leave the last quarter empty. This, in effect, gives you four different cooking temperatures: high, medium, low and "off" Once you get used to this charcoal arrangement on an open grill, you'll find it very useful.

If your uncovered grill has a rotisserie unit, by all means use it for cooking any whole poultry or fish and large cuts of meat, such as roasts. Given their uneven shape and lack of uniform thickness, cooking such foods on an open grill is practically impossible without a rotisserie.

Never position the food on the spit directly over the coals. It's a drip pan that you want directly under the meat, with the coals banked around the back and the sides. Put the meat on when the coals are good and hot and use the windscreen to do just that: screen the food from any prevailing breeze.

Expect spit-cooked foods to take longer to cook than foods cooked directly over the grill — but the wait will be worth it, especially if you use what falls into the drip pan as a baste every 15 minutes or so.

COVERED GRILL TECHNIQUES

Cooking on a covered kettle grill with the lid in place allows it to be used in two ways: grilling foods *directly* over the coals, or *indirectly,* by positioning the food away from the coals. This can be accomplished by shoving all of the coals to one side of the charcoal grate, on either side of the grate (leaving the center open), or the way I often do, with the coals centered in the middle of the charcoal grate and the food in a ring around (not over) the fire.

The literature provided with the popular Weber kettle grill recommends the direct method of cooking for any food that cooks in less than 25 minutes. I respectfully disagree. The cook has far more control using the indirect method, with the lid in place, for almost any food. The method I've found most successful is to start the food away from the direct heat of the coals and gradually inch it closer to the fire each time you turn it, ending up directly over the coals for a final, brief "browning stage." Cut-up pieces of chicken, among the most difficult of food to grill to golden, crisp perfection without the slightest bit of burning, consistently turn out perfect using this method.

That said, is there ever a time when it is advisable to cook something in a kettle grill, directly over the coals, *without* its cover in place? Again, I respectfully disagree with the folks at Weber-Stephen, who firmly advise against ever using their unit without the lid on. The exceptions include any food that cooks in a matter of minutes (or seconds). Oysters in the shell, thin fish fillets, bread and paillards (meat pounded into very thin slices) are a few items I regularly cook on an uncovered kettle grill, directly over the coals.

I also break with their advice when cooking beaf steaks. I cook the steaks over a good, hot fire, directly over the coals, without the lid in place. Using the lid when cooking steaks greatly increases the potential for overcooking—something no steak-lover would ever want to happen.

Using a Covered Grill

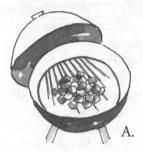
A.

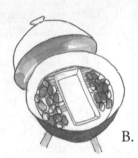
B.

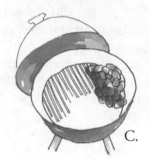
C.

The manufacturers of covered grills call grillinging away from the coals indirect cooking; I think it may be charcoal roasting. No matter what you call it, cooking away from the coals is one of the best ways to ensure a perfectly cooked meal. It demands three things: cleaning out the bottom of the grill prior to starting the fire so the draft holes can function properly, putting the cover on after positioning the food on the cooking grill and, in most instances, leaving both top and bottom vents completely open.

There are three ways to go about indirect cooking: A. position a pile of coals in the center of the fire grate and put the food in a ring around the fire on the cooking grill; B. divide the coals into two equal amounts, use a drip pan (filled with liquid or not, as you wish) in the center, with the food over the drip pan and C. pile all of the coals on one side of the fire grate and the food on the opposite side on the cooking grill — this works particularly well for long, slow cooking methods and the addition of smoking chips; be sure to turn the lid so the draft holes are on the opposite side of the fire; this will help pull the smoky aroma across the food.

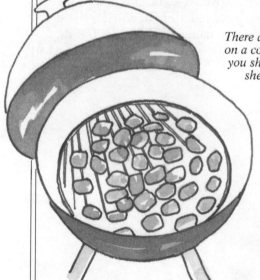

There are a few instances when cooking directly over the coals on a covered kettle grill is the preferred way to go. In the main, you should reserve this method for foods that cook in a jiffy: shellfish, bread, sausages and very thin cuts of meat.

Should you leave the top on or off? That's a judgment call best left to individual chefs. Be advised, though, if you put the lid in place, whatever it is that you're cooking directly over the coals may cook more rapidly than you might expect. This is why the instructions in this book do not recommend that you use the cover when cooking steaks; if you know your grill well, however, feel free to do so, as this actually produces a more succulent piece of meat.

If you want to use a kettle grill (one with a stationary fire grate) without the cover, just make sure to add a few extra coals to get the desired temperature at the level of the cooking grill.

CHARCOAL ROASTING

When you grill food on a covered grill using the indirect method, you are, in effect, charcoal *roasting* rather than charcoal *grilling*. Not only do a majority of foods turn out better this way (as opposed to grilling directly over the coals), an added and important benefit is achieved, namely, the elimination of fat dripping from the meat onto the coals.

Long before scientific research determined that this was unhealthy, Gerbase Markham, in his book, *The English Housewife* (published in 1668), cautioned against cooking directly over coals because, "the smoak occasioned by the droppings of the meat will ascend about it and make a stink." I don't know about you, but I have been served a fair share of meat cooked directly over the coals, redolent with the "stink" Mr. Markham advised against.

For large cuts of meat, such as roasts, whole large fish and whole poultry, indirect grilling in a covered grill is virtually the only outdoor cooking method that will produce excellent results (with the exception of using a rotisserie, which also qualifies as "charcoal roasting").

Before the advent of the modern gas and electric oven earlier in this century (and the coal-fueled stoves prior to that), large cuts of meat were always cooked indirectly over a fire, usually suspended on some type of rotating spit. Once cooks opted for the convenience of cooking these same cuts of meat indoors in their gleaming new ovens, the quality of the food suffered dramatically — a fact lost on most contemporary home chefs. In 1924, Henry Finck, an earnest commentator on food preparation, made the following statement: "In place of roast meat, most families now have to put up with baked meat."

When I pull a leg of lamb, turkey or prime rib off the covered kettle grill, it does my sense of history good to know that it was prepared in the preferred, time-honored method — charcoal roasted. I say leave the oven for what it does best — namely, baking pies, breads, cakes and cookies.

Three Ways to Charcoal Roast

Charcoal roasting, either in a covered grill or on a rotisserie, is reserved for those large cuts of meat — roasts, whole fish or poultry — that are almost impossible to cook directly over the coals. This is the way meats were cooked for countless generations prior to the invention of the electric or gas oven and, prior to that, the coal oven. If you really want to know how good a roasting hen, a whole salmon or a leg of lamb can taste, try using one of these methods.

1. Position the coals on both sides of the fire grate, with a drip pan in the middle. Place the meat on the cooking grill directly over the drip pan and put the cover in place. Leave top and bottom vents completely open and don't forget that meat thermometer.

2. On covered grills, you can alternately put the food in a roasting pan in the middle of the cooking grill, with the coals on the sides of the fire grate. This is a particularly good method to use for foods, such as veal roasts, when you want to save the juices for a sauce. Neither method 1 or 2 will require any basting but be sure to keep your eye on the meat thermometer (stuck into the thickest part of the meat), taking the food off the grill when it is 5 to 10 degrees shy of the desired temperature.

If you don't have a covered grill, you can still enjoy the pleasures of charcoal roasting with a rotisserie unit. Put a drip pan directly underneath whatever it is that you're cooking, with the coals banked towards the back and the sides of the pan. Without a lid, you'll find it necessary to baste the food every 10 to 15 minutes to keep it most and succulent. Use whatever falls into the drip pan and you'll be rewarded for your diligence.

SPIT COOKING

If you were referred to this page from the encyclopedia, you can either read through the following general instructions for spit-cooking or consult the list below and turn directly to the specific information on whatever it is that you're spit-cooking.

Beef, standing rib roast, *see Beef, Veal and Venison, page 48*
Beef, tenderloin, *see Beef, Veal and Venison, page 48*
Boar, *see Spit-Roasting Whole Animals, page 51 and Pig, page 54*
Capon, *see Poultry, page 50*
Capretto, *see Spit-Roasting Whole Animals, page 51 and Goat, 53*
Chicken, *see Poultry, page 50*
Cod, *see Fish, whole, page 49*
Duck, *see Poultry, page 50*
Fresh ham, *see Pork, page 50*
Goat, *see Spit-Roasting Whole Animals, page 51 and Goat, 53*
Goose, *see Poultry, page 50*
Halibut, *see Fish, page 49*
Lamb, leg, *see Lamb, page 49*
Lamb, whole, *see Spit-Roasting Whole Animals, page 51 and Lamb, page 53*
Pheasant, wild, *see Poultry, page 50*
Pig, suckling, *see Spit-Roasting Large Animals, page 51 and Pig, page 54*
Pig, large, *see Spit Cooking on the Ground, page 52 and Pig, page 54*
Pork, loin roast, *see Pork, 50*
Pork, ribs, *see Pork Spareribs, page 50*
Ribs, *see Pork Spareribs, page 50*
Rock Cornish game hens, *see Poultry, page 50*
Salmon, *see Fish, page 49*
Turkey, wild, *see Wild Turkey, page 51 and Poultry, page 49*
Veal, rolled roast, *see Beef, Veal and Venison, page 48*
Venison, *see Beef, Veal and Venison, page 48*

Manufacturers of covered grills are quick to point out that a rotisserie unit is not necessary when you use one of their grills with the lid in place. Weber-Stephen, manufacturers of the popular Weber kettle grill, actually makes a rotisserie attachment for their 22-inch grill, a fact that they deliberately underplay. The unit includes a wide metal ring for inserting between the bottom half of the grill and the top. Although it looks very odd, it works like a charm. There's a certain truth in the grill manufacturer's claim that a covered grill "turns the heat and not the meat," but there are several situations where a rotisserie is just the thing. Most obvious is if the only grill you own is an open model, rather than covered. There are also foods, such as suckling pigs and large turkeys, which are too large to cover with a lid. And then there are all manner of wild game and domestic poultry that don't seem to taste as good when cooked any other way than when turned on a spit.

Successful spit roasting is a matter of properly positioned coals, keeping the fire going and, most importantly, the balancing act: before cooking any food, it must be balanced on the spit so it turns evenly.

The Fire

In general, spit-cooking is best done over moderate coals, although beef roasts and fish are better cooked over a hot fire. Position the coals on the back half of the grill. The coals should extend at least three inches past either end of whatever it is that you're spit-roasting. Place a drip pan under the front half of the meat to catch its juices.

To keep the fire at an even temperature for long cooking times (such as for a suckling pig), add 5 or 6 briquets or small pieces of lump charcoal to the fire every 30 minutes or so. Don't wait until the original fire has died down too far before adding the additional charcoal; it will cause an uneven fire temperature as the coals die down and heat up again. Some people keep a bucket of live coals ready to avoid this problem. (See *Keeping the Fire Going,* page 34.)

Balancing and Tying

It is very important that the spit pass through the center of gravity of whatever you plan to roast. Otherwise, the meat will flop around, cook unevenly and put an unnecessary strain on the rotisserie motor. Tips for balancing specific meats are noted in each entry that follows.

Any type of fowl or rolled roast should be trussed or tied before roasting. Your butcher will tie a beef, pork or veal roast for you; you'll probably have to truss any poultry yourself (see *To Truss or Not To Truss,* page 243). Heavy-duty cotton string is best.

After the meat has been placed on the spit, gently rotate it with your hands to check for balance. If it flops or rolls unevenly, remount and retie it. A little extra effort at this stage makes all the difference in spit cooking. Most rotisserie units come with adjustable weights for counter-balancing uneven loads. They attach right on the spit and can be very useful for large or irregularly shaped cuts of meat.

Spit Roasting Tips

As with grilling any type of large roast or fowl, a meat thermometer takes the guesswork out of spit roasting. Standard cooking time charts cannot take air temperature, wind, or a variable heat supply into account, so it's best to not even consult them when cooking spit-roasted foods. This makes the use of a thermometer doubly important.

…Spit Cooking, *continued*

Slant a lightweight thermometer into the thickest part of the meat, making sure it doesn't touch any bones or the spit itself. If necessary, secure the thermometer with wire or string. Cook to the desired temperature (consult the chart on page 39 or individual entries in the encyclopedia section). Remember, though, that meat continues to cook after it is removed from the heat, so take it off when it is 5 to 10 degrees shy of the desired temperature. Allow the meat to rest on a carving board (one with a reservoir to catch the juices) for 20 minutes or so before carving. The resting period will make carving easier and give the internal temperature of the meat a chance to come up to the desired level.

Although it may sound rather esoteric, it is important that the spit turn in a certain direction. And no, it doesn't have anything to do with on which side of the equator you live. The top of whatever it is you are spit-roasting should move away from the cook and the bottom towards you. By turning in this direction, the fat drips off the meat and into the drip pan on the side facing the cook, making basting a simple proposition. Once you've spit-roasted something, you'll see that this makes perfect sense. Most rotisserie motors attach on either side of the grill, so changing the direction of the rotating spit is a simple matter of reversing the side to which the motor is attached.

WHAT TO COOK ON A SPIT

Any large cut of meat, such as roasts, all types of poultry (both domestic and wild) and large whole fish are the most likely candidates for spit cooking. When something grand is called for, spit roasting is the only way to go with a whole animal such as kid, lamb or pig. What follows are specific instructions for cooking a variety of meats on an open grill. Information on cooking whole animals is found on page 51.

Beef, Veal and Venison

Boneless or rolled roasts are easiest to balance. For beef, rolled rib roasts, tenderloin roasts, prime, rump and sirloin roasts are all excellent. For veal, ask for a rolled roast. The best cuts of venison for spit-roasting are the tenderloin and a rolled roast. If you're spit-roasting a beef tenderloin, ask the butcher to add a layer of fat to the roast before tying it, a process known as barding; venison roasts should be larded (see *Larding vs. Barding,* page 129).

Roasts with bones still intact are harder to balance but not impossible. Remember that the object is to try and run the spit through the center of gravity, no matter how "off-kilter" it may appear. This may mean piercing the meat at a diagonal to distribute the weight of the bones on either side of the spit. Beef standing rib roasts can be spitted this way (see illustration on page 55). The counter-balance weights provided with most spits come in handy with bone-in roasts.

If you're using top-quality beef, little seasoning is required. If the meat does not have a covering of fat, rub it liberally with olive oil, dust with coarsely ground black pepper and baste it with melted butter, olive oil or melted beef fat (if available) for an excellent beef flavor. If the meat has even a partial covering of fat, no additional basting should be necessary. Roast venison in front of a hot fire and baste frequently with the drippings in the drip pan. No matter how you like other types of meat cooked, venison is best served medium-rare — and hot off the spit. Over- or undercooking this meat is not advised.

Spit the meat as evenly as possible. By all means use a meat thermometer (see page 39 for recommended temperatures). Start the rotisserie turning when the coals are covered with a light gray ash and are at the "hot" stage. Keep your eye on the thermometer and get ready for some great eating.

Fish, Whole

Whole cod, halibut, salmon, tuna and striped bass are just a few fish that turn out beautifully on a spit. In general, moderate to oily, firm-fleshed fish are best for spit-roasting.

Run the spit through the fish, from one end to the other, securing it with cotton string or wire in three or four places, depending on the size of the fish. Start the cooking process while the coals are still hot, rather than at the moderate stage. Baste with melted butter that has been flavored with fresh lemon juice (juice of one lemon to ½ cup of butter), every 5 to 10 minutes. Due to the variations in size, it is difficult to provide much in the way of timing guidelines for spit-roasted fish. The use of a small, instant-reading thermometer, however, will take the guesswork out of spit-roasting a whole fish. When common sense or experience tell you the fish is almost done, stop the rotisserie and insert the thermometer through the thickest portion of the fish, almost to the bone. Remove the thermometer the fish from the fire as soon as the temperature reaches 145 degrees F. The individual flakes of fish will separate readily and be opaque almost to the bone.

Lamb

Lamb is, and always has been, considered the choicest meat for cooking over the coals, especially when done on a spit. Whole lamb (see page 53), legs (bone-in, or boned and tied), boned and rolled lamb shoulder roasts — even racks of lamb — can be spit roasted. Because lamb is so good cooked less than well-done, be sure to use a meat thermometer. Remove the lamb from the fire when the temperature reaches 135 degrees F. for rare; 140 degrees F. for medium.

A bone-in leg of lamb may be the trickiest to balance on the spit. Ask your butcher to remove the aitch and shank bones to make inserting the spit easier, running it parallel to the remaining bone.

Classic preparation includes studding the lamb with slivers of fresh garlic and basting it with a sauce made of equal parts olive oil and dry red or white wine, flavored with cracked fresh black pepper and either rosemary or oregano.

Pork

Pork is right up there near the top of spit-roasted meats. Favorite cuts include rolled shoulders, loin roasts, double loins tied together, tenderloins and a boned fresh ham. Don't start cooking until the coals have just reached the moderate stage, keep the fire temperature as even as possible by adding additional charcoal (preferably already hot, see *Keeping the Fire Going,* page 34) every 30 minutes or so and baste approximately every 15 minutes with one of the suggestions under *Mix and Match Marinade,* page 147. Be sure to use a meat thermometer when cooking pork and don't overcook the meat (see *The "T" Word,* page 187).

Pork Spareribs

Interestingly, pork spareribs may cook up better on the spit than any other way. So hard to keep from burning when grilled over the coals, spit-roasting allows a long, slow cooking process, rendering the fat away, without burning the exterior of the ribs.

Weave the spareribs onto the spit accordion-style, as shown in the illustration on page 55. If you use a tomato- or sugar-based sauce, or the Chinese-style marinade (page 289), any of the barbecue sauce variations (page 297 to 298) or the hot fresh plum marinade (page 291), baste the ribs during the last half of the cooking time instead of marinating. This will keep the sugars in the sauce from burning on the ribs. Total cooking time for ribs over a moderate fire will be approximately 1½ hours.

Poultry

Poultry, such as game hens, chickens, capons, pheasants, turkeys, ducks and geese, turn a beautiful golden brown (with a crisp skin) when roasted on a spit. Ask anyone who knows and they will tell you the preferred method for cooking poultry is spit-roasted over the coals. It's the standard against which all other forms of cooking poultry is compared.

Large birds, such as turkeys, geese, large chickens and capons, should be spitted head to tail, with the spit running through the body cavity of the bird.

Smaller birds can be lined up on the spit as shown in the illustration on page 55. The secret is to tie the legs and wings securely to the bird's body before spitting, so its appendages won't flop around on the rotisserie. When securing the legs and wings, pull the neck skin up over the cavity and attach it with small skewers or toothpicks. Once the holding prongs have been tightened, run a couple of long skewers through the birds, top and bottom, parallel to the spit, so they all turn at the same time. If your grill is large enough, you may be able to spit two or more birds end to end, as shown in the illustration on page 55.

The following cooking times are approximate. Best bet is to use a meat thermometer, inserted into the thickest part of the thigh, not hitting any bones. All poultry should be cooked to an internal temperature of 185 degrees F. An unstuffed, 10- to 24-pound turkey will take approximately 2½ to 4½ hours to cook; unstuffed chickens (2½ to 3½ pounds) will cook in 1½ to 2 hours; unstuffed Cornish game hens approximately 1 to 1½ hours; domestic ducks and geese (4 to 5 pounds) 2½ to 3 hours. Any poultry can be spit-roasted with or without stuffing. Cooking time will be approximately 45 minutes longer for stuffed birds.

Cover the wings and legs with aluminum foil if they start to darken too early in the spit-roasting process.

Wild Turkey: Count on 25 minutes per pound for spit-roasting a wild turkey above a hot fire. Remove the barding during the last 10 minutes or so of cooking, allowing the bird to brown nicely.

Wild Pheasant: Wild pheasant will cook above a bed of hot coals in approximately 15 to 20 minutes per pound. Baste frequently with oil or butter seasoned with your favorite herb.

SPIT-ROASTING WHOLE ANIMALS

When the occasion presents itself, there's nothing quite like spit-roasting a whole pig, lamb or goat (kid). These are situations when cooking becomes part of the day or evening's entertainment, so be prepared to have all eyes on *you,* if you're the cook. Spit-roasting a whole animal is one of the most primitive forms of cooking and nothing to shy away from using the following guidelines. The first is for spit-roasting over a large open grill; the second for spit-roasting on the ground.

Spit-Roasting Large Foods on An Equally Large Grill

1) Prepare the kid, lamb or pig according to the directions given in the individual entries that follow. Remove the meat from the refrigerator 3 to 4 hours prior to cooking. Cover the meat and allow it to come to room temperature. Failing this step, plan on an additional hour of cooking time.

2) Make basting sauce (see specific entries for suggestions).

3) Place heavy-duty aluminum foil pans in the fire grate, directly under the area where the meat will be cooking. Fill pans half-full of water. These "drip" pans will help prevent flare-ups and, as the liquid in the pans evaporates, help keep the meat moist.

4) Place briquets or lump charcoal on either side of the drip pans, in 6-inch wide rows, approximately 4 inches deep, extending 6 inches beyond both ends of whatever it is you will be cooking. Place an additional row of charcoal, connecting the other two rows, beyond where the shoulders of the animal will be located. Ignite charcoal.

...Spit Cooking, *continued*

5) In a separate grill or other fireproof container, ignite an additional 10 pounds or so of charcoal. Keep a ready supply of hot coals to add to the fire every 30 to 45 minutes as the original coals burn down.

6) Truss the meat to the spit. This may require wiring the meat to the spit in three or four places.

7) Loosely tie the flank area. Cover the mid-section (between the leg and the shoulder) with heavy-duty aluminum foil to retard cooking. Remove the foil during the last 45 minutes or so.

8) Once the coals reach the moderate-hot stage, put the spit into the rotisserie and start cooking. Baste frequently during the cooking process with basting sauce.

9) Consult individual entries in this section for approximate cooking times.

Spit Cooking on the Ground

For this process you will need:
1) 1 oak spit, 2" x 2" x 7'
2) 1 electric 1/2-hp motor gear, reduced to six revolutions per minute. Mount the motor on a time wheel with a square receptacle on the shaft to accept one end of the spit.
3) 1 metal, Y-shaped support for the end of the spit that's opposite the motor. This is best made from iron and can be commissioned from a local blacksmith.
4) 1 small roll of baling wire, thoroughly cleaned before use
5) 1 pair of 8-inch pliers
6) 1 metal garden rake
7) 60 to 80 pounds of charcoal

1) Prepare the kid, lamb or pig according to the directions given in the individual entries that follow. Before cooking, remove the animal from the refrigerator, cover and allow it to come to room temperature, a process that will take approximately 3 to 4 hours. Failing this step, plan on an additional hour of cooking time.

2) Make basting sauce (see specific entries for suggestions).

3) Make a place on the ground to start the fire. The space should be 12 to 18 inches larger on all sides than the animal you intend to spit-roast.

4) Arrange the Y-shaped support at one end and the rotisserie motor at the other, making sure that the spit fits correctly between the two.

5) Truss the meat to the spit. This may require wiring the meat the spit in three or four places.

6) Place briquets or lump charcoal in a pile and ignite. Once they are covered with a fine gray ash, use the rake to arrange in a single row on the far side of the spit. The row of coals should be at least 6 to 8 inches wide and extend 6 inches beyond both ends of whatever it is you will be cooking.

7) In a separate grill or other fireproof container, ignite an additional 10 pounds or so of charcoal. Keep a ready supply of hot coals to add to the fire every 30 to 45 minutes as the original coals burn down.

8) Put the spitted beast in place. Adjust so the coals are approximately 9 inches from meat for the first 30 minutes; approximately 7 inches from the coals after that. Baste frequently during the cooking process with basting sauce (see specific entries for suggestions).

Goat (Kid)

A young goat, or kid, makes for good eating; an older goat is one tough customer. Rub the dressed goat well with a half-and-half mixture of olive oil and white wine. Sprinkle both the outside and inside (the cavity) with pepper, garlic powder and a combination of chopped fresh rosemary and marjoram.

Spit and cook over a moderate fire, about 8 inches from the coals, until the meat thermometer registers 145 to 150 degrees F. Because the meat is so lean, it must be basted frequently (every 10 minutes or so) with olive oil, flavored with rosemary and marjoram, if desired.

Lamb

Count on approximately ¾ to 1 pound of dressed weight lamb per person. If you're spit roasting on the ground, you can cook a lamb as large as 40 or 50 pounds; if you're spit roasting over a grill, the size of the grill will dictate the size of the lamb.

Start by removing the shank bone from the front legs. Tuck the front legs between the rib cage and the skin. Fasten the lamb on the spit, from front to back. Secure with baling wire (pre-washed), winding your way around the lamb, beginning with the hind legs and ending at the head.

For a 40- to 50-pound lamb, ignite approximately 40 pounds of charcoal (use a proportionally less amount for smaller lambs). Once the coals are covered with a light gray ash, arrange them as suggested above. Insert the spit into the rotisserie and adjust the height so the coals are approximately 9 inches away from the lamb. After 30 minutes, adjust so the coals are a little closer, approximately 7 inches from the lamb.

Baste the lamb every 30 minutes or so with olive oil flavored with lemon juice, freshly ground pepper, garlic and rosemary, if desired. As the lamb starts to brown, arrange the coals so they are concentrated below the front and hind quarters of the lamb. Depending on a variety of conditions, a 40- to 50-pound lamb should be done to medium-rare in approximately 3½ hours.

Pig

You can spit-roast almost any size pig (or boar) you want, from 12 to 40 pounds, depending on the size of your grilling equipment and the size of the crowd you plan to feed. If it's much larger than 20 pounds, consider spit-roasting it on the ground, following the directions given on pages 52. When you order your pig, count on approximately 1½ pounds of dressed pig per person.

Thread the spit through the pig's mouth, along its backbone and out the tail end. Secure the pig with holding forks. If necessary, pass several U-shaped pieces of wire through the rib cavity and out the top of the pig's back so the wire, when tightened, secures the backbone to the spit.

The pig's legs will either extend forward or backward, or be bent under and stuck into pockets cut in the chest and stomach. Once positioned, they are difficult to move. If the legs are extended forward and backward, tie the front legs together; tie the back legs together, then secure both to the spit with string or wire. If the legs are tucked in pockets in a kneeling position, it may be necessary to partially truss the pig with string to achieve a proper balance.

Check the balance of the spitted pig by spinning the spit. Adjust trussing or wiring to make it spin as evenly as possible. Wrap ears and tail in aluminum foil. Prop the pig's mouth open with a small piece of wood. Place the pig on the spit supports once the coals have reached the moderate stage. Position a drip pan under the pig.

The pig should be basted every 10 to 15 minutes with a half-and-half mixture of melted butter and vegetable oil, flavored with dried sage, if desired. If you want to impart a particular flavor to the meat, baste with any of the marinades listed on pages 289 to 295.

Cook the pig until a meat thermometer inserted in the thickest portions (shoulder or rump) registers 160 to 170 degrees F. After about half the cooking time, wrap the belly section with aluminum foil. This will help prevent it from over-cooking while the thicker portions finish up.

Spitting Techniques

You will always be better off using a drip pan under any spitted food, if only because it allows you to baste it in its own juices. If you feel so compelled, add a little of your favorite herb or wine to the drippings for extra flavor.

Pork ribs, the devil to cook to succulent perfection directly on the grill, baste themselves on a spit. All that's necessary is to thread them accordion-style and maybe baste them every now and then.

A rolled roast is one of the easiest of all things to cook on a spit, given its uniform shape. Whether it's beef, pork or veal, all that may required is inserting a few slivers of garlic directly into the meat before it's spit. If it's an exotic flavor you're after, marinate before grilling and use the leftover marinade as a baste.

Few people think of spitting a whole fish. But it works out beautifully. Baste the fish, if you desire, cook it over a good hot fire and take it off as soon as the flesh reaches 145 degrees F. on an instant-reading thermometer.

Depending on how many birds you have to grill, you can spit them back to back or cheek to cheek — just make sure that they're evenly balanced and well secured before grilling.

Balancing any food is the trickiest part of cooking on a spit. Sometimes, as with this standing rib roast, you'll have to defy logic and put the pit through at an angle to find the center of gravity. Get this part right, and both you and your rotisserie motor will be much happier.

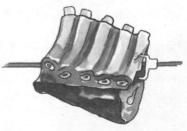

SKEWER COOKING

Almost every food mentioned in the encylopedia section of this book can be cut up and grilled on skewers. While it doesn't taste dramatically different than food grilled in any other form, there are a number good reasons for cooking food on skewers: 1) skewered food is easy to handle on the grill (in fact, grilling chunks of a dense meaty fish like swordfish or shark on skewers is a great way to build confidence for grilling fish steaks and fillets), 2) when made up of boneless pieces of meat and slices of vegetables, there's little or no waste, 3) serving is a snap when each person receives a skewer or two on their plate.

Skewer Cooking Tips

• Whatever you put on skewers, be it vegetables, meat, poultry, fish or fruit, should be cut into more or less uniform pieces for even cooking.

• If you prefer meat that's cooked rare or medium rare, tightly pack the pieces onto the skewers. Conversely, if you prefer meat that's more well-done, keep a little space between each piece of meat on the skewer.

• To keep skewered food from spinning around as you turn them on the grill (especially round items like slices of zuchinni), use two skewers that run parallel through the food. There are also a number of commercially available skewers featuring two parallel prongs (see illustration at right).

• Soak bamboo skewers in hot water for 30 minutes or so before using them on the grill. This helps to keep the ends from burning off.

• It won't make any difference in the taste, but try cutting meats such as pork, chicken and beef into strips rather than cubes. Thread the strips onto the skewers keeping them tight together or loose; tightly threaded strips of meat are not so likely to dry out on the grill.

• If you plan to serve skewered meat and vegetables for the same meal, put them on separate skewers. It may not be as attractive in terms of presentation, but each type of food can be cooked to perfection, rather than hitting a "happy medium" where the meat is done but the bell peppers and onions are not.

• To take food off the skewers, hold onto one end of the skewer, with the other end held against a plate. Using a fork or tongs, start by pushing about a third of the food off the skewer, working your way up the rest of the skewer in increments. It is almost impossible to push all of the food off the skewer at one time, especially if it has been packed on tightly.

Skewering Techniques

Any meat can be cut into cubes (anywhere from 1 to 1½ inches square) or in strips and strung onto skewers. Whether the meat is cubed or cut into thin slices doesn't affect the taste or texture, but the strips accept the flavors of a marinade a little more readily. If you like your meat on the rare side, pack it onto the skewers tightly; this will also help keep it moist. If you prefer your meat well done, leave a bit of space between the pieces.

If you're serving an entired skewered meal of meat and vegetables, resist the temptation to combine the foods on a single skewer. Although it's more attractive that way, it's almost impossible to have the different foods cook to your liking. When cooking skewered vegetables, in fact, it's best to keep one type to a skewer, as each will have a slightly different cooking time.

There are many foods, such as shrimp and cherry tomatoes, that will spin around on a single skewer, making it very difficult to turn and cook them on both sides. This problem can be solved easily by using two parallel skewers.

For the griller who has everything, there are a variety of two-pronged skewers available. They solve the problem of spinning foods as noted above. The model on the far right even has a little "pusher" to slide the food off after it has been cooked.

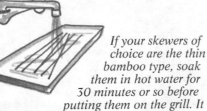

If your skewers of choice are the thin bamboo type, soak them in hot water for 30 minutes or so before putting them on the grill. It helps prevent the ends from completely burning off during cooking.

EXPERIENCE IS THE BEST TEACHER

Grilling is a notoriously inexact method of preparing food, with everything from the weather, to the type of grill used, to the mood of the cook undermining any attempt at consistency. With that in mind, I shamelessly reprint here (with the permission of the publisher) a great idea from that master of outdoor cooking, the late James Beard. The idea, which makes perfect sense to me, was found in Beard's *Cook It Outdoors,* originally published in 1941. He advised the following:

"…make a chart for yourself and list the various types of food you grill and the type of fire and the average cooking time. You will find this a perfect reference sheet and doubly valuable if you have had two or three drinks and can't quite remember how long you gave the ham steaks last time. Each individual grill has different attributes and experience is the only teacher."

Food	Cooking Time	Type of Fire

Food	Cooking Time	Type of Fire

Food	Cooking Time	Type of Fire

Food	Cooking Time	Type of Fire

ENCYCLOPEDIA

A

ABALONE

As rare as it is, abalone falls into the esoteric food category; if you choose to grill it, make that doubly esoteric.

Most prevalent on the Pacific coasts of California, Japan, Mexico and Australia, this univalve (meaning that it has only one shell, unlike mussels, clams and oysters, which are bivalves) is rarely seen in other markets of the world. To go "abbing" along the coast of northern California is to experience one of the region's most delightful culinary expeditions. Finding abalones, and then prying them off the rocks to which they tenaciously cling, is hard work, made more uncomfortable by the fact that the weather and the water are almost always bitterly cold. The reward comes with only a couple of these large creatures, whose shells must be 7¼ inches or more across to legally harvest them, at least in California. Not only that, but there's a limit of four abalone per person! Being so carefully monitored, you can begin to understand their rare appeal. With regulations like that, even old fence posts would become prized delicacies.

The meat inside (which is in the form of a large, very tough steak) must be pried loose and then thoroughly scrubbed to remove its black coating. Some people choose to cut this layer off, but by doing so lose a considerable amount of the precious meat. Next, slice the steak ¼ to ⅜ inches thick, and pound with a wooden mallet to within an inch — make that an eighth-inch — of its life. This is best accomplished between a couple of layers of waxed paper and with gentle pounding, just like the waves on the shore.

The time-honored method of cooking abalone is to dip the pounded pieces in egg or flour, or first in flour then beaten egg and, lastly, in finely ground saltine crackers. Have your large skillet nice and hot, with a

"To go 'abbing' along the coast of northern California is to experience one of the region's most delightful culinary expeditions."

I once heard about an intriguing method for preparing abalone, purportedly developed by the Indians who inhabited the coasts of California. The method, as related, involved nailing the just-gathered abalones to a vertical surface, shell and all. As the abalone gradually loses it grip on life, it supposedly relaxes (if you can call it that), elongating right out of the shell. Once in this state, it (again supposedly) is tender enough to be cooked without pounding. I've never known anyone willing to risk ruining even one abalone in trying this method, but like I said, it is intriguing.

Another quick method for tenderizing abalone is definitely not an old Indian custom. This one involves removing the entire muscle from the shell, cleaning it, positioning it on a sturdy wooden surface and —whap!— hitting it broadside with a 4x4. Rumor has it that this tenderizes the whole abalone in one fell swoop, at which point it can be sliced and prepared any way you wish. I should be quick to point out that I've never done this myself, seen it done, nor do I personally know anyone who has tried it; it may simply be another abalone myth. Abalones are like that.

liberal layer of bubbling butter and sauté for about 20 to 30 seconds per side. A true delicacy! If you ever find yourself in a northern California coastal town, see if you can find someone to prepare a breakfast of scrambled eggs and sautéed abalone — one of the most obscenely delicious combinations ever to be concocted.

As good as sautéed abalone is, it can also be grilled, but with much different (yes, chewier) results. A purist may initially scoff at this method, but I know more than one abalone expert who no longer prepares it any other way *except* grilled.

If you want to try this method, soak the pounded slices of abalone in a mixture of a little Japanese rice wine vinegar, a scant squeeze of fresh lemon juice, a few grinds of pepper, a little chopped fresh cilantro and very finely diced, fresh, hot chili pepper (the amount and type of chili pepper is up to you, depending on how much excitement you can stand). The delicate flavor of abalone is easily overwhelmed, so don't leave it in this mixture for more than ten minutes or so.

Build a hot fire and liberally oil the grill. Cook the pieces of abalone directly over the coals for about 30 to 60 seconds per side, just long enough to heat them through and produce those appealing grill marks. This is the type of food that legends are made of, so you might as well make a big deal of it: have everyone close at hand, very chilled champagne already poured and pass out this rare treat, hot off the grill.

AHI

In the Hawaiian Islands, where it is plentiful, the natives call yellowfin tuna, ahi. All types of tuna are grilled in virtually the same way. For grilling instructions, see Albacore, the entry that follows.

ALBACORE

If you've never encountered albacore (which is a member of the *Thunnus,* or tuna, family) in the fish market before, you might be a little taken aback. Although the lightest of the tunas, which includes yellowfin, bluefin and bonito, albacore is nonetheless a fairly dark-fleshed fish — nothing at all like what you see in a can. Once you put the tuna on the grill, however, a transformation takes place: the flesh becomes much lighter and quite firm.

After you've witnessed this change and tasted the results, you'll never be put off by the sight of raw tuna again. Members of this family are truly among the best choices of fish to grill, either as steaks or cut up into 1-inch cubes and strung on skewers.

The distinctive flavor of all tunas is complemented by any number of marinades. Try Greek marinade (page 290), herb marinade (page 291) or lemon-white wine marinade (page 292); marinate for 30-45 minutes. Or serve it with cilantro lime butter (page 305), Niçoise butter (page 306) or confetti salsa (page 301). Steamed rice (page 337) and black-eyed peas (page 318) make for good side dishes.

1) Keep the fish refrigerated until about 30 minutes before grilling.

2) Ignite as many briquets or as much lump charcoal as it takes to make a bed of coals a little larger in size than what the fish will take up on the grill.

3) Put the cooking grill over the coals and allow it to become hot before putting on the tuna; fish will stick to a cold grill. Use a wire brush to clean the hot grill (if necessary) and coat it with vegetable oil, using a large basting brush.

4) Cook the tuna directly over a bed of hot coals, with the cooking grate 4 to 6 inches above the fire on adjustable grills. If you're using a covered grill, don't put the cover down.

5) Grill the tuna for 10 minutes per inch of thickness. For example, a 1-inch-thick steak would take 10 minutes to cook — 5 minutes per side. Plan on turning the fish only once — half the total cooking time on each side.

6) While virtually all fish tastes best hot off the grill, the tuna family holds up deliciously at room temperature or

Albacore is truly one of the best choices of fish to grill.

When grilling any type of tuna, I usually cook a couple of extra portions and then squirrel them away in the refrigerator. The first time wasn't intentional, but that was before I found out how good a salade Nicoise is with leftover grilled tuna — not to mention a leftover grilled tuna sandwich.

For salade Nicoise, start with a bed of your favorite lettuces. Arrange a few small, boiled new potatoes, a couple of handfuls of cooked green beans and halves of hard-boiled eggs around the outside of the plate. Speciality food shops carry canned French haricot vertes, the traditional and "proper" green bean to grace a salade Nicoise. Your everyday grocery store should have canned new potatoes. Normally, I'm not much on canned vegetables, but both of these are very good. They are better if you refrigerate them before putting them on the salad.

Break the leftover tuna into good-sized chunks and put on top of the lettuce. Mix up some vinaigrette (see page 71) and pour over the tuna and other accompaniments. Top with a few anchovy fillets (if you like them) or capers (if you don't).

Serve with warm, crusty French bread and a chilled Sauvignon Blanc or Chardonnay. Mighty fine warm-weather dining!

There's nothing to making a grilled tuna sandwich; just use your favorite bread, a little lettuce, and a healthy amount of mayonnaise and Dijon mustard. If the grilled tuna isn't too thick, use it whole; if not, break it into chunks. Makes the canned variety look a little pale by comparison.

even cold. If you have any leftovers, see *Intentional Leftovers* at left for a great way to prepare salade Nicoise — delicious when made with cold grilled tuna!

See Fish, page 133, for more information.

ANGLER

Alternately known as monkfish, goosefish or lotte, angler is a member of the shark family. It is one of the most outstandingly ugly creatures of the deep, looking very much like something from *20,000 Leagues Under the Sea*. Unfortunately (or perhaps fortunately), you'll rarely see what angler really looks like, because only the tail section reaches fish markets; angler's huge and brutish head is thrown overboard before the fishing boats ever reach port.

You can't, however, judge a fish by its looks: angler's dense white flesh is mild and sweet, often termed "poor man's lobster." On both sides of the Atlantic, angler is considered to be one of the finest eating fish to come from the sea. Angler can be cut into small pieces (like scallops) for putting on skewers, the tail meat can be cut crosswise into "steaks," or a portion of the tail can be butterflied. Ask your fishmonger to cut it into whatever form you want, but not more than ¾-inch thick.

Marinate the angler for 30 to 45 minutes in Dijon marinade (page 289), fresh ginger-garlic marinade (page 290), pesto marinade (page 293) or herb marinade (page 291). Or, simply brush with vegetable oil, sprinkle with paprika and serve the grilled fish with fresh lemon wedges and a little chopped parsley. If it's a special dinner, consider grilling plain (oiled and dusted with paprika) and serve with the elegant beurre blanc sauce (page 300), flavored with your favorite fresh herb.

A simple side dish of boiled new potatoes (page 320), steamed parslied rice (page 337) or galette of potatoes (page 323) goes well with the rich flavor of angler. Any steamed, fresh vegetable would be appropriate.

1) About 30 minutes before cooking, take the angler out of the refrigerator.

2) Ignite as many briquets or as much lump charcoal as it takes to make a bed of coals a little larger in size than what the fish will take up on the grill.

3) Fish will stick to a cold cooking grill, so put the grill over the coals and let it heat up before putting on the angler. Once the grill is hot, use a wire brush to clean it. With a large basting brush, coat the grate with vegetable oil just before you're ready to cook the fish.

4) With the cooking grate 4 to 6 inches above the coals on adjustable grills, cook the angler directly over a hot fire. Do not use the cover on covered grills.

5) Grill the fish for 10 minutes per inch of thickness, turning only once, halfway through the total cooking time.

6) Most fish should be served piping hot and angler is no exception. After it's cooked, land the angler on a platter that you've heated for 15 minutes in a 250-degree F. oven. Everything else that you're planning to serve with the fish should be ready to go before putting the angler on the grill.

See Fish, page 133, for more information.

APPLES

Apples are usually considered dessert food, but when grilled, they take on a different, more rustic character. Be advised that grilled apples may not appeal to everyone, but I consider them first-rate as a side dish, especially with almost any type of pork.

To prepare as a side dish, peel, core and quarter the apples, and squeeze a little fresh lemon juice over them to keep them from turning brown. Toss the apples around in a bowl with enough melted butter to coat, and place them on the grill at the same time as the main course. Keep the apples to the sides of the fire, away from direct heat. Turn every ten minutes or so, basting with melted butter if they begin to stick to the grill. Depending on the heat of the fire, the apples should be cooked

Apples take on a rustic character when grilled, and are especially good with any type of pork.

through in about 30 minutes. For easier handling, the apples can be cut into ½-inch thick slices and placed in a hinged-wire basket (see page 214). If you're cooking two courses at once, however, it may not be possible to find room on the grill for this apparatus.

If it's a dessert you're after, stick with an old standby, like foil-wrapped baked apples. Peel the top third of the apple, core and fill the cavity with a little butter, a few walnuts and raisins, a sprinkle of cinnamon and maybe a little real maple syrup. Double wrap individual apples in foil and cook directly over the coals for 30 to 40 minutes, or until a knife inserts easily into the apple. This procedure can be done after the main course has been taken off the grill; the apples will be ready for eating just about the time the dishes have been done.

APRICOTS

Just because something can be grilled doesn't necessarily mean that it *should* be. I feel this way about most fruits because, quite frankly, there are much better ways of preparing them — like in pies. Apricots deserve mention here for two reasons: they are excellent served with grilled ham steak (page 147) and grilling improves the rather insipid flavor of most store-bought apricots.

I don't know what's happened to the apricots in this country; probably the same thing that's happened to tomatoes. Where once they were small, intensely flavored, and of luscious texture, they are now large, hard and practically tasteless. Or am I only remembering the ones we used to pick every June from that ancient apricot tree behind our cabin at Clear Lake?

Here's how to grill today's apricots: split them in half, remove the pit and brush them with melted butter. Warm the apricots on the grill, skin side down and away from the direct heat of the coals. This will only take a few minutes per side. Just before serving, baste again with butter and move the apricots directly over the fire to leave those telltale grill marks and to brown slightly — no more than 1 minute per side. The word "ambrosial" may be a bit too strong, but these sure are good.

Grilling improves the rather insipid flavor of most store-bought apricots. They're excellent served with grilled ham steak (page 147).

ARTICHOKES

Even though I like the idea, I have not been impressed with the reality of grilled artichokes. I've tried them split in half, basted with olive oil and grilled, but the whole thing left me cold. And I've had fresh artichoke hearts, parboiled and marinated in olive oil, lemon juice and garlic, grilled directly over the coals until just brown. They were okay, but it hurts this California boy's heart to see the rest of the artichoke (all those outer leaves) go to waste.

Artichokes are a treat that should be enjoyed just as they are. It's far better, in my book, to simply boil or steam them. Boiled artichokes can be a little soggy, but steaming them results in perfection, even though it takes practically forever.

Serve hot, cold or at room temperature with drawn butter, mayonnaise or vinaigrette (at right). These are particularly good with that other spring delicacy, lamb.

ASPARAGUS

One has to draw the line somewhere; for me it's drawn around both artichokes (see above) and asparagus. I don't consider either one of these fine vegetables truly suitable for grilling. Steamed or boiled asparagus is the way to go, served with wedges of lemon, drawn butter, mayonnaise or vinaigrette (at right).

A Good Vinaigrette

Knowing how to make a good vinaigrette dressing not only frees you from using one of those dubious bottled offerings, it also allows for customizing in any way that suits your palate. The following is just the ticket for tossed green salads and steamed vegetables like artichokes, asparagus and broccoli. It's easiest to make in a small glass jar with a tight-fitting lid.

Makes enough vinaigrette for a salad for 4 people.

¼ teaspoon of salt
A good grind of black pepper
2 tablespoons of red wine vinegar
6 tablespoons of good quality olive oil
1 tablespoon of water
2 teaspoons of Dijon mustard

Put all ingredients in the jar, put lid in place, and shake vigorously. To customize the vinaigrette, add ¼ cup loosely packed fresh herbs — thyme, sweet marjoram, chives, parsley, salad burnet, summer savory or basil — to the mixture. A pressed clove of garlic can also be added, as well as a teaspoon or so of fresh lemon juice or balsamic vinegar. If you add the lemon juice or balsamic vinegar, subtract an equal amount of vinegar from the recipe.

If you want to make vinaigrette in a larger amount (it will keep in the refrigerator for a week or so), the following recipe makes 2 cups of vinaigrette.

1 teaspoon of salt
Several grinds of black pepper
½ cup of red wine vinegar
1½ cup of good quality olive oil
4 tablespoons of water
2 tablespoons of Dijon mustard

B

BABYBACK RIBS

Just for the record, babyback ribs do not come from baby pigs. They are smaller than traditional spareribs, and more tender, being found further back on the animal, right next to the loin. See Pork, ribs on page 192.

BANANAS

The familiar yellow banana found in grocery stores across America makes surprisingly good grilling fare, as does the banana's close cousin, the plantain (page 183).

While plantains are often cooked as a part of the main course, the common yellow banana should be reserved for dessert. I prefer to start with bananas that are covered with black spots — a stage most people consider overripe. Any earlier in the ripening process, and grilled bananas tend to have an insipid taste instead of that rich, sweet flavor of ripe fruit.

If you are planning to grill bananas for dessert, don't close down the grill after cooking the main course. Let the coals keep burning; there should still be plenty of heat left to cook bananas after dinner.

There's nothing to grilling bananas: simply put them on the grill, directly over the coals, until the peels turn completely black (not *charred,* mind you, just black in color) and the flesh has had a chance to heat through. This should take only 5 to 7 minutes, even over a low fire. Use care when taking bananas off the grill; once cooked, they have a tendency to split open. Before they are peeled, grilled bananas are not the most appetizing of sights, so you might want to consider handling them while your guests are in another room.

Although they can be eaten right out of the peel, you'll have far more takers if you have dishes of premium

"While plantains are often cooked as a part of the main course, the common yellow banana should be reserved for dessert."

vanilla ice cream already scooped up, and top them with slices of the still-hot banana. Add a dollop of whipped cream and a sprinkling of toasted almonds. Sinfully delicious!

BARRACUDA

The so-called "great" barracuda *(Sphyraena barracuda)* found in Atlantic waters is not so great for eating; in fact, its flesh is toxic. The Pacific or California barracuda *(S. argentaea)* is edible and excellent for cooking on the grill. Unfortunately, it is rarely seen in fish markets.

For a fish classed as fatty, barracuda is relatively lean. Steaks and fillets are the cuts generally available. A liberal brushing of vegetable oil and a sprinkling of paprika on both sides is all that's needed prior to cooking, although after cooking you may want to serve it with a sauce, as barracuda stands up well to a variety of zesty flavors. Try confetti salsa (page 301) or Nicoise butter (page 306).

Simple side dishes are best. Try steamed rice (page 337), pommes frites (page 331), or grilled potato wedges (page 196). A combination of steamed or sautéed fresh vegetables would be an appropriate accompaniment.

1) Allow the steaks or fillets to come to room temperature by taking them out of the refrigerator about 30 minutes before grilling.

2) Determine how much space the steaks or fillets will take up on the grill, and ignite as many briquets or as much lump charcoal as it takes to make a bed of coals a little larger in size.

3) Put the cooking grill over the coals and let it become good and hot (fish will stick to a cold grill). Next, use a wire brush to clean the grate, if necessary, and coat it with vegetable oil using a large basting brush.

4) Place the steaks or fillets directly over a bed of hot coals, and cook them for 10 minutes per inch of thickness, turning just once. For example, a 1-inch-thick steak will take 10 minutes to cook — 5 minutes per side. Do not put the cover down on covered grills.

Eating Out of Doors

Ruth Dean, a pre-eminent landscape architect during the early part of this century, had some interesting ideas regarding the use of gardens. Listen to what she had to say about eating meals "out from under roofs," orignally published in the July 1921 issue of The Garden Magazine:

"Take the question of eating outdoors. The plainest of meals becomes a bit of a feast, if it is spread under the grape arbor, but this is a festivity so easily had that few but our children and 'foreigners' perceive it. Mr. Thomas A. Janvier, in his book on old New York, speaks of coming into a French settlement on West 21st Street and beholding a 'gay Gallic company breakfasting under its own vine and ailanthus tree with such honest lightheartness as can be manifested only by French folk, eating something — eating almost anything out of doors.'"

In her article, Miss Dean went on to urge people to "shake off the house entirely and get out from under roofs," when it came time to eat a meal. It wasn't enough for her that people ate in their morning rooms or back porches; she wanted her clients to eat "out among the lilacs."

I think she has a point. A meal that has been cooked outdoors should be eaten outdoors whenever possible. When sitting around a table under the trees, everyone seems a little more relaxed, slows down a bit and lingers after the meal to just chat and enjoy the surroundings.

Here's to the notion that the "honest lightheartedness," which Mr. Janvier asserts can only be manifested by French folk, would be adopted by more people of all extractions while "eating something — eating almost anything out of doors."

5) Fish should be served hot off the grill — within seconds, if possible — so have everything else ready to go before putting the barracuda on the grill. Heated plates help keep the fish hot; slip them into a 250-degree F. oven for 15 minutes, along with a platter for the fish.

See Fish, page 133, for more information.

BASS, CHANNEL OR RED

The channel or red bass is a favorite of good cooks in the New Orleans tradition. More commonly called redfish, you'll find it on page 203.

BASS, STRIPED

I can remember when striped bass were relatively plentiful in the San Francisco Bay. More than once we spent the early morning hours on that cold, gray, foggy bay, returning home a few hours later with a few fish, ready for the grill, and a tired fishing group ready to thaw out in the warm Napa Valley sun. Striped bass (or stripers, as the're sometimes called) was prized not only for its flavor, but for the fight it put up on the other end of the line.

Striped bass was introduced as a game fish from the Atlantic coast to the Pacific. The species was thought to be exclusively anadromous (spawning in freshwater, living the rest of the time in salt water), but stripers have successfully been introduced into a number of large freshwater lakes where they live full-time.

Because striped bass are not fished commercially, at least in the Pacific, you'll have to catch one to taste its firm, sweet flesh. The fish can become very large, up to 50 pounds, but stripers in the 3- to 12-pound category are much more common. Stripers can be cut into steaks or fillets for grilling; if they are under approximately 10 pounds, they can be grilled whole.

The natural taste of striper is so good, it seems a shame to mask it with a marinade. A liberal brushing of vegetable oil and a sprinkling of paprika on both sides is

"More than once we spent the early morning hours on that cold, gray, foggy bay…"

all that's needed prior to cooking. Once the fish comes off the grill, give it a few squeezes of fresh lemon.

The cavity of a whole bass can be filled with a few handfuls of chopped onion, celery, parsley and sliced lemons. Close the opening with sutures (use the same needle and cotton thread as described in *To Truss or Not to Truss,* page 243), or by weaving a couple of small skewers across both sides of the cavity. Rub vegetable oil over the outside of the fish and dust well with paprika.

Serve with pommes frites (page 331), boiled new potatoes (page 320), or steamed parslied rice (page 337). A big platter full of garden fresh tomatoes sounds good, as do marinated cucumbers (page 327).

1) Take the fish out of the refrigerator about 30 minutes before grilling.

2) Ignite as many briquets or as much lump charcoal as it takes to make a bed of coals a little larger in size than what the fish will take up on the grill. Put the cooking grill in place and let it heat up. Once it's hot, clean it (using a wire brush) and oil it (using a large basting brush and vegetable oil).

3) Grill the bass directly over a bed of hot coals, with the cooking grill 4 to 6 inches above the fire on adjustable grills. If you're cooking fillets with the skin intact, put the fish on the grill skin side down first. Cook for 10 minutes per inch of thickness, measured at the thickest point. Turn the fish only once — half the total cooking time on each side. Don't use the lid on covered grills.

4) Serve the bass hot off the grill on a platter that has been heated for 15 minutes in a 250-degree F. oven. Everything else should be ready to go before grilling.

See Fish, page 133, for more information.

BAY SCALLOPS

The bay scallop is a close cousin to the much larger sea scallop. Both are great for grilling and are covered on page 215 under the heading of Scallops.

Eating Out of Doors II

The late Helen Evans Brown is one of my favorite food writers. Her writing on food contains a wonderful spirit — a natural commitment to the joys food can bring to our lives. Inspired by her way of life in Pasadena, California, Helen Evans Brown sought to inspire others, no matter where they might live, to experience some of the same pleasures. It was a worthwhile and benevolent crusade, one that had tremendous impact on a whole generation of readers. From her Patio Cook Book (published by The Ward Ritchie Press in 1951 and no longer in print), comes the following passage:

"All over America the patio has become the pleasantest part of summer living. A patio, to Mr. Webster, is 'an inner court, open to the sky.' Not so to anyone who owns a patch of lawn, a square yard of concrete, or an acre of paved terrace. This is THE PATIO. This is the place where warm leisurely days begin and end, where breakfast coffee is a drink sublime, and where the simplest supper, served under the stars, becomes a memorable meal. Of all the outdoor pastimes it is the outdoor dining that is enjoyed the most."

Beef, brisket

Brisket is one of the best, most flavorful cuts of beef for capital-B *Barbecue*. Here we enter treacherous waters, because each region of the country lays claims to the best method for producing the best barbecued brisket. It's been said that the hottest seats in hell are reserved for people who won't take sides in a controversy. If that's the case, my reservation is being made with the following statement: I think everyone's right. The best barbecue just happens to be the one you grew up with.

Although the procedure I've outlined below is sure to offend some aficionados, I believe it contains the basic process by which anyone can cook a tasty brisket. Please note, however, that it is open for customizing, particularly in the seasoning and sauce departments. Before you get started, four basics apply to cooking a brisket:

First, don't look for a completely lean brisket. There should be a ¼-inch thick layer of fat on the back side of the meat. This layer, in addition to the fat inside the brisket, is what keeps it from drying out during its long cooking process — a process that renders virtually all of the fat from the meat.

Second, don't rush the cooking process. Brisket is best cooked in a covered grill over a very low fire (around 200 to 250 degrees F.). At this temperature, a brisket will take anywhere from three to ten hours to cook. Lest you think one of the numbers just given is a typographical error, rest assured, they are presented as intended. All brisket is going to be "well done;" that's not the point. The number of hours you cook a brisket depends on how tender you want the meat, how easily you want it to fall apart, and how dark and crusty you like the outside layer — which is a matter of regional tradition and personal taste. More than one person will tell you that the dark, crusty exterior is the best part of the brisket, or that any brisket that isn't fork-tender is undercooked.

Third, don't sauce the brisket while it's cooking. A dry rub is the preferred pretreatment; sauce is for putting on *after* you take the brisket off the grill.

Last but not least, properly cooked brisket demands the use of a covered grill. Many home barbecue cooks like to add handfuls of soaked hickory, oak or mesquite wood chips to the coals to produce a smokier-tasting brisket. If this is the flavor you desire, soak the wood

"Here we enter treacherous waters, because each region of the country lays claims to the best method for producing the best barbecued brisket."

chips in warm water for about 30 minutes before putting them on top of the glowing briquets. A handful on top of each bunch of briquets should be sufficient. Add more smoking chips each time you add briquets, depending on how smoky a flavor you want.

1) Preseason the meat using the Barbecue-style dry rub found on page 309. After massaging the dry rub evenly into the brisket, shake off any excess, place on a platter at room temperature for 60 minutes. If you have the time, wrap the brisket in plastic wrap and store it in a refrigerator for 6 to 8 hours or overnight.

2) Ignite 10 to 15 briquets. Once they are covered with a light gray ash, separate them into equal amounts and push to opposite sides of the fire grate. Place a disposable aluminum pan in the center of the fire grate and fill halfway with water. Put the cooking grill in place.

3) Place the brisket fat side up on the cooking grill, over the drip pan. (Whether or not you wrap the brisket in foil is up to you; some people do so for the entire cooking time, others don't wrap the brisket at all, and still others wrap it in foil only for the first half of the cooking time. Personally, I think the foil helps keep the meat moist.) Put top in place, leaving the bottom vent completely open and top vent about half open.

4) To maintain a low but constant temperature, add 10 more lit briquets to the grill, 5 on each side, every hour or so (see *Keeping the Fire Going*, page 34). If you choose not to wrap the brisket in foil, baste the meat each time you add more coals. The basting liquid can be anything you choose—flat beer flavored with a little chili powder, a mixture of equal parts vinegar and water, or a very dilute solution of barbecue sauce and water.

"...don't sauce the brisket while it's cooking. A dry rub is the preferred pretreatment; sauce is for putting on after you take the brisket off the grill."

5) When the brisket has reached the desired degree of doneness (it will be thoroughly cooked in 3 hours or so, but as I've said, some cooks leave briskets on the grill for as long as 10 hours), remove it from the grill and allow it to rest for about 15 minutes.

Slice at an angle, across the grain, into thin slices. Serve with your favorite barbecue sauce (for suggestions, see page 297), coleslaw (page 321), dill pickle slices, cold beer and the lowest-quality white bread you can find (see *A Cross Cultural Phenomenon*, page 149).

BEEF, GROUND

Something happens to many home cooks when it comes to grilling that all-time favorite, the hamburger. For some reason they buy quality ground beef (which is way too lean), make the patties way too thick and, forgetting that the meat shrinks alarmingly once cooked, they usually make them way too small. The result is almost always a piece of dry, shrunken, overcooked ground beef that in no way resembles that juicy, flopping-over-the-sides-of-the-bun burger of Wimpy's dreams.

To create a nice, juicy hamburger, forget the top-of-the-line ground round or sirloin; opt for the budget ground chuck instead. Look carefully at the diameter of the buns you intend to put the burgers on. As you shape the patties, make them about an inch larger in diameter to allow for shrinkage. And don't make them so thick! Take a lesson from the fast food joints: If someone wants a lot of beef, make a double or triple burger, but don't try to combine all that beef into one patty — it'll be the devil to cook without completely drying out. Make a patty more than ½-inch thick, and you're asking for trouble.

Cook the patties directly over a hot fire, with the cooking grill 5 or 6 inches above the coals. Do not, no matter how sorely you are tempted, press down on the hamburger patty with your spatula. You will lose valuable juices and start a conflagration in the process.

Grill for 2 minutes on the first side and 5 minutes on the second side for medium burgers. As a rule, don't turn more than once. If need be, don't be afraid to use the sharp edge of the spatula to gently cut into the burger to check how it's doing.

Warm liberally buttered buns on the grill, away from the fire. As you take the burgers off the grill, move the buns into position directly over the coals and watch them like a hawk. In just a few seconds they will be perfectly and deliciously toasted. (That butter makes for a memorable burger.) You know what to serve with the burgers.

"Take a lesson from the fast food joints: if someone wants a lot of beef, make a double or triple burger, but don't try to combine all that beef into one patty."

BEEF, HEARTS

There was a time when hearts and other "variety meats," as they are euphemistically called, were far more popular than they are today. Beef, veal, lamb and pork hearts can all be successfully grilled. All can be marinated, and all should be cooked rare; longer cooking will toughen the meat. Good marinades include teriyaki marinade (page 295) and red wine marinade (page 294). Beef hearts should be cut in about ½-inch-thick slices. If not marinated, brush the slices liberally with oil or melted butter. Cook directly over a hot fire, with the cooking grill 5 or 6 inches above the coals if you're using an adjustable model. The sliced hearts will be cooked rare in about 2 to 3 minutes per side, depending on their size. Serve with baked potatoes (page 317) or steamed parslied rice (page 337).

BEEF, RIBS

When I was a kid, these big, meaty beef ribs were always a special treat, not only because they were exceptionally flavorful, but because my parents called them "dinosaur bones." Very exotic fare for a ten-year-old.

Beef ribs are the same ones found on a standing rib roast. There are two ways to go about grilling them: Use the leftover ribs from a rib roast or, alternately, buy the ribs by themselves, straight from the butcher. You'll need to plan ahead if you're going to grill leftover ribs, and leave enough meat on the bones when you carve the roast — otherwise your grilled rib dinner will be pretty slim pickings. If you start with uncooked beef ribs, they can be prepared three ways:

Method 1 — Use a dry rub before grilling and serve a sauce with the ribs after they have been cooked. This method appeals to those who like that old-fashioned, traditional barbecue flavor. Try any of the dry rubs suggested on pages 309 to 310. Serve with your favorite bottled barbecue sauce or use one of the recipes found on pages 297 to 298.

Method 2 — Marinate the ribs ahead of time for 2 to 3 hours and then grill, basting with the leftover marinade. This works only for non-traditional barbecue marinades (basically, any marinade that isn't tomato-red in color). Try all-purpose marinade (page 289) or red wine marinade (page 294). Both produce very flavorful results, but *not* in the barbecue style. If you try to grill ribs (or any other meat) that have been marinated in a tomato-based sauce, it's almost impossible to keep the sauce from burning during the cooking process.

Method 3 — Grill the ribs without any seasoning until almost done, and then mop with a traditional barbecue sauce during the last 10 minutes or so on the grill. This method produces less intensely spiced ribs than the first method, but still with that old-timey flavor. The few minutes the coated ribs are on the grill allows the sauce to set and adhere, but avoids the problem of charring. Additional sauce can be heated and poured over the ribs at the table. Use your favorite bottled brand or one of the recipes given on pages 297 to 298.

Serve the ribs hot off the grill with grilled and filled potato skins (page 197) or grilled potato wedges (page 196) and a nice tossed salad or coleslaw (page 321).

Remove the ribs from the refrigerator about 30 minutes before cooking so they'll be at room temperature when they go on the grill.

If cooking over an open grill, ignite enough briquets to create a single layer a little larger than what the ribs will take up on the cooking grill. Wait until the coals die down to the moderate stage (see *How Hot is Hot,* page 39) before placing the ribs directly over the coals. The cooking grill should be 4 to 5 inches over the fire. Turn the ribs every 15 minutes or so. They should be done in 45 to 60 minutes.

On covered grills, use the indirect method (see page 42), with the briquets on both sides of the grate and a drip pan between the coals. When the coals are covered with a light gray ash, place the ribs on the cooking grill, directly over the drip pan. Put the lid in place and keep both top and bottom vents completely open. The ribs will be done in about 1 hour. Turn once, approximately halfway through the cooking time.

If you are grilling leftover beef rib bones, the procedure is quite different. Because the ribs have already been cooked, all you need to do is season them and then grill to the desired degree of crispness. The easiest method is to brush the cooked ribs with a little melted butter and place them directly over the coals, with the cooking grill

"Dinosaur bones" — *very exotic fare for a ten-year-old!*

about 5 to 6 inches above a hot fire. Cook for 5 minutes on each side, baste with your favorite barbecue sauce, and continue to grill for an additional 5 minutes per side. These ribs are so good they hardly qualify as leftovers; for some, the ribs are better eating than the roast itself.

BEEF, SHISH KABOB

Beef, cut into chunks and strung on skewers, is popular and delicious grilled fare, not to mention the fact that skewering is one of the easiest methods of preparation. Many different cuts of beef can be used. For information on how to grill skewered beef, see *Skewer Cooking* on page 56.

BEEF, SHORT RIBS

Short ribs, which come from the end of the beef ribs mentioned on page 82, have a reputation for being fatty They are also extremely flavorful. Younger cooks seem to think that the flavor of meat is in the meat itself. While that's true up to a point, it's the fat and the juices from bones that impart a great deal of flavor into the meat, a fact that gave rise to that old saying "the closer the bone, the sweeter the meat."

A long, slow cooking process will render virtually all of the fat away from any cut of meat. What's left, especially in the case of short ribs, is flavorful indeed. Short ribs can be made even more distinctive by marinating them first. Most people favor a traditional barbecue sauce. Use your favorite bottled sauce or follow the recipes on page 297 to 298. For something different, try hot fresh plum marinade (page 291), Mexican-style marinade (page 293) or red wine marinade (page 294). Marinate the ribs for 4 to 6 hours, or overnight in the refrigerator.

Side dishes for these savory morsels should be kept simple: big baked potatoes (page 317), with butter, sour cream and chives, of course; cowboy beans (page 321); grilled corn on the cob (page 118) and maybe a simple tossed salad. There's nothing subtle about a meal like

"Beef, cut into chunks and strung on skewers, is popular and delicious grilled fare, not to mention the fact that skewering is one of the easiest methods of preparation."

this, so why not go all out and finish off with big pieces of devil's food cake and let everyone just waddle home.

The long slow-cooking process good short ribs necessitates the use of a covered grill.

1) Remove short ribs from the refrigerator approximately 30 minutes before grilling.

2) Ignite approximately 40 to 50 briquets.

3) When the coals are covered with a light gray ash, separate them into equal amounts on opposite sides of the fire grate. Allow the coals to reach the moderate stage then place a disposable aluminum drip pan in the center of the fire grate and fill about halfway with water. Put cooking grill in place.

4) Arrange the short ribs on the cooking grill directly over the drip pan. Put lid in place. Leave bottom draft holes completely open; top draft holes about half open.

5) Turn the short ribs every 20 to 30 minutes. Total cooking time will be approximately 2 to 3 hours. Baste the short ribs with leftover marinade or sauce during the last 20 minutes of cooking time, if desired. Don't worry if the fire seems to be dwindling towards the end; a low and slow cooking process suits short ribs just fine. The ribs will be done when they are nicely browned and most all of the fat has been rendered away. Serve hot off the grill.

BEEF, STANDING RIB ROAST

Like whole roast turkeys, once you try a standing rib roast that's been cooked on a grill, you may never go back to cooking one in the oven again, no matter how special the occasion. And for very sound reasons: Not only does it relieve some of the activity in the kitchen, but experienced home cooks and professional chefs alike are quick to point out that cooking large joints of meat over open coals is truly *roasting*, whereas cooking a roast in the oven amounts to *baking* — an important distinction given the difference in the end results.

"...it's the fat and the juices from bones that carry a great deal of flavor into the meat, a fact that gave rise to that old saying 'the closer the bone, the sweeter the meat.'"

To roast a large cut of meat, you will need a covered grill or an open grill with a rotisserie attachment (see *Spit Cooking*, page 46). Either method produces similar, delicious results. Other than that, all that is needed is the best quality piece of beef you can find, a little freshly cracked pepper, and a disposable aluminum drip pan.

A whole standing rib roast has seven ribs — enough to feed the neighborhood — and is generally available only upon special request. Butchers, catering to today's smaller households, usually cut the standing rib roasts into smaller sections, between two and five ribs. Old-timers will tell you that the first three or four ribs of the standing rib roast are the best (which led to the name *prime ribs),* although this distinction seems to have been lost. If you're interested in leftovers (and who isn't?), plan on 1 pound (precooked weight) of meat for each person.

Serve with baked potatoes (page 317), galette of potatoes (page 323), grilled carrots (page 99), grilled onions (page 174) or grilled whole tomatoes (page 232). For some reason, spinach souffle goes well with this roast, and you can't make one any better than the one you find in the frozen food section of your grocery store. Give it a try. And while you're at the store, pick up a fresh jar of horseradish, which tends to lose its punch if it's been opened and stored in the refrigerator for too long. If you prefer a mild horseradish sauce, see the recipe on page 301.

1) Remove the roast from the refrigerator at least 30 minutes before cooking; dust with as much freshly cracked pepper as you desire.

2) Ignite approximately 55 to 65 charcoal briquets.

3) Once coals are covered with light gray ash, divide equally and push to opposite sides of the fire grate. Position a drip pan between the coals, in the middle of the fire grate. Put cooking grill in place.

4) Insert a meat thermometer into the center of the roast. Place roast on the middle of the cooking grate, directly over the drip pan. Put lid in place, leaving both top and bottom vents completely open.

"…experienced home cooks and professional chefs alike are quick to point out that cooking large joints of meat over open coals is truly roasting, whereas cooking a roast in the oven amounts to baking."

5) Length of cooking time will depend on the size of the roast, the conditions, and how well-done you want the meat. To cook the roast to medium, count on 15 to 20 minutes per pound for indirect cooking on a covered grill, and approximately 30 to 35 minutes per pound when spit-roasted. Best bet is to check the thermometer every 20 or 30 minutes, remembering that the internal temperature of the meat increases much faster towards the end of the cooking process.

6) Remove the roast when it is 5 to 10 degrees shy of the desired temperature (140 degrees F. for rare, 160 degrees F. for medium, and 170-180 degrees F. for well done). Transfer the roast to a cutting board, cover it loosely with foil and allow it to rest for 15 to 20 minutes.

7) Using a sharp carving knife, cut the bones away from the meat (save them, if desired, for barbecued beef ribs, page 79). Carve the meat into thick slices (American-cut) or thin (English-cut), as you and your guests prefer.

BEEF, STEAK

At some point during the past 40 years, a big, juicy steak cooked on the backyard grill came to symbolize the good life in America. That particular image may be changing with the times, but a grilled steak still makes for awfully good eating. There are some times, at least for me, when nothing else quite fits the bill. If you are only an occasional steak-eater, you might as well make it a great steak, right? Here's what to look for:

First off, a thick steak — at least an inch thick or thicker. An inch-and-a-half used to be considered ideal for most steaks. This may seem a little excessive by today's standards, but remember the old adage, "nothing succeeds like excess"? (The only exception to "the thicker the better" rule is when you're cooking up sirloin steaks for steak sandwiches — three-quarters of an inch thick is just fine for these.)

Second, the meat itself should be bright red and the fat, creamy white.

Third, look for meat with thin streaks of fat running through it, a sought-after trait known as "marbling."

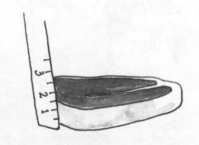

An inch-and-a-half used to be considered ideal for most steaks. This may seem a little excessive by today's standards, but remember the old adage, "nothing succeeds like excess"?

You can handily take care of all three of the above considerations simply by patronizing the best butcher shop in town. I figure if you don't patronize these places at least once in a while, they'll go the way of the Duesenberg. And then where will you be when you want that perfect tenderloin of beef for your Christmas Eve dinner?

A generation ago, it was common practice to buy very large, very thick (up to two or three inches thick) steaks and serve them in thin slices for a crowd. Favorite cuts for this method of presentation included porterhouse, strip, sirloin and chateaubriand. This may be a practice worth reviving, as long as you can get everyone to agree on how they like it cooked, although I admit I've long since stopped asking, and simply cook everyone's steak — individual or group — medium-rare. The slices are excellent served with Béarnaise sauce (page 298).

If the other members of your family aren't big steak fans and you are, wait until you're home alone some evening; steaks serve the single diner well, in both body and soul. These are special times when you can read a book while eating, pour on all the bottled steak sauce (or catsup) you want without fear of someone questioning your upbringing, and wash it all down with a good bottle of red that no one besides yourself would really appreciate anyway.

Finally, much could be said about the relative merits of one cut of steak over another. In the end, it's really a matter of personal preference, and nothing I could say here would make you believe that a rib eye steak was actually better than filet mignon. Steaks can, however, be divided into those that can (and should) be cooked without marinating, and those somewhat tougher cuts that benefit from tenderizing in one way or another.

Excellent marinades for steaks include all-purpose marinade (page 289), red wine marinade (page 294), and teriyaki marinade. Marinate the steaks for 2 to 4 hours.

Steaks for Cooking au Naturel
Club
Filet mignon
Kansas City
Loin

Flare-ups

Carol Truax is one of the most thoroughly delightful food writers ever to put her thoughts on paper. From The Cattleman's Steak Book (now out-of-print) comes this soigne method of dealing with flare-ups:

"A man, by tradition, fancies himself a fire-maker and outdoor chef. To ensure little or no trouble, you'd better lay the fire yourself and use briquets with some surefire spray or an electric lighter.

"…If you have a persistent male cook, provide him with asbestos gloves and a pair of tongs, NO FORK, so the steak won't get holes punched in it to let the juices run out. Don't admit it, but a woman or a moderately bright child of either sex can cook the steak, provided you tell him or her the exact number of minutes to cook the steak. Don't however let several cooks go to work at once.

"…Don't make a huge fire, and don't let the fire get too high. If there are blue flames, probably caused by drippings, put them out by sprinkling with a little water from a bottle, a meat baster or a water pistol you have borrowed from your moderately bright child. Lacking a child, you can drop a small piece of ice out of your martini on the offending flame."

New York
Porterhouse
Rib
Shell
Sirloin (may also be marinated)
Strip
T-Bone
Tenderloin

Steaks to Marinate Before Cooking
Chuck
Eye of round
Flank
Round
Sirloin
Skirt
Top round

Choose your favorite cut and serve it up with a big baked potato (page 317), pommes frites (page 331), or — if you're not trying to impress anyone except yourself — some crispy Tater-tots hot out of the oven, a green salad with a few crumbles of Roquefort cheese (remember, you're living it up), and whatever vegetable suits your fancy.

The following procedure works for plain steaks as well as those that have been marinated.

1) Take the steak out of the refrigerator about 30 minutes before grilling. It should be at room temperature when it goes over the fire.

2) Ignite enough coals to create a single layer a little larger than the steak or group of steaks you will be cooking. This could be anywhere from a dozen briquets in a hibachi for a single T-bone to 55 or 65 briquets for a half-dozen strip steaks.

3) Trim excess fat from the steaks, but leave ¼ inch or so to help keep the steak juicy. Use the trimmed fat to grease the hot grill before putting the steaks in place. If you haven't marinated the steaks, rub both sides of the meat with a little olive oil and dust with as much freshly ground pepper as desired. Press the pepper into the steak

"Choose your favorite cut and serve it up with a big baked potato (page 318), pommes frites (page 334) or — if you're not trying to impress anyone except yourself — some crispy Tater-tots hot out of the oven."

with the heel of your hand. To help retain the meat's juices, do not salt the steak.

4) Once the coals are covered with a light gray ash, arrange in a single layer, sides touching.

5) Set the cooking grill in place, 5 to 6 inches from the fire if you're using an adjustable model. Stick one of the trimmed pieces of fat on a long-handled fork and grease the cooking grill.

6) Place the steak directly over a hot fire. Generally speaking, it's best to turn the steaks only once — that's how you get a nicely seared exterior. If flames become a problem, squirt them with a squirt bottle filled with water (if you can manage to keep it from being stolen by a member of the junior set, a squirt gun works admirably for this purpose), or simply move the steak away from the coals for a moment or two.

7) The timing guidelines given at right are just that — *guidelines*. There are so many variables in grilling that it's difficult to put down hard and fast rules. Experience will eventually be the best guide of all, but lacking that, read over the guidelines — at least it's a starting point. In general, never leave the grill while cooking steaks; the minute or so you take running into the kitchen can make the difference between medium-rare and medium.

Over time you will develop your own means for telling when certain steaks are done. Two time-honored methods involve *pressing* the steaks — either with your finger or the backside of the tines of a long-handled fork. The latter makes you look like an old pro, but takes a little practice. Take my advice, start by using your finger.

The fundamentals of this method are as follows: A rare steak is soft to the touch; a well-done steak is tough, almost hard. All designations in between vary between the two extremes. Start by pressing your finger on an uncooked steak, just to feel how soft a completely raw steak is. Put the steak on the grill, sear for a couple of minutes on each side, then press down again, using your finger: this will be what a *very* rare steak feels like. Keep pressing the steaks every few minutes and you will see

Steak Cooking Times

Please remember, the following are only guidelines. All steaks (with the exception of very thick steaks, as noted below) should be cooked directly over a hot fire. The cooking grill should be about 3 to 5 inches above the coals.

To tell whether the fire is at the stage for cooking, hold your hand approximately one inch over the cooking grill and quickly spell out the word "Mississippi." If you can hold your hand in place without screaming, the fire is just right.

The following times are for cooking on an open grill. Although you can cook steaks on a covered grill with the lid on, I don't recommend it — it's just too easy to overcook them. Far better to just use the covered grill without the lid in place, and with the bottom vents completely open.

1-inch-thick steaks will take approximately 10 to 12 minutes to cook to the rare stage (5 to 6 minutes per side); 14 to 16 minutes for medium (7 to 8 minutes per side).

1½-inch-thick steaks will take approximately 12 to 14 minutes to cook to the rare stage (6 to 7 minutes per side); 18 to 20 minutes for medium (9 to 10 minutes per side).

2-inch-thick steaks should be cooked over moderate to hot coals. They will take approximately 16 to 20 minutes to cook to the rare stage (8 to 10 minutes per side); 24 to 30 minutes for medium (12 to 15 minutes per side).

A great steak begins to be less than great once it goes beyond the medium stage; the meat toughens and begins to dry out.

just how quickly it goes from one stage to another. If the steak doesn't spring back to the touch at all, you've got a piece of well-done shoe leather on your hands.

BEEF, STEAK, FLANK

It wasn't that long ago that butchers couldn't give flank steaks away. Today, with increased demand for lean cuts of meat and the rise of interest in stir-fry cooking (to which they are well-suited), flank steaks have become much more popular — and expensive.

In their favor, flank steaks are one of the tastiest cuts of beef, take well to marinades (owing to their large surface area), and cook up in a hurry. Without the tenderizing effect of a marinade, however, flank steaks can be tough. Almost any marinade is appropriate; some of the best include all-purpose marinade (page 289), Mexican-style marinade (page 293), red wine marinade (page 294), teriyaki marinade (page 295), or *A Secret Sauce* (page 89). Marinate for 2 to 4 hours. While you're at it, you might as well marinate and cook an extra one; flank steak has an alarming habit of disappearing off the cutting board, slice by slice, before it ever gets to the table. And it's excellent cold the next day for sandwiches.

Classic side dishes include baked potatoes (page 317), cowboy beans (page 321), galette of potatoes (page 323) and home-alone beans (page 325).

Because the cooking time is so short, and the cut so even in thickness, flank steaks are best cooked directly over the coals. On adjustable grills, position the grate about 4 to 5 inches above the coals. If you don't have a an adjustable grill, make up for the fact that the coals are so far away from the cooking grate by using the cover while cooking. Both methods work perfectly well.

1) Remove the flank steak from the refrigerator approximately 30 minutes before grilling and allow it to come to room temperature.

2) Ignite approximately 40 to 50 briquets (enough so when spread out, the surface area is a little larger than the steak itself). Once the coals are covered with a fine gray ash, spread them in an even, single layer.

When carving a thick steak, keep your knife at a 45-degree angle, a process known as cutting on the bias.

3) Position the flank steak on the grill directly over a hot fire, and spoon a little of the marinade on the meat. For covered grills, put the lid in place, leaving both top and bottom vents completely open.

4) After 5 minutes, turn the flank steak and spoon additional marinade over the top. Cover the grill and cook for 5 additional minutes for rare; 7 to 8 minutes for medium-rare. If you prefer your meat well-done, turn the steak again, and cook an additional 3 to 5 minutes.

5) Take the steak off the grill and allow it to rest for 5 or 10 minutes on a cutting board — one that won't let the valuable juices get away. (Now's the time to put that auxiliary steak on the grill.)

6) Using a sharp knife, carve the flank steak into thin slices, starting from one of the short sides of the meat. Keep the knife at a 45-degree angle, a process known as cutting on the bias (see illustration on page 88).

BEEF, TENDERLOIN

I've roasted any number of these elegant cuts of beef on a covered kettle grill; they also cook up beautifully on a rotisserie (see *Spit Cooking*, page 46). A whole tenderloin usually runs five to six pounds, enough to feed ten to twelve people. There is nothing simpler to cook on the grill, and few things more impressive. Next time the occasion calls for something special, try a tenderloin and sit back and relax while it cooks.

While several marinades are well-suited to beef, I'm not convinced that a tenderloin really needs any marinade. If you decide otherwise, consider all-purpose marinade (page 289) or red wine marinade (page 294). I have settled on simply rubbing the tenderloin with olive oil, maybe inserting a few slivers of garlic here and there into the meat, and dusting well with freshly cracked pepper.

With the emphasis on lean these days, most butchers are quick to cut away almost all of the fat on a tenderloin of beef. Because we have these roasts so infrequently, I want them to be as flavorful and moist as possible, so I

A Secret Sauce

Every once in a while, you run across something that really deserves wider recognition. A couple of years ago, I received a bottle of "Dale's Steak Seasoning" in the mail. I had never seen the product before. It looked very dark and, when I opened it, smelled very intense. I put it on the shelf and didn't think about it for a while.

I have no idea what the conditions were that finally led to my pulling it off the shelf and using it on a flank steak (I think), but I've been hooked on it ever since. The label advises some caution in the amount you use and the length of time you let the meat sit in the liquid. I took the caution seriously, and simply brushed it on with a basting brush — liberally, mind you, but definitely not the same amount you would use as a marinade. I let the steak sit for about 30 minutes at room temperature, and then covered the steak with a fair amount of coarsely ground, fresh black pepper. I've been following the same procedure for a wide variety of steaks ever since. Couldn't be any simpler or more delicious.

The recipe for Dale's Steak Seasoning was given to the late Jake Levine by a Korean woman while Jake was stationed in Hawaii during World War II. He returned to Birmingham, Alabama, after the war, and started producing the sauce. Jake's son, Michael, continues the tradition today.

If you can't find Dale's Steak Seasoning locally, write: Dale's Sauces, P.O. Box 130684, Birmingham, Alabama 35213. Or call (205) 833-6330. Dale's will ship full cases (twelve 16-oz. bottles) anywhere via UPS.

"I have settled on simply rubbing the tenderloin with olive oil, maybe inserting a few slivers of garlic here and there into the meat, and dusting well with freshly cracked pepper."

ask my butcher to add an extra layer of fat and tie it in place, a practice known as barding (tying fat to one side of the roast; start grilling fat side up). After cooking, the additional fat can simply be thrown away, but it adds a great deal of flavor to the finished product.

Excellent side dishes include whole grilled tomatoes (page 232) and galette of potatoes (page 323). Those two are so good with the beef that I'm going to leave the suggestions at that. If desired, mix up a little horseradish sauce (page 301) or the classic, Béarnaise sauce (page 298). A nice tossed salad, a distinguished red wine, and you're ready to serve the most discerning of guests.

1) Remove the roast from the refrigerator about 30 minutes before grilling; dust with freshly cracked pepper. Insert slivers of fresh garlic into the roast here and there, if desired.

2) Ignite approximately 55 to 65 charcoal briquets.

3) Once coals are covered with light gray ash, arrange them in one of the following ways, depending on the type of grill you're using:

For covered grills, divide the coals equally and push them to opposite sides of the fire grill. Position a drip pan between the coals, in the middle of the fire grate, and put the cooking grill in place.

For uncovered grills, arrange the coals in a single layer, sides touching.

4) On adjustable grills, position the cooking grate 4 to 5 inches above the coals.

5) Insert a meat thermometer into the thickest part of the roast, so the face of thermometer is looking out from the short, thick end of the meat.

6) On covered grills, begin by putting the roast directly over the coals and searing it on all sides, a process that takes 5 to 10 minutes. If you had extra fat put on the roast, don't let a fire erupt and burn the outside of the meat. The point is to produce a nice, brown exterior and seal in the juices. Once the roast has been seared, place it on the middle of the cooking grill, directly over the drip

pan. Put the lid in place, leaving both top and bottom vents completely open.

For uncovered grills, wait until the coals reach the moderate stage and simply place the roast on the cooking grill directly over the fire. Turn every 10 to 12 minutes.

7) Length of cooking time will depend on the size of the roast, the conditions, and how well-done you want the meat. Begin checking the thermometer after about 30 minutes, remembering that the internal temperature of the meat increases much faster towards the end of the cooking process than it does in the beginning.

8) Remove the roast when it is 5 to 10 degrees shy of the desired temperature (140 degrees F. for rare or 160 degrees F. for medium). Transfer it to a cutting board (one that will catch the juices), cover loosely with foil, and allow it to rest for 10 to 15 minutes. You can carve the meat into slices 1 inch to 1½ inches thick and serve like individual filet mignon steaks, or into thin slices — whichever way you and your guests prefer.

BELGIAN ENDIVE

Belgian endive has many aliases, but it is most commonly sold under the simple name of endive. It is surprisingly good grilled. See Endive on page 130.

BELL PEPPERS

There has been a veritable explosion of interest in all kinds of peppers in the last few years. The familiar green bell pepper has been joined by a host of other family members: yellow ones, red ones — even purple and chocolate brown ones, skinny ones, long ones, fat ones, big ones and little ones. The diversity of colors and shapes is matched by differences in flavor, from mildly pungent to atomic-powered.

The smaller, hot to very hot chili peppers are rarely grilled, being best used fresh. The larger, milder peppers, whatever the color, are great grilled. To do so, wash the

"The smaller, hot to very hot chili peppers are rarely grilled, being best used fresh. The larger, milder peppers, whatever the color, are great grilled."

peppers, core and seed them, and then slice in whatever way suits your taste. If the slices are small, string them on a skewer before grilling. Brush with a little oil or a marinade that contains oil. Grill the peppers directly over moderately hot coals. If the coals are still at the very hot stage, cook them just at the edge of the fire. Try not to char the peppers; the point is to heat them through until they wilt a bit. Take the peppers off the grill while they still have a little crunch to them.

Take advantage of the variety of colors available and grill green, red, orange and yellow peppers at the same time. The expensive, dark purple peppers turn a rather common shade of green once they are heated through. Peppers of assorted colors make a beautiful display on any plate. Some cooks put the grilled peppers in a bowl just before serving and toss with a little good quality olive oil, a dash of balsamic vinegar, salt to taste and maybe a little chopped fresh herbs, such as basil, thyme or oregano. Very good eating!

If your intent is to roast and peel peppers, put whole peppers right over a very hot fire and turn until all sides are completely charred. Put the charred peppers in a double (or triple) thick paper bag, twist the top closed, and let them sweat for 10 minutes or so.

Using a small sharp knife, remove the stem end and peel the charred skins away from the peppers. Slice into thin strips, scrape off the seeds and prepare, as above, with a little olive oil and vinegar. These are superb, simply mounded on top of crusty pieces of French bread, or on grilled French bread (page 95) spread with a little grilled goat cheese (page 100) — an hors d'oeuvre that many would just as soon have as a main course.

Bison

Much leaner and with three to four times less cholesterol than beef, bison has found favor with those who have been told to cut back on their consumption of red meat. Because it is so lean, bison needs special handling on the grill. Large cuts, like roasts, are better cooked on the stove using a moist-heat method, as you would a pot roast. Ground bison and steaks can be successfully grilled, as long as you don't overcook them.

Bison is so popular that demand often outstrips supply, which, in turn, makes bison very expensive.

The best advice for bison steaks is to sear them very quickly on both sides and then finish grilling at a lower temperature than you would beef steaks. On adjustable grills, raise the cooking grill until it's about 6 inches away from the coals; on covered grills, move the steaks away from the coals after searing, and finish cooking using the indirect method with the lid in place.

Bison burgers don't need to be seared first, but, like bison steaks, they should be cooked over lower heat than what you would use for beef.

Once the bison is on the grill, watch it carefully. With such a low fat content, the meat can quickly go from juicy to dry. Because bison's real claim to fame is its good flavor and low fat and cholesterol levels, it doesn't make much sense to marinate it before grilling, or to serve it with a rich sauce.

BLUE CRAB

The blue crab is native to the south Atlantic coast and the Gulf of Mexico. This is the crab that sheds its shell when it finds the old one too tight. During the short period of time before the new shell hardens, blue crab becomes the prized "soft-shelled" crab — surprisingly good grilled. For more information, see Soft-shelled crab, page 220.

BLUEFIN

Bluefin is a member of the tuna family, which also includes albacore, bonito and yellowfin. All types are excellent on the grill and are cooked in virtually the same way. For grilling instructions, see Albacore, page 66.

BOAR

Only three areas of the country play host to wild boar: the Ozarks, northern California coastal areas, and the Southwest. The Ozark variety is domesticated pig turned wild after more than a century of freedom; the California boar is the real McCoy — European wild boar

"…the California boar is the real McCoy — European wild boar escapees, originally imported many years ago to stock a private reserve."

escapees, originally imported many years ago to stock a private reserve. The Southwest is home of to animal known as the javelina or peccary, technically a wild pig.

If you are lucky enough to come home with any of these wild pigs, they all make for fine eating, but are so lean that individual cuts fare poorly on a charcoal grill. All are excellent prepared whole and cooked on a spit (see page 46).

BOLINA

Bolina is a member of the large Pacific rockfish family. It is considered the best of the lot. For grilling instructions, see Rockfish, page 207.

BOLOGNA

I don't know that I'd serve it to a visiting head of state, nor would I make a main course out of it, but for *puu-puus* (Hawaiian for hors d'oeuvres), it's not bad. Don't mess with those skinny presliced pieces; opt instead for the bologna the butcher sells and cut it yourself into about three-quarter-inch slices. Grill the bologna right over the coals until it starts to sizzle at the edges. Remove the bologna from the grill, cut it into small wedges, then drop it onto waiting saltine crackers (with a squirt of mustard, if you like). Hand it out to the kids to stave off the hungries. As soon as the kids have run off again, make a couple for yourself. Not half bad with a sundowner.

BONITO

Bonito (also called bonita) is just one of the members of the tuna family, which also includes albacore, yellowfin and bluefin. When raw, bonito is even darker in color than albacore, but like albacore, once you put it on the grill, the flesh becomes much lighter and quite firm. Cooking methods for all members of the tuna family are virtually the same. For grilling instructions, see Albacore, page 66.

BREAD

Anyone who doesn't occasionally grill up some thick slices of good bread is missing out on one of life's major pleasures. The trick is to start with either homemade bread or a good quality, crusty, toothsome, Italian or French loaf. Cut it into slices between ¾ to 1 inch thick, and place on the grill. If you put it directly over the coals on an open grill, watch carefully so the bread toasts rather than burns — usually less than one minute per side.

If you're using a covered grill, timing is not quite as critical. Place the bread at the edges of the grill, away from the fire, and put lid in place. Check frequently and remove when lightly toasted on both sides. The goal is not to dry the bread out, but to get a crisp exterior and a moist, warm, fragrant interior. If you want to go over the top, try the bruschetta, at right. When they said "a loaf of bread, a jug of wine and thou," this is the bread they were talking about.

BRILL

Brill is another name for the highly esteemed petrale sole. Ranging in size from one to five pounds, the smaller petrale sole are the ones you want to grill. See Sole, page 221.

BUFFALO

You say buffalo and I say bison…actually the term buffalo legitimately applies to any number of animals, while bison is the brute of the American plains. Whatever you choose to call it, American bison is increasing in popularity every year. To find out why, see Bison, on page 92.

The hybrid "beefalo," which made quite a splash a few years back, seems to have all but disappeared. Some sources claimed the herds are being built up again; others said there weren't enough takers for the hybrids, and production dwindled.

Bruschetta

I may be all wet, but for my tastes, one of the most satisfying things to grill over an open fire is bread — as long as it's good bread — a dense, crusty loaf made in the Italian or French style. A good, rustic loaf of homemade (or store-bought, if it's available) sourdough bread ranks right near the top, as well.

In Italy, where they know all about these simple pleasures, bread, toasted, with the addition of olive oil and garlic, is known as bruschetta (or bruschette). The bread is cut about 1 inch thick, grilled until lightly toasted (the inside should still be soft and chewy), rubbed with a cut clove of fresh garlic and drizzled with the best olive oil you can find.

As good as it is with just olive oil and garlic, you can embellish bruschetta with fresh slices of vine-ripened tomatoes, thin slivers of Parmesan cheese (Reggiano is the name to look for when buying Parmesan), or slices of fresh mozzarella, tomato and a few leaves of fresh basil. This is so good, you may forget about dinner.

C

CABEZON

Those who fish commercially rarely go looking for cabezon, but people who angle for the fun of it love this ugly creature. It's great fun to catch, and good to eat, as well. Although the angler fish is uglier (see page 68), there are many similarities between the two. Both have a low fat content, and mild, fairly firm flesh.

Most fish with a low fat content are a little difficult to handle on the grill. The fact that cabezon is relatively firm helps, as does marinating it for about 30 minutes in a marinade that includes oil.

Cut the cabezon into fillets or steaks before marinating. Try Southeast Asia-style marinade (page 294), teriyaki marinade (page 295), or simply brush with vegetable oil, sprinkle with paprika and serve the cooked fish with fresh lemon wedges and a little chopped parsley. If it's a special dinner, consider grilling cabezon plain (oiled and dusted with paprika) and serve with the elegant beurre blanc sauce (page 300), flavored with your favorite fresh herb.

A simple side dish of boiled new potatoes (page 320), steamed parslied rice (page 337), or a galette of potatoes (page 323) goes well with the flavor of cabezon. Any steamed, fresh vegetable would be appropriate.

1) Take the cabezon out of the refrigerator about 30 minutes before cooking. The fish should be at room temperature when it goes on the grill.

2) Make a bed of coals (or lump charcoal) that's a little larger in size than what the fish will take up on the grill, and ignite. Fish will stick to a cold grill, so put the cooking grill in place and allow it to become good and hot. Clean the grate, using a wire brush, and coat it with vegetable oil just before you're ready to cook the fish.

"Those who fish commercially rarely go looking for cabezon, but people who angle for the fun of it love this ugly creature. It's great fun to catch, and good to eat, as well."

3) Cook the fish directly over a bed of hot coals. If the fillets have the skin intact, put them on the grill skin side first. Cook for 10 minutes per inch of thickness, measuring at the thickest part. Turn the fish only once. Don't put the cover down on a covered grill.

4) This entrée should be served hot off the grill — within seconds, if possible — so have everything else ready to go before putting the fish on the grill. Serve the cabezon on a platter that has been heated for 15 minutes in a 250-degree F. oven.

See Fish, page 133, for more information.

CALAMARI

Around the Mediterranean, where they really know how to cook it, squid goes by some variation of the name calamari: kalamari, calmar, calamaro and calamar, depending on what country you happen to be in. Calamari is also the name you'll find squid listed as on most restaurant menus. But a squid is still a squid, no matter how unappealing the name may be. For more information, see Squid, page 224.

CAPON

This young, neutered rooster used to be considered the paragon of fine poultry. Weighing in at a formidable eight to twelve pounds with a disproportionately large breast, well-fatted flesh, and good flavor from its diet of corn, a roasted capon proudly graced many a Sunday table just a generation or so ago.

Unless you're lucky enough to have a specialty poultry shop in your area, you are most likely to find today's capons in the frozen food department of your local supermarket. If at all possible, search out a fresh bird; if not, a frozen one will do.

Serve with grilled and filled potato skins (page 197) or garlic mashed potatoes (page 324) and sautéed peas

Around the Mediterranean, where it's frequently grilled, squid goes by some variation of the name calamari: kalamari, calmar, calamaro or calamar.

Poultry Lacers

Although it's not necessary to truss any bird for the grill, it certainly makes for a neater package. The method outlined on page 243 is the traditional method, but the little wires you can buy in any variety or grocery store are a quick substitute. They are particularly handy for stuffed birds, as they make sure the stuffing stays put.

After stuffing, thread the wires across the opening; cut a 24-inch-long piece of cotton twine and lace back and forth as shown in the illustration; pull tight and knot.

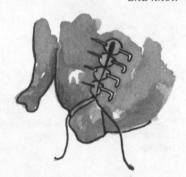

with lettuce (page 336). Chill a bottle of one of those big California chardonnays, or their elegant uncles from France, a Mersault or Montrachet. This is the type of eating that could put you in a time warp, and a very pleasant time at that. Cold leftover capon makes sliced chicken sandwiches the likes of which Dagwood's midnight dreams are made.

If you have a rotisserie attachment for your grill, roast the capon on the spit (see *Spit Cooking,* page 46) so you can baste it frequently as it turns, to produce a tender, beautifully brown bird. Lacking a rotisserie, roast the capon in a covered kettle grill; it will turn out equally delicious.

1) Remove the capon from the refrigerator 30 minutes before grilling.

2) Ignite approximately 55 to 65 briquets or an equal amount of lump charcoal.

3) Thoroughly wash the capon in cold water; pat dry using a towel. Truss (see *To Truss or Not to Truss,* page 243), or simply tuck the wings under the back and tie the legs together using a piece of cotton string. Place the bird in a baking pan or a disposable aluminum pan.

4) Rub the capon with softened butter or olive oil. Sprinkle with salt, pepper and a little poultry seasoning or the herb mixture known as herbes de Provence (available at most well-stocked grocery stores). Insert meat thermometer into the thickest part of the thigh, without hitting the bone.

5) When coals are covered with a gray ash, push equal amounts to opposite sides of the fire grate. Replace cooking grill and place roasting pan and capon in the middle of the grill. Cover, leaving both top and bottom vents completely open.

6) After about 1 hour, begin checking the temperature. Depending on the size of the bird, it can be done in anywhere from 1½ to 2½ hours, when the thermometer registers 175 to 180 degrees F. (Remember, the temperature increases much faster towards the end of the cooking

time than it does in the beginning.) When done, remove the bird from the grill, place it on a carving board or platter and cover with a foil tent. Allow to rest for about 15 minutes.

7) Carve the capon at the table or serve already cut, using the easy dismantling method described on page 102.

After everything a capon has been through, you should really honor it by making a simple sauce. The Classic Sauce for Poultry, found on page 112, is delicious and easy — it's made right in the roasting pan.

CAPRETTO

Any goat that you'd want to grill is going to be young and correctly called "kid." It's rather horrifying, however, to say, "I'm grilling a kid tonight." Although the Italian name *capretto* sounds much more appetizing, "Goat" is where you'll find some additional information (see page 140). There you will be referred to *Spit Cooking*, page 46, because that's the best way to grill a goat. It's a circuitous route, but it will be outstanding once you get to the end results.

CARROTS

When was the last time you thought about putting a carrot on the grill? I'll admit to being a little skeptical at first, but I can tell you with confidence that they are absolutely delicious, cooked whole over the coals. I've yet to serve them to anyone who hasn't thought they were great. It seems that the earthy flavor of any vegetable that spends its formative years underground is particularly well suited to the rustic, slightly smoky flavors imparted by charcoal grilling. Consider cooking potatoes, carrots and onions at the same time as any big roast, just like you would in the oven. I think you'll like the results.

Those big fat carrots you find in the wintertime are great for boiling or steaming, but favor the skinnier

Did You Hear the One About…

Henrietta lived in a hen house with a lot of her hen friends. But Henrietta was not content with her life, and frequently spoke of breaking out. She was especially keen on paying a visit to the roosters nearby. Henrietta's friends advised against such action, but Henrietta was determined.

One night, Henrietta dug a tunnel out of the hen house, all the way over to the rooster pens. She was gone all night.

Henrietta made it back to the henhouse just before dawn the next morning. Her friends were shocked at her appearance: ruffled feathers, dark circles under her eyes and a vacant expression.

"What happened? What was it like?" they anxiously asked.

"Wouldn't you know," Henrietta replied, "the other end of the tunnel came up in a capon's cage, and he kept me up all night telling me about his operation!"

"Those big fat carrots you find in the wintertime are great for boiling or steaming, but favor the skinny young carrots for grilling."

young carrots for grilling. Forget peeling them; simply use a plastic scouring pad and scrub them briskly under cold water. Keep them in a bowl of cold water until it's time to put them on the grill. Depending on how hefty they are, the carrots will probably take at least 15 to 20 minutes to cook; longer if they are large. Place them directly on the grill, at the edges of the fire, but not directly over the coals. Baste with butter or olive oil during the cooking process.

Because you're the cook, it's perfectly legitimate to take a taste test now and then, but don't let anyone else, or there won't be any for supper. Take the carrots off the grill while they still have some "tooth" to them.

CHEESE

Other than the cheese you put on "cheesy-burgers," it's very difficult to cook cheese directly on a charcoal grill. The only kinds that can be grilled with any success are chevres (either domestic or imported goat cheeses), and then only when they're fairly firm and dry. Make no mistake about it, grilled goat cheeses are superb, but they are also very tricky to handle.

Grilling cheese is not a maneuver for the faint at heart. Summon up all your confidence and just do it. It will be worth the effort.

Start by marinating a whole "log" of chevre in a good-quality olive oil, freshly ground pepper and maybe a sprinkling of dry oregano. Turn it over several times to make sure it is well-coated in oil. Next, dip the cheese into finely ground, dry bread crumbs, then back for a dunk in the oil. Although it's not absolutely necessary, you may find the cheese easier to handle on the grill if you refrigerate it at this stage for at least 30 to 45 minutes.

Place the cheese on on an oiled grill, directly over a hot fire. The point is to simply heat the cheese and brand it with those telltale grill marks, a process that should take no more than 5 or 6 minutes. Watch it carefully; as it heats up, the cheese will want to melt through the grill. Before this can happen, roll the cheese along the grill, keeping it directly over the fire, using an oiled spatula. Cook for another minute or so.

Have the marinade platter at the ready. Take the cheese off the grill as quickly as you can. Serve as an hors d'oeuvre with crusty French bread (perhaps toasted on the grill) and a bowl of good Mediterranean olives or sprinkle chunks of the cheese atop a simple salad at the end of the meal. This is a messy, anxiety-producing process, but it results in very good eating.

CHICKEN, BREAST
(Bone and Skin Intact)

Chicken breasts were made for the charcoal grill. Cooked with the skin on and the bone in gives the delicate white breast meat a little more flavor and succulence than those that have been skinned and boned. Given enough time, chicken breasts will absorb seasonings and flavors admirably: plan on a 6- to 8- hour soak in a marinade, or about 3 to 4 hours for the flavors contained in a dry rub to penetrate.

Virtually any of the marinades or dry rubs described on pages 289 to 310 can be used with chicken breasts — it simply depends on the mood you're in. A few of the all-time favorite marinades include Dijon marinade (page 289), Greek marinade (page 290), or pesto marinade (page 293). The versatility of chicken also applies to side dishes (see pages 316 to 338 for recipes).

1) Marinate the breasts for 6 to 8 hours before grilling time, or the night before. About 30 minutes before cooking, remove the breasts from the refrigerator and allow them to come to room temperature. If using a dry rub, start the process 3 to 4 hours ahead of grilling time.

2) Ignite approximately 40 to 50 briquets. When the coals are covered with light gray ash, push them into the center of the fire grate, creating an even layer. If you're using an adjustable grill, position the cooking grill 5 to 6 inches above the fire.

3) On covered kettle grills, place the breasts, skin side up, on the cooking grill in a circle around the coals — not directly over them. Cover the grill, leaving both top and

Chicken — What's in a Name?

When it comes to chickens, it's a good idea to know the differences between the types and ask for what you want by name. You'll produce a better meal if you use the chicken best-suited to the method of preparation you have in mind. Generally speaking, the younger the chicken, the better they are for the grill. The categories are as follows:

Poussin: 1 to 1½ pounds, approximately 35 days old. Essentially a baby chicken; used to be known as "spring chicken."

Broiler: Up to 2 pounds, approximately 40 days old. Not generally available, except by special order.

Fryer: 2 to 4 pounds, approximately 45 days old. Most chickens sold cut up in "family packs" (or as they are called here in the midwest, "Pick of the Chick"), are fryers.

Young Roaster: 4 to 5 pounds, approximately 48 days old. Usually sold whole.
Roaster: 5 to 8 pounds, approximately 60 days old. Sold whole.

Stewing/Baking Hens: 3½ to 5 pounds, approximately 14 months old. In the old days, these used to be old laying-hens, but the modern laying hen is such a scrawny breed, it would never make it in the consumer market. Today's stewing hen is the parent of a broiler, usually sold whole.

Capon: 8 to 12 pounds, approximately 75 days old. Surgically neutered male chicken, prized for its disproportion-ately large breast. Roosters used to become capons through the unwitting ingestion of hormones, a practice today considered unlawful, not to mention…well, not to mention.

Free-range Chickens: Chickens raised the old-fashioned way, as opposed to being mass-produced in chicken "factories." (See Meet Rocky Jr. and Sr. on page 109.)

Poultry Dismantling

Poultry dismantling is just that: taking apart the pieces. Although there's nothing elegant about it, it results in a platterful of perfectly carved meat pieces. Just be sure to do it in the kitchen.

Start on one side and cut the wing from the body through the joint. This isn't hard if you actually pull up on one end of the wing as far as you can; the joint will become very apparent. Do the same for the leg and thigh: pull out on the leg so the thigh separates a bit from the body. Cut through the joint, where the thigh bone meets the body of the bird. That done, cut through where the leg meets the thigh. Repeat this process for the other side of the bird.

There's nothing to cutting the entire breast away from the carcass once the other pieces have been removed. Start by pressing the knife up against the breastbone, gradually tilting the knife out as it meets the rib cage.

Place the breast skin-side up on a cutting board and cut into slices against the grain, starting at either of the short ends. Cut what meat you can from the leg, thigh and wings or place them intact on a platter with the sliced breast meat and let people gnaw to their hearts' content.

bottom vents completely open. On uncovered grills, place the breasts directly over the coals, skin side up.

4) Total cooking time will be approximately 20 to 24 minutes. Start by cooking the breasts, skin side up, for 7 minutes, then turn. If you're cooking in a covered kettle, keep the breasts in approximately the same position after turning, away from the coals. On an open grill, watch for flare-ups once the skin side is down; move breasts away from the flames if the heat becomes too intense.

5) Cook for an additional 7 minutes and turn again, but this time, if you are cooking in a covered kettle grill, place the breasts directly over the coals.

6) Cook for another 3 to 5 minutes. Turn again (the breasts will be skin side down now), and cook for a final 3 to 5 minutes. At this point, the skin side should be a golden brown — not *burned* — especially if you are using a covered kettle grill. If you're concerned about the degree of doneness, remove one from the grill, make a neat incision with the tip of a sharp knife into the thickest part of the meat. It should be opaque white to the bone, without a trace of pink.

CHICKEN BREAST
(Boneless and Skinless)

Boned chicken breasts are now widely available at most large markets. Shoppers pay a premium for this convenience, but it sure saves time when you're in a hurry. Without the bones or skin, the breasts cook very quickly, which is another way of saying, if you don't watch them carefully, they will dry out in a hurry.

There are three basic ways to prepare boneless chicken breasts: as they come from the package, cut into chunks or strips and grilled on skewers, or pounded flat (to about ⅛-inch thick), creating what the French call a *paillard* (see *Pounding Paillards* at right). The first two methods require 10 to 12 minutes grilling time; the paillards cook faster than you can say *"êtes-vous sûr que ce type sache vraiment ce qu'il raconte?"*

Because there isn't anything to interfere with absorption, boneless and skinless chicken breasts readily absorb the flavors of a marinade or dry rub. One hour at room temperature in either is plenty; any longer, and the acidic component of the marinade (wine, lemon juice or vinegar) will begin to break down the fibers of the chicken, producing mushy breasts — definitely to be avoided.

Whole or skewered, these tender morsels lend themselves to any of the marinades or dry rubs described on pages 289 to 311. Particularly pleasing are the Asian-inspired recipes, such as fresh ginger-garlic marinade (page 290), lime-garlic marinade (page 292), and Southeast Asia-style marinade (page 294).

Paillards need only to be brushed with oil, dusted with salt and pepper, and served with a light, elegant sauce, such as beurre blanc (page 300), napped, as they say, over the top. Virtually any of the side dishes on pages 316 to 338 will provide a nice accompaniment to grilled chicken breasts.

Because they are so small, boneless and skinless chicken breasts can easily be cooked over one of those little hibachis; covered kettle and open grills also work fine. If you're cooking the breasts on skewers, please read the short section on *Skewer Cooking*, found on page 56.

1) Ignite 40 to 50 briquets, not more than necessary to create a bed of coals about the same size as what you will be cooking.

2) Once the coals are covered with a light gray ash, spread them out to create an even layer, sides just touching. Put the cooking grill in place and allow to heat for a few minutes.

3) Just before grilling, brush the breasts liberally with vegetable or olive oil — even if you have marinated the breasts in a mixture that contains oil. Place breasts or skewers directly over the coals. If you're using a covered kettle grill, put the top on, leaving both top and bottom vents completely open. Cook for 5 minutes.

4) Turn carefully, using a pair of tongs or a thin-bladed spatula (the breasts have a tendency to stick) and cook for

Pounding Paillards

Paillards — flattened, very thin pieces of boneless meat — fall into the "luncheon" category. They can be formed from beef, veal, pork, lamb or chicken. I'm not quite sure why, but to me, the process seems far more suited to chicken and veal than to beef or pork. Be that as it may, paillards cook up in an instant over a hot grill, and must be well-moistened with melted butter or vegetable oil (even if they've been marinated in a mixture that includes oil) so as not to stick to the grill. Drizzled with a light sauce, paillards are elegant, and especially attractive to those watching their weight.

To form a paillard from a chicken breast, start with half of a breast, with the small muscle (the one with the white ligament in it) removed. Put the breast between two sheets of oiled waxed paper or plastic. Pound evenly with a mallet (don't tell anyone, but a certain member of my household has actually been known to use a croquet mallet — which is not the kind of mallet being referred to here) or the side of a wide cleaver. Pound until the breast is about 1/8- to 3/16-inch thick.

If you want, the paillards can be marinated after flattening. Because they are almost all surface area, 20 to 30 minutes in the marinade is all that's necessary. Suitable marinades can be found at left, in the entry for boneless chicken breasts. Cooking time will be approximately one minute per side.

How's that for fast food?

5 additional minutes, at which point the breasts should be done.

Note: If you're cooking paillards, simply lay them on the grill directly over the coals, and cook for about 45 seconds to 1 minute on each side, depending on the heat of the fire. To turn them, you'll almost definitely need a thin-bladed spatula.

CHICKEN, GIZZARDS

My old Webster's defines gizzard as "the muscular enlargement of the alimentary canal of birds…has unusually thick muscular walls and a tough horny lining for grinding the food." In other words, if a chicken had a stomach, the gizzard would be it. Gizzards are generally included in the little packet inside a whole chicken (along with its neck, heart and liver). In larger markets, chicken gizzards are sold packaged, often in combination with chicken hearts. However, if you want to grill gizzards in any amount, you may have to ask your butcher to procure them for you.

The gizzard's tough outer membrane can either be trimmed off using a small, sharp knife or softened by parboiling in water for about 5 minutes. (Trimming more than a few gizzards is tedious work; I opt for parboiling.) After that, the gizzards should be marinated for at least 2 hours, strung on skewers and grilled. They can handle a strong-flavored marinade; try red wine marinade, page 294.

1) Parboil the gizzards in salted water for a few minutes. Drain and allow the gizzards to cool before marinating them for 2 to 4 hours.

2) Ignite approximately 25 to 35 briquets, depending on how many skewers you will be grilling. Once the coals are covered with a fine gray ash, spread them into an even layer. On adjustable grills, position the cooking grill about 3 to 4 inches from the fire.

3) Thread the gizzards on small bamboo skewers and

Particularly pleasing, when preparing chicken for the grill, are the Asian-inspired marinades, such as fresh ginger-garlic (page 290).

brush them with vegetable oil. Grill directly over a hot fire, for 2 to 3 minutes on each side. On covered kettle grills, cook with the lid on, and leave both top and bottom vents completely open. Cooking time will be approximately the same using a covered or open grill.

CHICKEN, GROUND

The first time I grilled ground "chicken burgers," I did so for a couple of 11-year-olds, figuring they'd be the toughest critics. They came back for seconds, and the one remaining patty was quickly cut up and devoured by the hovering adults before the kids could come back for thirds. Chicken burgers are good!

I had expected ground chicken meat to be somewhat dry and crumbly, and not at all appetizing. The following procedure produces moist patties that hold together well. Patted into circles, they're perfect for hamburger buns; shaped into ovals they're ideal for putting into pita bread (which can also be heated on the grill), along with a little olive oil, plain yogurt, chopped tomatoes, onions and sliced cucumbers.

Buy as many split chicken breasts as you need, figuring approximately one split breast per patty. Bone and skin the breasts, remove tendons and any cartilage, and process the meat in a food processor (using a metal blade). Be careful not to over-process. If you don't have a food processor, the breast meat can be chopped easily and quickly with a heavy, very sharp kitchen knife. Put the meat on a chopping board and chop — first in one direction and then in the opposite. The end result should be slightly coarser than ground hamburger meat. Put the chopped chicken in a bowl and add a little heavy cream (about one tablespoon per half breast), salt, ground white pepper, and a little seasoned salt. Mix well, using your hands.

Melt a few tablespoons of butter. The ground chicken is quite sticky, so start the patty-making process by rubbing a little of the melted butter on your hands; shape the meat whatever way you want, approximately ½-inch thick. Place on a ceramic plate and brush with the melted butter. Do not, I repeat, *do not* place patties on

The ground chicken burgers you make at home and cook on the grill bear no resemblance to anything offered at the "drive-thrus." They're tender, moist and flavorful, and kids love them.

I've marinated a few chickens in my time, in some pretty good marinades. But by the time they had been grilled and consumed, I was always left with the feeling that I had done something wrong.

The ingredients that made up the marinade were good and flavorful, the chicken smelled great while it was marinating, and I always left the chicken to soak for the requisite period of time. But, to me, the chicken never tasted as if it had absorbed as much flavor as it should have.

In talking this over with a few people, a simple explanation ensued: The chicken's thick and (let's face it) fatty skin acts as a barrier to any type of liquid — no matter how long the chicken soaks.

Having discovered that, I no longer felt that I was repeatedly making some sort of elementary culinary mistake, and the following solutions were devised:

...continued on page 107

waxed paper; talk about sticking! The patties will be easier to handle on the grill if you refrigerate them for at least 30 minutes prior to cooking.

Grill the patties directly over a hot fire for approximately 2 or 3 minutes per side. Toast buttered buns or pita bread brushed with a little olive oil on the grill while the chicken patties cook. Serve hot. It's unlikely that you'll have any leftovers, but if you do, cold chicken patties make good sandwiches.

CHICKEN, HEARTS

Like chicken gizzards, if you want to grill these in any quantity, you may have to put in a special order with your butcher. Chicken hearts are so small, the only practical way to cook them is on skewers. Chicken hearts make great appetizers, just right for quick cooking before the main course goes on the grill.

1) Marinate the hearts for 3 to 4 hours (try teriyaki marinade, page 295).

2) Ignite approximately 25 to 35 briquets, depending on how many skewers you will be cooking, or simply use those already started for the main course.

3) Once the coals are covered with a fine gray ash, spread them into an even layer. If you're using an adjustable grill, position the cooking grate about 3 to 4 inches from the fire.

4) Thread the hearts on small bamboo skewers and brush them with vegetable oil.

5) Grill for 3 to 4 minutes per side, directly over the coals. On covered kettle grills, cook with the top on, and both top and bottom vents completely open. Cooking time will be approximately the same using an open or covered grill.

CHICKEN, LEGS

At some point in the last few years, packagers of chickens decided that it made sense to pack chicken parts separately. It makes great sense when you're feeding large groups, especially if there are kids involved. Rare is the child who doesn't favor "drumsticks," not to mention a fair number of adults who savor the moist dark meat the leg offers.

If you plan on marinating the legs, start the night before you will grill: legs take a long time to absorb the flavors of a marinade, unless you skin them first. Any of the marinades found on pages 289 to 295 will work admirably; if it's a junior function, try one of the barbecue sauces on pages 297 to 298 or Chinese-style marinade (page 289). Both of these qualify as basting sauces rather than marinades, so don't apply until the last 10 minutes of cooking time; the high proportion of natural sugars in both sauces will caramelize and burn if you mop it on too early.

1) About 30 minutes before grilling, remove the chicken legs from the refrigerator.

2) For a dozen or so chicken legs, start approximately 40 to 50 briquets, more or less depending on the number you plan to cook. When the coals are covered with a light gray ash, arrange them in the center of the fire grate, sides touching. If your grill is adjustable, lower the firebox to about 5 inches below the cooking grate.

3) On a covered kettle grill, arrange the legs in a ring around the fire, rather than directly over it. Put the cover down, leaving both top and bottom vents completely open. If you're using an open grill, Wait until the coals die down to the moderate stage, then place the legs directly over the fire. Watch carefully for flare-ups, and move the chicken away from the coals if the flames become too intense.

4) Turn the legs every 7 to 10 minutes, for a total cooking time of about 30 to 40 minutes on an open grill, and about 50 minutes using the indirect method on a covered grill. Attention, covered kettle grillers: Move legs (the chicken's, not yours) a little closer to the fire

...continued from page 106

1) *Skin the chicken before marinating it. Skinned chicken will absorb the flavors of almost any marinade in a couple of hours.*

2) *Use a dry rub on the chicken, eat the skin and the seasoning, and be satisfied. This principle holds true for moist rubs, such as Jamaican Jerk (see page 195) and strong-flavored basting sauces (traditional red barbecue types) — which flavor the chicken admirably, simply because the concoctions are so strongly flavored.*

3) *Mix up a flavored butter (the butter must be at room temperature for this), lift up the skin of the chicken, and insert the butter between the skin and the flesh, attempting as complete coverage of the flesh as possible (no easy task, this).*

4) *Buy a bulb baster with an injection needle and inject the flavors through the skin and into the meat. This method is objectionable on all sorts of levels, but it's the one that produces the most flavorful bird. See Demon Bulb Baster, on page 207, for more information.*

after each turn until, on the last turn, the legs are directly over the coals.

5) If you're basting the legs, start applying the sauce after the third turn and watch carefully to make sure the sauce doesn't burn. Move the meat away from the fire if this is a problem.

CHICKEN, LIVERS

Chicken livers have long been a favorite snack food served hot off the grill. A classic preparation method is to skewer the livers with small pieces of bacon between each liver. Another time-honored favorite is to marinate the livers in teriyaki marinade (page 295), completely wrap each liver in bacon and place on skewers with alternating chunks of water chestnut.

If you use either of these methods, you'll find the bacon far easier to handle if you first partially cook it in complete strips; remove the bacon from the pan (or microwave) as it starts to brown slightly, cut it into individual pieces, then wrap the livers. Just before grilling, baste the wrapped, skewered livers with melted butter or bacon grease, and lightly dust with salt and pepper.

Delicious, and even more simple, is to thread the livers on skewers, brush with melted butter, and dust with salt and pepper. Grill and serve hot with a generous sprinkling of fresh cilantro and wedges of lime. Wonderful as a first course!

1) Rinse the livers in cold water and pat them dry. Cut each liver in half, discarding any tough membrane or connective tissue. Marinate for 2 to 3 hours, if desired, then place the livers on skewers.

2) Ignite approximately 25 to 35 briquets, depending on the number of skewers you're grilling, or simply use coals that are started for the entrée. When the coals are covered with a light gray ash, arrange them in an even layer, sides just touching. On adjustable grills, position the cooking grill about 3 to 4 inches from the fire.

A favorite method for preparing chicken livers is to marinate the livers in teriyaki marinade (page 291), completely wrap each liver in bacon and place on skewers with alternating chunks of water chestnut.

3) Place the livers on small bamboo skewers and brush them with melted butter. Grill directly over the coals, for 2 to 2½ minutes per side. On covered kettle grills, cook with the top on, and both top and bottom vents completely open. The cooking time will be approximately the same using either type of grill.

CHICKEN, PAILLARDS

For information on these thin, pounded pieces of chicken, see Chicken, breast (boneless and skinless), page 102, and *Pounding Paillards,* page 103.

CHICKEN, THIGHS

For moist and meaty eating, chicken thighs are hard to beat. Covered with skin on only one side, thighs will accept the flavors of a marinade more readily than legs or wings. Most processing plants leave far too much skin and fat on the thigh; trim off the excess before grilling. Although they can be boned and skinned, it's quite an ordeal for such a small morsel of meat, not to mention the fact that it's the skin and the bones that add most of the succulence to this piece of chicken. I say, leave them intact.

Any of the marinades or dry rubs found on pages 289 to 311 are suitable for chicken thighs. Because dark meat has more flavor than white breast meat, chicken thighs can stand up to stronger flavorings. Try fresh ginger-garlic marinade (page 290), Mexican-style marinade (page 293), teriyaki marinade (page 295), Jamaican jerk (page 195) or any of the others that suit your fancy.

1) If marinating the chicken thighs, start 3 to 4 hours before cooking time (or the night before). Remove them from the refrigerator about 30 minutes before grilling.

2) For a dozen or so chicken thighs, start approximately 40 to 50 briquets, more or less depending on the number you plan to cook. When coals are covered with a light

Meet Rocky Jr. and Sr.

Knowing very much about how modern chickens are mass-produced, I'm sorry to admit, is a little like knowing too much about how mass-produced sausages are made.

But not all chickens are raised that way, at least not on Bart and Pat Ehman's farm in Sebastopol, California. The Ehmans started out by raising baby lambs for a number of specialty restaurants in San Francisco. A few years ago, one of the chefs put in a request for a few free-range chickens. The Ehmans complied, and the rest is history: Today they sell more than 40,000 free-range chickens a week.

One question should be answered right up front, namely, "Can you really tell the difference between a mass-produced chicken and a free-range one?" The answer is a resounding "Yes." Free-range chickens are given no antibiotics, no growth enhancers, and fed no animal by-products. "What they eat ultimately determines what they taste like," says Bart Ehman. "Our chickens eat a diet composed of corn and soybeans — just like the 'scratch' old-timers used to throw out to their chickens around the farmyard."

The Ehmans sell chickens in two different sizes: the Rocky Range Chicken, which is approximately ten weeks old and averages 5 pounds, and the Rocky Jr., about 7 weeks old, weighing in at about 3 pounds. "The Rocky Range Chicken is almost too big for the grill, unless you want to cook it slowly on the rotisserie. The Rocky Jr., however, is perfect for grilling," say the Ehmans.

The two Rockys are certified by the U.S.D.A. to be genuine free-range chickens. Look for them at your specialty butcher or health food store.

If you are using a covered kettle grill, arrange the thighs in a ring around the fire, rather than directly over it.

gray ash, arrange in the center of the fire grate, sides touching.

3) Position the cooking grill about 5 inches above the fire (if the grill is adjustable).

4) On a covered kettle grill, arrange the thighs in a ring around the fire, rather than directly over it. Put the cover down, leaving both top and bottom vents completely open. If you are using an open grill, wait until the coals die down to the moderate stage, then place the thighs directly over the fire. Watch carefully for flare-ups; move the chicken away from the coals if the flames become too intense.

5) If you're basting the thighs with a tomato-based marinade or sauce, start applying after the third turn and watch carefully to make sure it doesn't burn. Move the meat away from the fire if this becomes a problem.

6) Turn the thighs every 7 to 10 minutes, for a total cooking time of about 30 to 40 minutes on an open grill; and about 50 minutes using the indirect method on a covered grill. If you're using a covered grill, move the thighs a little closer to the fire after each turn until, on the last turn, the thighs are directly over the coals.

CHICKEN, WHOLE

Crispy brown and steaming, proudly sitting on a platter, perhaps floating on a sea of polenta and surrounded by a bunch of grilled, basil-flecked tomatoes, a whole roast chicken is an impressive sight indeed. While I've always found it difficult to produce a nicely browned, whole roast chicken in the oven, no matter how much I baste it, they almost always turn out picture-perfect when cooked in a covered kettle grill — with little or no basting. But beware: A whole roast chicken, no matter how beautiful, proves true that old adage, "Seeing is deceiving; tasting is believing."

Let's face a couple of facts. First, today's mass-produced chickens are so short on flavor that they could almost be called bland. Second, it's nearly impossible to get a whole chicken to accept the flavors of a marinade, no matter how long you marinate it. A whole chicken, encased as it is in its naturally fatty skin, is nearly impervious to liquids, including marinades.

There are two ways around this "tasteless" problem. The first is to buy a free-range chicken, for the simple reason that it will actually taste like a chicken. If you find it difficult to utter such currently fashionable phrases as "free-range" in public, get around it by asking the butcher for "one of those old-fashioned, barnyard chickens over there." (See *Meet Rocky Sr. and Jr.,* page 109.)

The second alternative is to inject flavors into the chicken, rather than soaking it in a marinade in vain. Although the term "inject" may conjure up some fairly diabolical images, and the mere sight of a bulb-baster outfitted with an injector needle might cause neighbor children to flee home for days, injecting marinades is a method that produces definite and delicious results. See *The Demon Bulb Baster,* page 207.

Classic side dishes include risotto (page 333), polenta with Parmesan (330), steamed parslied rice (page 337) or galette of potatoes (page 323). Any vegetable in season will do, but consider grilled whole tomatoes — they're excellent in combination with roast chicken, even when the tomatoes are less than perfect (see page 232).

A covered grill is needed for the following procedure. If you have an open grill, flatten the chicken(see at right) and grill it directly over a bed of hot coals, with the cooking grill about 6 inches above the fire. Cook for a total of 60 minutes, turning every 10 minutes or so. Or, use a rotisserie attachment (see *Spit Cooking,* page 46).

1) Remove the chicken from the refrigerator about 30 minutes before grilling.

2) Ignite approximately 55 to 65 briquets.

3) Thoroughly wash the chicken in cold water; pat dry using a towel. Truss (see page 243), or simply tuck the wings under the back and tie the legs together using a piece of cotton string. Place the bird in a baking pan or disposable aluminum pan.

Flattening Poultry

More properly, this process should be called "flattening birds," because the same method works on all types — from chickens and turkeys to wild pheasant and quail.

Grillers of senior status know the many benefits of flattening any bird before cooking; it just takes the rest of us a while to catch up. In fact, if you quiz these old pros, they will, almost down to a one, tell you that flattening birds is the preferred method of preparation for grilling poultry, bar none.

A flattened bird is easier to handle on the grill than one left whole or cut into pieces. With an almost uniform thickness, undercooking or overcooking is less of a problem. With the bones and skin intact, the end result is a more succulent, flavorful bird. And when the bird is opened up flat, it accepts the flavors of a marinade more readily.

All birds, from a giant turkey to a miniscule quail, are flattened the same way. Start by removing the backbone, just below the rib cage on both sides. This can be done with a very sharp boning knife (the type with a long, skinny blade) or with a good pair of poultry shears.

Turn the bird breast side up and press down on it with the palm of your hand. Obviously, the amount of pressure you apply will differ, depending on the size of the bird, but expect some of the rib bones to break when flattening small types.

That's it!

4) Mix the desired marinade. Particularly tasty and well-suited for chicken are Dijon marinade (page 289), Greek marinade (page 290), and lemon-white wine marinade (page 292). Using a bulb-baster with an injection needle attachment, inject about 1 tablespoon of the marinade into the meaty portions of the chicken: breast, thighs, and legs. Reserve leftover marinade to make sauce, if desired (see below).

5) Rub chicken thoroughly with softened butter or olive oil. Sprinkle with salt and pepper. Insert a meat thermometer into the thickest part of the thigh, without hitting the bone.

6) When the coals are covered with a gray ash, push equal amounts to opposite sides of the fire grate. Replace the cooking grill and put the chicken (in its roasting pan) in the middle of the grill. Cover the grill, leaving both top and bottom vents completely open.

7) After about 45 minutes, check the temperature. Depending on the size of the bird, it should de done in 1 to 1½ hours, when the thermometer registers 180 to 185 degrees F.

8) When the chicken is done, place it on a carving board or platter and cover it with a foil tent. Allow the bird to rest for about 10 minutes. If you're making the optional sauce, be sure to retain the juices in the roasting pan and carving board.

9) Carve the chicken at the table or serve already cut up, using the easy dismantling method described on page 102.

Classic Sauce for Poultry

From start to finish, this shouldn't take more than five to seven minutes. More instructions than are perhaps necessary are presented here for the benefit of the uninitiated. After you've done it a few times, the process will become second nature; the resulting sauce (some might call it gravy) will be so good, you'll wonder why you never tried it before. In addition to the juices left in the roasting pan, you'll need:

"Although the term 'inject' may conjure up some fairly diabolical images…injecting marinades is a method that produces definite and delicious results."

2-3 tablespoons of flour
  1 can of regular strength chicken stock (or home made, if you have it)
  ½ cup dry white wine
    Leftover marinade, if desired

1) Carefully tip the roasting pan and remove all but a couple of tablespoons of fat, skimming it off with a large spoon. The flavorful juices will remain below the layer of rendered fat.

2) Place the pan directly on a burner set at medium-high; bring to a low boil. Use a large fork or wire whisk to quickly scrape up any browned bits of chicken.

3) Sprinkle 2 tablespoons of flour, one at a time, into the mixture. Cook for 1 to 2 minutes, stirring quickly and constantly. Take off heat if the roux (that's what this mixture of fat and flour is called) starts to get too dark.

4) Whisk in 1 cup of chicken stock, ½ cup of dry white wine, reserved marinade, plus any juices that have accumulated on the carving board. Return the sauce to the heat and allow it to come to a low boil. Cook for a couple of minutes, whisking the entire time.

5) If the sauce is too thick, add more chicken stock or water. If it's too thin, allow it to cook for a few more minutes. Taste. Add salt and pepper if necessary. If the sauce tastes too strong, add water, about ¼ cup at a time, and cook to desired thickness. Although it's not necessary, the sauce will look a little more finished if you pour it through a strainer before serving.

"While I've always found it difficult to produce a nicely browned, whole roast chicken in the oven, no matter how much I baste it, they almost always turn out picture-perfect when cooked in a covered kettle grill — with little or no basting."

CHICKEN, WHOLE, ON A ROTISSERIE

It was for the simple pleasure of watching a couple of plump, spitted chickens turning over a bed of glowing coals that I purchased an open grill with a heavy-duty rotisserie unit — this in addition to the two covered kettles already gracing my back porch. I've always felt that it was all right to be passionate about something, as

There are some friends you consult for gardening advice, others for help in raising your kids, and a few from whom you might expect some great investment tips. Like the Oracle of Delphi, rare is the friend you can consult in any emergency, be it intellectual, aesthetic or practical.

I'm very fortunate in counting one of these rare birds as a friend. His name is JP and his motto is, "Ask me. I know. I'm an artist." I respect his opinion almost as much as I respect his attitude. Attitude, with a capital "A," is the point of this homily.

I dropped by JP's house unannounced one day for some advice. It was around three o'clock in the afternoon. On the way through his studio I noticed a handsome platter of grilled chicken wings.

"Have some. They're good," he offered. "Yes, they are," I replied with my mouth full. "Are you having a party?" I asked, feeling a pang of guilt that I might be eating the hors d'oeuvres intended for someone else. "No. No party." he said. "Haven't you ever heard of Ceremonial Cooking?"

I had never heard of Ceremonial Cooking. But I caught the drift.

For myself, at least, I had learned yet one more lesson from JP: If you like to cook, you don't always have to be hungry or have any other reason to do so. Enjoyable ceremonies are always meant to be shared, just like wisdom — and chicken wings.

long as that something kept you at home.

Using a rotisserie is one of the best ways to prepare a whole chicken, not to mention many other large cuts of meat, poultry and fish. For more information, see *Spit Cooking*, page 46.

CHICKEN, WINGS

Chicken wings have become popular fare these days. Any of the marinades found on pages 289 to 295 will work with chicken wings; Indian yogurt marinade (page 291), Mexican-style marinade (page 293), teriyaki marinade (page 295) or Southeast Asian-style marinade (page 294) are particularly good. Marinate for 3 to 4 hours or overnight. If you're serving them as a main course, count on at least five or six chicken wings per person. Wings are also a good subject for *Ceremonial Cooking* (at left).

1) Remove the wings from the refrigerator about 30 minutes before grilling.

2) For 20 or so chicken wings, start approximately 40 to 50 briquets, more or less depending on the number you plan to cook. When the coals are covered with a light gray ash, arrange them in the center of the fire grate, sides touching. If your grill is adjustable, position the cooking grill about 5 inches above the fire.

3) On a covered kettle grill, arrange the chicken wings in a ring around the fire, rather than directly over it. Put the cover in place, leaving both top and bottom vents completely open. If you are using an open grill, wait about 10 minutes or so for the coals to reach the moderate stage, then place the wings directly over the fire. Watch carefully for flare-ups, moving the chicken away from the coals if the flames become too intense.

4) Turn the wings every 7 to 10 minutes, for a total cooking time of about 25 to 30 minutes. If using a covered kettle grill, move the wings a little closer to the fire after each turn. On the last turn, the wings should be directly over the coals.

5) If you are basting the wings, start applying the sauce after the third turn and watch carefully to make sure the sauce doesn't burn. Move the meat away from the fire if this becomes a problem.

CHINOOK

Chinook is most often sold as King Salmon, a name befitting its rank as the finest salmon available. For more information, see Salmon, page 209.

CLAMS

As far as I'm concerned, grilled clams fall into a culinary gray area. It's not that they're not good; they are. It's just that there are better, easier ways to prepare clams (such as steaming them). Successful grilled clams demand fresh, small, tender clams and split-second timing on the grill. If you cook them too long...well, the word "vulca- nized" comes to mind.

If you decide to proceed, the washed clams can simply be put on the grill, directly over a very hot fire. They will be ready to eat, right out of the shell, when the shells conveniently open on their own — usually in just a few minutes. Toss any clams that don't open. This, by the way, is an outstanding preparation method for oysters (see page 175).

Clams will be ready to eat, right out of the shell, when they conveniently open on their own , usually in just a few minutes.

Shelled clams can be threaded on small bamboo skewers and grilled. Insert pieces of partially cooked bacon between the clams, if desired, to add flavor and help keep them from drying out. Plan on only 2 to 3 minutes of total grilling time.

Place the clams on skewers. To help avoid overcook- ing, pack them on rather tightly. Ignite about 30 to 35 briquets. Once the coals are covered with a light gray ash, spread them in an even layer, sides touching. On adjust- able grills, position the fire grate about 5 inches from the cooking grill. If you're using a covered kettle grill, cook the skewered clams without the top in place.

Brush the skewered clams liberally with melted

butter just before putting them over a hot fire. Cook about 1 to 1½ minutes per side. Serve hot with wedges of lemon and melted butter for dipping, if desired.

Cod

Owing to its plenitude and its white, very mild flesh, cod is the most popular fish in the world, and has been for generations. Most of it comes from the Atlantic, with only one species, the Pacific or True Cod, being found in Pacific waters.

Cod fillets can be cooked on the grill, but because they are so lean, they should be basted liberally with vegetable oil or melted butter before and during the grilling process. Add a sprinkling of paprika to both sides of the fish before grilling. If you want to use a marinade, try herb marinade (page 291), flavored with your favorite herb. Marinate for 30 to 60 minutes — no longer.

Classic side dishes for cod include boiled new potatoes (page 320), creamed spinach, (page 322), pommes frites (page 331) and steamed parslied rice (page 337).

Whole cod, when you can find it, can be tied to a spit and cooked on a rotisserie. This is a very impressive main dish and the essence of simplicity, once you've secured the fish to the spit. See *Spit Cooking*, page 46, for more information.

My favorite way to cook a mild, lean fish such as cod is to wrap individual portions in grape leaves and grill the little bundles right over the coals. The leaves add a nice tang, and the fish can be seasoned however you wish before wrapping in the leaves. Handling the leaf-wrapped packets on the grill is infinitely easier than struggling with a lean fillet that wants to stick, no matter what precautions you've taken. For more information, see *Leaf-wrapped Packets* on page 117.

For grilling cod fillets, use the following procedure:

1) Keep the fish refrigerated until about 30 minutes before cooking.

2) Determine how much space the fillets will take up on the grill, and ignite as many briquets or as much lump

"Whole cod, when you can find it, can be tied to a spit and cooked on a rotisserie. This is a very impressive main dish…"

charcoal as it takes to make a slightly larger bed of coals. Put the cooking grill in place and let it heat up. (Fish will stick to a cold grill.)

3) After the cooking grill is hot, use a wire brush to clean it. Coat the gill with vegetable oil, using a large basting brush.

4) If the fillets have the skin intact, place them skin side down on the cooking grate. Grill the fish directly over a bed of hot coals. Do not put the cover down on covered grills.

5) Cook the fillets for 10 minutes per inch of thickness, measured at the thickest part. Turn the fish just once — half the total cooking time on each side.

6) Serve the cod on a platter that has been heated for 15 minutes in a 250-degree F. oven. Have the rest of your dinner ready to go, or have someone else finish up in the kitchen while you're tending the fish.

See Fish, page 133, for more information.

COHO

Even though it is ranked #2 among salmons (just behind King Salmon), Coho makes for mighty fine grilled fare. See Salmon, page 209.

CORBINA

Corbina is also sold as corvina (making one wonder whether there's a cultural difference involved, or just a typographical error), and sometimes as drum. As a saltwater fish of moderate fat content, corbina is excellent cooked on the grill. This fish is most often sold as fillets.

Not as pronounced in taste as members of the tuna family, it nonetheless stands up well to a strong-flavored

Leaf-wrapped Packets

Grilling fish wrapped in grape leaves is an old Mediterranean custom, one well worth developing in this country. Actually, fish isn't the only thing Mediterranean cooks wrap up and grill: Lamb (with bits of goat cheese and herbs) and whole quail also get this treatment.

Grape leaves are available fresh, of course, wherever grapevines are growing nearby. They are also available preserved in a brine, in jars, probably at your local specialty market. Either way, it's the largest, young, tender leaves that are used. If you use brined leaves, remove some of the saltiness by blanching them very briefly (less than a minute) in a pot of boiling water, and then immediately rinsing them in cold water. While you're refreshing the leaves, soak a few yards of cotton string in water.

Cut the fish into individual serving pieces, around 6 ounces each. Lay out a few grapevine leaves, overlapping by half, on a platter. Position one of the fish pieces in the center of the leaves. Add a scant teaspoon of good olive oil, maybe a little fresh lemon juice, and a sprinkling of your favorite herb — oregano is good.

Wrap the leaves around the fish. If they don't cover the top, add a couple more leaves. At this point, they won't be very cooperative. This is where you'll probably need the help of another pair of hands and that wet string. Tie the bundles, as best you can, with the strings running perpendicular to one another. Brush them with olive oil and put on the grill, directly over the fire.

Follow the rule of 10 minutes per inch of thickness (measuring the entire bundle), but turn often enough so the leaves don't char. The leaves are edible, and add a pleasant, piquant, almost lemony flavor to your delicate fish.

marinade or any of the compound butters found on pages 305 to 306. For marinades, try fresh ginger-garlic marinade (page 290), herb marinade (page 291) or Southeast Asian-style marinade (page 294). Do not marinate for longer than 30 minutes.

Classic side dishes include steamed parslied rice (page 337), "baked" basmati rice (page 316), or grilled new potatoes (page 196). Grilled whole tomatoes (page 232) or any steamed fresh vegetable would also be appropriate.

1) Keep the fish refrigerated until about 30 minutes before cooking.

2) Put the cooking grill over the coals. Clean it, if necessary, using a wire brush. Coat the grill with vegetable oil before putting on the fish.

3) Grill the fish directly over a bed of hot coals. If you have a covered grill, cook the fish without putting the cover in place.

4) Cook the fish for 10 minutes per inch of thickness. Turn the fish just once, halfway through the total cooking time.

5) Corbina, as with most fish, should be served piping hot, on a platter that has been warmed in the oven.

See Fish, page 133, for more information.

CORN

When fresh corn is at its midsummer peak, it's a real convenience to cook it on the grill, if for no other reason than it means one less pot of boiling water to overheat the kitchen.

Corn can be cooked either wrapped in foil or right in its husks. Either way, unless it was picked straight from the garden, it will benefit from soaking in cold water for about 20 minutes before grilling. Corn is usually cooked as a side dish, simply sharing grill space with the entrée.

"For a midsummer meal, consider making corn the main course and let everyone get their fill of this seasonal treat."

But for a midsummer meal, consider making corn the main course and let everyone get their fill of this seasonal treat.

Some cooks like to brush a little softened butter mixed with their favorite seasoning on the corn before wrapping it up and grilling it. By doing so, the corn comes out of the husks already buttered and ready to eat. Plan on approximately 15 to 20 minutes total grilling time.

For Foil-wrapped Corn

1) Shuck and de-silk the corn. Soak in cold water for 20 minutes.

2) Tear off squares of aluminum foil, and place each ear diagonally in the center. Spread softened or melted butter or margarine on each ear. Roll the foil around the ears and close it up by twisting the ends.

3) For covered kettle grills, cook the corn at the edges of the fire, turning 3 times, once every 5 to 7 minutes. This will leave room on the cooking grill for whatever else you might be preparing. On open grills, place the corn directly over the coals. If your grill is adjustable, position the cooking grill 4 to 5 inches above the fire.

For Corn in the Husk

1) Bend the leaves back gently to de-silk the corn. Cut 1 inch or so off the end of the ear. Soak ears in cold water for 20 minutes.

2) Rub the ears with softened butter or margarine, if desired, and fold the leaves back in place. Twist the husks tightly at the cut end, and tie them closed with a piece of cotton string (soaked in the water at the same time as the corn) or a thin strip of corn husk.

3) For covered kettle grills, cook the corn at the edges of the fire, turning 3 times, once every 5 to 7 minutes. On open grills, place corn directly over the coals. If your grill is adjustable, position the cooking grill 4 to 5 inches above the fire.

Staging a "Feed"

I'm not sure where the custom originated, but having a "feed" of one sort or another makes for fun entertaining. Nebraska corn feeds are legendary, as are the crab feeds that take place all around northern California. I've heard of asparagus feeds, and one friend of ours combines a corn feed with a barbecue — for a few hundred of his closest friends.

The essence of a feed is simplicity, namely a huge quantity of the featured food. Given that the purpose of a feed is to indulge (or perhaps overindulge), you can hardly have too much of whatever it is you are serving.

Our friend starts his feed in the early spring by planting a couple of acres of white sweet corn. The date for the corn feed depends solely on when the corn ripens. Once ripe, out comes the huge grill for hamburgers and the equally huge cauldron that can hold a hundred or so ears of corn at a time.

Once the guests arrive, they are invited to wander into the corn patch, pick and shuck their own ears, and throw them into the bubbling water. Sure, a few hamburgers are consumed, but most people are content to sit at one of the long tables and eat ear after ear of the freshest and sweetest corn imaginable. Pass the butter — quick!

COUNTRY-STYLE PORK RIBS

Country-style pork ribs come from the first five ribs of a pig, high up on the back. As such, they have a portion of both back and rib bones attached. Much different from the classic spareribs used for barbecue, country-style ribs are nonetheless delicious when cooked on the grill. For more information, see Pork, ribs, page 192.

CRAB

The first time I ever had grilled Dungeness crab was at a restaurant in northern California. I happened to be dining with my father, a second-generation seafaring San Franciscan. When the hot grilled crab arrived at the table he looked at it as if something had just landed from Mars. "What, in God's name, is that?" he asked incredulously. "Grilled crab, " I replied. "I don't believe it!" was his only response.

Although the grilled crab was interesting, my father was right: a purist would never consider grilling Dungeness crab. Crabs are bought on the waterfront, freshly boiled, and eaten chilled with plenty of sourdough French bread, mayonnaise, lemon and beer (or white wine, if you must).

But let's talk about crabs for a minute. In addition to the comparatively large Pacific Coast Dungeness crabs, there are the small rock crabs of the northeast, the enormous Alaskan king crab and snow crabs, and the marvelous stone crabs of Florida. Then there are the delicious blue crabs of the Atlantic and Gulf coasts, which occasionally shed their shells and become, for a short period of time, the famous soft-shelled crab, eaten soft shell and all (an act that continues to bewilder old San Franciscans to this day).

Crabs are a delicacy; as such, the cooking method used to prepare any crab should preserve their unique and subtle flavor. Without meaning to sound strident on this subject, I'm going to side with the traditionalists and say that the only suitable method of cooking crabs is to boil them and eat them cold — with the exception of soft-shelled crabs, which can be successfully grilled

"...a purist would never consider grilling Dungeness crab."

(see page 220). Over the years, many recipes have been suggested for grilling already-cooked crabs. Here again, I don't see the point of grilling an already perfectly cooked crab; further preparation will only detract from the quality of the crab, rather than enhance it.

That said, if you still want to grill a crab, here's how to do it: Procure the live crabs; kill them; clean them; and marinate them, if desired, in the refrigerator for 1 hour or more. Any spicy Asian or Indonesian marinade, such as fresh ginger-garlic marinade (page 290) or Southeast Asian-style marinade (page 294) would be good. Grill the crab over an open bed of hot coals, about 3 or 4 minutes per side, or until the shells turn red.

If you want detailed instructions on how to kill and clean live crabs, ask your fishmonger. But truthfully, wouldn't you really be happier with a nice chilled, already cooked and cleaned crab, ready for cracking and eating?

The delicious blue crabs of the Atlantic and Gulf coasts occasionally shed their shells and become, for a short period of time, the famous soft-shelled crab, eaten soft shell and all.

"If there are no hunters in your family, this shouldn't stop you from obtaining quality deer meat. Deer are now raised on preserves…"

D

DEER

If there are no hunters in your family, this shouldn't stop you from obtaining quality deer meat. Deer are now raised on preserves, and with a little advance warning, your butcher should be able to obtain whatever cut you desire. For more information, see Venison, page 252.

DOLPHIN, DOLPHINFISH, DORADO

This fish not only has too many names, but many consumers aren't sure it's a fish at all when they see the name "dolphin" anywhere near it. Rest assured; it's a fish, *not* the mammal. Increasingly, it is being sold under its Hawaiian name, mahi-mahi. For more information, see Mahi-Mahi, page 167.

DOVE

These small birds are valued for their dark and flavorful meat. Grilling doves directly over the coals is a fine way to prepare them. Depending on their size, count on at least one or two birds per person.

Doves can be grilled whole, but they are easier to handle and cook properly if they have been split and flattened (see *Flattening Poultry,* page 111). Either way, wash the doves well and dry. Rub them inside and out with softened butter, and season with finely ground pepper. Attach a piece of bacon around the bird with a toothpick; if flattened, place the bacon over the breast area.

With the cooking grill about 5 to 6 inches from the coals, grill the birds directly over a hot fire. Depending on their size, doves will cook in 15 to 20 minutes. Turn to cook on all sides every 5 minutes or so. Serve on individual pieces of toast (which can be toasted on the grill) with a sprinkling of chopped parsley on top and wedges of lemon on the side.

DRUM

Drum seems an odd name for such a good fish, but that's what it is called in some areas. It is most often sold under the name corbina. For more information, see page 117.

DUCK

Most of the domestic ducks in this country come from Long Island. The ducks arrived on Long Island around 1873, via a Yankee clipper ship, having made the trip all the way from China. Today, Long Island produces so many ducks, and of such high quality, they are now exported to China — an interesting twist in the balance of world trade.

Most large supermarkets stock frozen ducks; alternately, you can order fresh ducks from your butcher. Whether they are called ducks or ducklings is a distinction that's hardly worth worrying about anymore; they're all young, usually under two months old.

Ducks generally weigh in at about 4 pounds each — enough for one hearty appetite or two weight-watchers. Once you subtract the bones and fat, there's not all that much meat on a domestic duck.

Grilled domestic ducks have an excellent flavor, and cooking them outdoors makes dealing with the relatively enormous amount of fat that will render from the birds a little easier to handle. Duck bones are very tender, making it easy to split and flatten the birds (see *Flattening Poultry*, page 111), or cut them into pieces, as you would a chicken.

Fattening Lean Meats

Upland game birds — dove, grouse, pheasant, pigeon, quail and wild turkey — are a notoriously lean clan. To keep them from drying out while on the grill, a common remedy has been to wrap either the whole bird or just the breast in bacon. While this does the job, some have complained that the bacon imparts too much of its own flavor to the bird. Here are a few other options:

If you want to stick with bacon but cut back on its saltiness, blanch the uncooked bacon in boiling water for 10 to 15 minutes, then rinse it in cold water.

Then there's salt pork, with all the saltiness of bacon but none of the smoky flavor. This, too, can be blanched. Cut it into thin slices (⅛- to 3/16-inch thick) before putting it in the boiling water.

If you can find it, unseasoned pork fat is preferred by many discriminating chefs. Ask at your butcher shop if they will hold some back for you, and try to get the largest pieces possible. Wrapping any food in unseasoned fat is a process known as barding.

You can omit the fat altogether by simply basting the birds like crazy while they cook on the grill. Use either melted butter or a mild-flavored vegetable oil.

The dense, rich flavor of duck lends itself well to a number of spices and seasonings. Try Chinese-style marinade (page 289), marsala marinade (page 292), or garlic, rosemary and rosé marinade (page 290). Plan on marinating duck for at least 6 hours, or overnight.

No matter what type of marinade you use, any grilled fruit makes an excellent accompaniment to duck. Try grilled pineapple (page 182), grilled apples (page 69), grilled apricots (page 70), or grilled melon (page 169). Other tasty side dishes include wild rice casserole (page 338) and sautéed peas and lettuce (page 336).

If you're wondering whether or not the breast meat of a flattened duck will dry out, the answer is a qualified yes. It will be drier than if you cooked it separately, but cooking on a covered grill will help it retain enough of its juicy succulence to make for a fine meal.

Cut-up or flattened duck will take much less time to cook than a whole duck — although the presentation won't be quite as impressive. Either way, a covered grill is all but essential to control flare-ups caused by the rendering fat. Rotisserie cooking is an excellent method for cooking ducks (see *Spit Cooking*, page 46).

For Split and Flattened or Cut-up Duck

1) Remove the duck from the refrigerator approximately 30 minutes before grilling, and allow it to come to room temperature.

2) Ignite approximately 40 to 50 briquets or an equal amount of lump charcoal. If you're using an adjustable grill, position the cooking grill about 6 inches above the fire.

3) *For a covered grill:* When charcoal is covered with a fine gray ash, separate into equal amounts, and push to opposite sides of the fire grate. To make clean-up easier, position a disposable aluminum drip pan in the center of the fire grate. Put the cooking grill in place.

Place the split and flattened duck on the grill, directly over the drip pan. If you're grilling cut-up pieces of duck, place them — with the exception of the breast portions — directly over the aluminum drip pan. Keep the cover on the grill, with both top and bottom vents completely open.

Most of the domestic ducks in this country come from Long Island. The ducks arrived on Long Island around 1873, via a Yankee clipper ship, having made the trip all the way from China.

Total cooking time for the split and flattened duck, or the legs and wings of the cut-up duck, will be approximately 40 minutes; individual breast portions will cook in just 10 to 14 minutes, depending on the size. Keep a close watch on the clock, and put the breasts on about 25 to 30 minutes into the cooking process.

Turn every 10 minutes or so. If the duck has not browned to your liking after about 30 minutes, move it directly over the coals for the last 5 to 10 minutes. This will also produce a crisper skin — something that sends some people into gastronomic delirium.

4) *For an uncovered grill:* Cook directly over hot coals. Place the flattened or cut-up duck skin side down and cook for no more than 5 minutes. Turn and cook for 6 to 8 additional minutes, basting with marinade, if desired. Continue to repeat this process for a total cooking time of 30 to 45 minutes. Breast portions will cook in just 10 to 14 minutes. Keep your water pistol handy to control flare-ups, and be careful not to over-cook the duck; the meat should be moist.

For a Whole Duck

Unless you have a rotisserie attachment for your uncovered grill (see *Spit Cooking,* page 46), whole ducks need to be cooked on a covered grill.

1) Remove the duck from the refrigerator about 30 minutes before grilling.

2) Ignite approximately 40 to 50 briquets or an equal amount of lump charcoal.

3) When the coals reach the hot stage (they will be covered with a fine gray ash), separate them into equal amounts and push to opposite sides of the fire grate. Position a disposable, aluminum drip pan in the center of the fire grate and put the cooking grill in place.

4) Position the duck, breast side up, directly over the drip pan. Put the lid in place, leaving both the top and bottom vents completely open.

5) Total cooking time will be approximately 2 hours.

Gen. Barton's Duck, via Beard

"Perhaps the finest duck I have ever eaten in all these years were prepared by General Harold Barton in California. They had been rubbed with olive oil and thyme the day before and oiled again the next day. He spitted them through the middle of a row, head to tail, put two steel knitting needles through them at either end, and finally put the spit clamps on so they would stand firm. They were revolved over good coals for exactly 23 minutes, and the fire was brought up for the last few minutes. He then flambéed them with warm Cognac, which produced quite a flame. They were allowed to rest a few minutes before being served."

These are good ducks!

From James Beard's American Cookery, one of the finest cookbooks around.

During the last 30 minutes, the duck may be basted with reserved marinade, if desired.

DUNGENESS CRAB

Dungeness crab is the deservedly famous crab of the Far West, being found from Baja California all the way to Alaska. Whether or not it (or any other hard-shelled crab) is suitable for grilling is the subject of the discussion found under Crab, page 120.

"Dungeness crab is the deservedly famous crab of the Far West..."

E

EEL

If you were wondering whether or not I actually cooked everything discussed in this book, I did — everything, that is, except eel. Not only is it hard to come by in my neck of the woods, but like those two other delicacies from the deep, lobster and crab, eel must remain alive right up to the time of cooking, which made procuring it doubly impossible. And if you thought killing lobsters was difficult, the procedure for doing in an eel is so macabre, I thought it best to omit it for the time being. While I've never had it grilled, I have eaten fried eel in Belgium and smoked eel in Holland; I found both versions to be very tasty.

Skewered, grilled eel is a favorite in Japan, where it is first split, the bone removed, and then marinated in a teriyaki-type marinade — so I know that eel can, in fact, be grilled. Someday, I hope to have the opportunity to grill eel firsthand, and do a better job of reporting on the procedure. If someone out there has cooked eel on a grill, I'd like to hear about it.

Eel, generally ignored by Americans, is a favorite food throughout most of Europe.

EGGPLANT

There are two ways to cook eggplant on the grill: whole or sliced. Each produces entirely different results, both delicious.

There are real advantages to cooking sliced eggplant on the grill, especially if you're counting calories. When sautéed in a skillet, eggplant is notorious for soaking up huge quantities of oil. Cooked over coals, either sliced or as cubes strung on skewers, all that's required is a brushing of olive oil to keep the eggplant from sticking to the grill.

Cut-Up Eggplant

Although it's not necessary, I prefer to skin the eggplant before grilling. Many recipes call for salting the eggplant to remove bitterness (a trait said to afflict the large purple eggplant, but not its smaller Asian counterparts). Frankly, I've never encountered a bitter eggplant, so I omit this step.

Cut the eggplant into ½-inch thick slices, in sections or, if you're cooking with skewers, into cubes. Drizzle olive oil over the eggplant; toss or turn pieces to completely coat all sides. The olive oil can be flavored with pressed garlic, a little balsamic vinegar, and whatever herb strikes your fancy. (Oregano and basil are both good choices.) Sprinkle with salt and freshly ground pepper, if desired.

Grill directly over the coals, with the cooking grate approximately 5 to 6 inches from a moderate to hot fire. Turn every 5 minutes or so for a total of 10 to 15 minutes. On covered grills, eggplant can also be cooked using the indirect method, away from the fire; it will just take a little longer. Either way, the point is to cook the eggplant until it is easily pierced with the tip of a knife — just tender on the inside.

Serve the grilled eggplant as is, with just a sprinkling of chopped parsley on top and a couple of lemon wedges on the side, or as the all-important ingredient for grilled ratatouille, found on page 332.

Whole Eggplant

Choose a couple of large eggplants (about 1 pound each). Wash the outside skin, dry, then rub them with a generous coating of oil. Next, pierce the skin in several places with a knife. Place the whole eggplant directly over a hot fire, with the grill about 5 to 6 inches from the coals. Turn, so all sides cook, until the skin is charred and the eggplant appears "inflated." This process could take from 45 minutes to 1 hour. The eggplant is done when it can be easily pierced with the tip of a sharp knife all the way through to the center. Use the grilled eggplant for the following recipe:

Middle Eastern-style Eggplant

Remove the eggplant from the grill and allow it to cool slightly. Cut it in half and remove the pulp; discard the

A large eggplant, grilled whole, results in a very delicious vegetable dish. The eggplant is grilled until the flesh is soft. The flesh is then scooped away from the skin and lightly mashed. Add a little olive oil, lemon juice and maybe a dash or two of cumin and cayenne, and you're on your way!

charred skins and any large clumps of seeds. Put the pulp in a bowl and beat it lightly with a fork. Top with a drizzle of good olive oil, a squeeze of lemon juice, a sprinkling of paprika (and/or cumin, if desired), and a little chopped fresh parsley. Very good with grilled lamb (page 154).

ELK

Elk, like most wild game, shouldn't be messed with too much. After all the work that has gone into procuring the meat, there's no need to devise a method of preparation that disguises it in any way. In other words, marinades used for elk steaks, chops and roasts should be kept at their most simple (or none at all), and sauces shunned altogether. Appropriate marinades include herb marinade (page 291) and wild game marinade (page 295).

Elk steaks and chops should be cut about 1 inch thick. One hour before grilling, liberally brush the meat with olive oil. Cook directly over the coals, with the grill about 5 to 6 inches from a moderate to hot fire. Elk is best served rare (being lean, it tends to toughen and dry out if cooked too long). Cooking time will be 4 to 5 minutes per side. Season with salt and freshly ground pepper, if desired. Serve with a dollop of softened butter on top of each steak or chop.

All of the root crops — potatoes, turnips, carrots and the like — are excellent accompaniments to an elk dinner. Particularly good are whole roasted carrots (page 99), galette of potatoes (page 323) and grilled new potatoes (page 196) with a sprinkling of rosemary. And you could hardly go wrong with a good Pinot Noir, Cabernet Sauvignon or a rich Zinfandel.

If you have an elk roast on your hands, you'll need a covered grill to charcoalroast it.

1) The roast should be at room temperature when it goes on the grill. Remove it from the refrigerator about 30 minutes before cooking.

2) Ignite approximately 50 briquets or an equal amount of lump charcoal.

Larding vs. Barding

In an era when fat is a four-letter word, the notion of larding seems positively loathsome to most people. Be that as it may, there are many cuts of meat — wild game in particular — that greatly benefit from the practice.

Larding differs from barding in that thin strips of fat are pushed through the meat, rather than simply laid on top of it. Roasts are the cuts of meat most often larded.

There are two ways to go about larding a roast. One is to simply make small, deep incisions in the roast (using the point of a thin-bladed boning knife), then poke pieces of fat into the incisions as deeply as possible. The other, more traditional method involves the use of a special tool called a lardoir. In essence, lardoirs are like large needles with a catch at one end to hold the long strips of fat. The needle is pushed all the way through the roast, taking the fat with it. It is customary to leave the short ends of the strips of fat (called lardons or lardoons) showing on either side.

A few tips: the fat used can be salt pork, blanched salt pork (see Fattening Lean Meats, page 123), bacon, suet or beef fat — but best of all is fresh pork fat. It helps to chill the lardons in the refrigerator before threading them through the meat. If you care to, flavor the lardons before inserting them into the meat by dipping them in your favorite seasoning — freshly and finely ground pepper, mashed garlic, rosemary — whatever appeals to you. The fat will do a good job of carrying the flavors into the meat.

"Elk, like most wild game, shouldn't be messed with too much."

3) Wipe the roast with a cloth dipped in wine. If you choose to lard the roast, see *Larding vs. Barding*, page 129. Rub the roast with olive oil and dust with finely ground fresh pepper.

4) Once the coals are covered with a fine gray ash, put the cooking grill in place. While the coals are still very hot, put the roast directly over the fire and quickly sear the entire outside. This won't take long, but demands strict attention. By all means, don't leave the roast unattended while it is directly over the coals. Remember, the point here is to brown the outside of the roast, not to char it. Remove the roast from the fire as soon as it has been seared; place it in a roasting pan, preferably one not much larger than the roast itself. Pour about 1 cup of dry white wine or dry vermouth over the roast.

5) Back to the grill. Separate the charcoal into two equal amounts and push to either side of the fire grate, leaving the center free of fire. Insert a meat thermometer into the thickest part of the meat. Put the cooking grate in place and set the elk roast (in the roasting pan) smack dab in the middle. Put the cover on the grill, leaving both the top and bottom vents completely open.

6) Start checking the thermometer after about 40 minutes, remembering that the internal temperature rises much more quickly towards the end of the cooking process than at the beginning. Baste with additional olive oil and juices in the roasting pan each time you check the temperature (every 12 minutes or so). For a rare elk roast, take it off when the thermometer reaches 135 degrees F., and allow to rest indoors on a platter, loosely covered with foil, until the thermometer reaches 145 degrees F. Slice and serve with the juices that accumulate on the platter.

ENDIVE

Here's a vegetable that should win an award simply for having the most names; it alternately goes by Belgian endive, Belgian chicory, French endive, witloof chicory

— or its nickname, endive. And then there's the question of pronunciation: You say endive (en-dive) and I say endive (on-deeve). Let's call the whole thing off... .

Endive is labor-intensive and time-consuming to produce. Roots of the chicory plant are dug up, usually at the end of the summer growing season, and most of the outer leaves are cut off. The root is then replanted in cool, dark, forcing beds. The tops are covered with sand to block out any light. The results are those whitish, torpedo-shaped, tight little bundles of crisp, slightly bitter, crunchy leaves so favored by gourmets. No wonder endive is expensive!

Normally found in elegant salads or as individual leaves filled with bay shrimp or Roquefort cheese at swish cocktail parties, endive is also a good candidate for the grill. Cut the endive in half lengthwise (separate into individual leaves); wash gently, and dry. Mix up a simple vinaigrette of olive oil, a dash of balsamic vinegar and a squeeze of lemon. Marinate the endive halves in the vinaigrette for 1 hour or more, turning a couple of times in the process.

Place endive on the grill cut side down, directly over a moderate to hot fire. The cooking grill should be 5 to 6 inches from the coals. Grill for about 3 minutes. Turn, baste with leftover vinaigrette, and cook an additional 3 minutes. Do not allow the endive to become charred. Endive can also be cooked using the indirect method on covered grills; cooking times will be approximately the same.

Serve hot or at room temperature with a beef roast (page 82); it's also delicious with veal roast (page 250) or chops (page 246).

Endive...those whitish, torpedo-shaped, tight little bundles of crisp, slightly bitter, crunchy leaves so favored by gourmets.

ENGLISH SOLE

Sole has been so popular for so long that fishmongers have used considerable latitude with the term. Most probably, the filet of sole sold at your market will actually be "English sole". In filet form, sole is far easier to handle in the skillet than on the grill. If, per chance it's pan-dressed, see grilling instructions under Sole, page 221.

"There's a natural affinity of anise flavor for fish. The best recipes for rich fish stocks almost always call for a little Pernod, an anise liqueur, and cooks in Provence, France, are quick to grill fresh fish over a fire of dried fennel stalks."

F

Fennel

This one is a relative newcomer to most American supermarkets. If you don't like the taste of licorice, skip over this entry: Fennel's claim to fame is its crisp texture and pronounced anise flavor.

Related to carrots, parsnips and parsley, fennel is an attractive plant with feathery foliage. Mature plants produce thick stalks that form a bulb-like structure (think of it as a fat head of celery). Both the ferny tops and the celery-like bottoms are used in cooking. In Italy, fennel is eaten raw in salads, chopped and sautéed in pasta, and braised as a side dish for meat.

There's a natural affinity of anise flavor for fish. The best recipes for rich fish stocks almost always call for a little Pernod, an anise liqueur, and cooks in Provence, France, are quick to grill fresh fish over a fire of dried fennel stalks. Until you've tried the combination of fish and licorice, it's a little hard to imagine, but it's a classic and worth trying.

The easiest way to grill fennel is to wash and trim it, and then quarter the tight cluster of stalks. If you don't cut the base completely away, the individual stalks will remain hooked together, making them much easier to handle on the grill. Soak the fennel in good-quality olive oil and salt it before putting over the coals. Wonderful with any grilled fish, veal roast, or grilled chicken.

1) Ignite 30 to 35 briquets, or use those already started for the main course.

2) When the coals are covered with a light gray ash, place quartered fennel pieces just at the edges of the fire, with the cooking grate about 4 to 6 inches from the coals; for covered grills, follow the same procedure, but cook with the lid in place.

3) Turn and brush with leftover olive oil every 5 to 7 minutes, for a total cooking time of 15 to 20 minutes, depending on how much of the fennel's natural crispness you want to retain. Each time you turn the fennel, move it a little closer to the coals, but don't allow it to burn: Charring will destroy fennel's delicate flavor.

FISH

Grilled fish is one of the true delights to come off a charcoal grill. It has increased in popularity to such an extent that it is now possible to buy an excellent assortment of fresh fish in almost every part of the country. Generally speaking, fish will be available in one of three forms: whole, fillet or steak.

Fish with moderate to high fat content, such as trout, salmon, mahi-mahi and tuna, are tops for cooking on the grill. Their natural oils help keep them moist during the hot process of grilling.

Leaner fish, such as perch, rockfish, cod and snapper, will also cook up beautifully on the grill. They just need a little extra attention to keep them from drying out over the coals.

Some fish, because of their very tender flesh or multitude of small bones, are not suitable for grilling. These include blackfish, bocaccio, buffalofish, butterfish, California pompano, carp, catfish, Pacific pompano, sablefish, and shad.

The first rule in grilling fish is to buy only the freshest fish. How can you tell? The skin of whole fish should be shiny and slimy, the eyes should be bright and the pupils clearly black — not clouded over or sunken — and, lastly, the fish should smell fresh.

Fillets and steaks should look moist, with no discoloration toward the edges. If you're in doubt, ask the butcher or fishmonger if you can smell the fish. (Don't worry, they'll actually respect you for being such a discriminating shopper.) It should smell clean and, if it's a saltwater fish, briny.

Faced with a display case full of fish, even inexperienced fish-shoppers can pick out the freshest of the lot. It's instinctive…which is one of the reasons even old

The Ten Best Grilling Fish

This is a subjective list, but it's one that has developed over time. The following fish have excellent flavor. Happily, they are also amongst the easiest fish to handle on the grill. The list is presented alphabetically, rather than in order of preference:

1) *Albacore (or any of the others in the tuna family)*
2) *Halibut*
3) *Mahi-mahi*
4) *Florida Pompano*
5) *Red Snapper*
6) *Salmon*
7) *Shark*
8) *Striped Bass*
9) *Swordfish*
10) *Trout*

In the main, these are firm-fleshed fish, which accounts for the ease in grilling them. If you're new to grilling fish, consider starting with one of those on this list. Halibut and swordfish, in particular, stand up well to any abuse to which the neophyte might subject them, with the exception of overcooking.

Remember the cardinal rule in cooking fish: 10 minutes per inch of thickness. Turn the fish only once, halfway through the cooking time. You can do it!

pros refuse to say what's on the night's menu before they've seen what's available.

Being flexible in the menu-planning department has other advantages, as well. It's been my experience that purveyors of fish can be fairly creative when it comes to naming what's in the display case. This is not as dishonest as it may sound, but simply a case where the monger knows more than you do, and can substitute names (not to mention develop interesting new ones), when they know one species of fish will taste and cook the same as another. I have also known fishmongers — those with their own fishing boats — to deliberately misname fish that were not supposed to have been caught commercially.

I have tried to include Encyclopedia entries for all types of fish that are available in this country, listing them by their various common names. (Please note that these are American common names; in Europe the same common name may refer to an entirely different species.) Because common names for the same fish differ according to custom — across the country and even from one end of town to another — you may find your fish cross-referenced under a different name.

No matter what it's called, with truly fresh fish in hand, you're already more than halfway to producing a delicious meal. After reading the general instructions shown below, which apply to any fish, find the listing for your particular fish in the Encyclopedia. Individual listings will include appropriate marinades, sauces and side dishes.

Most people will agree that plain grilled fish, served with wedges of fresh lemon and a little sprinkling of chopped parsley, is special enough. But when the mood or occasion calls for it, a sauce will catapult the meal into the "extra-special" category. One sauce that is appropriate to any fish is beurre blanc (page 300).

Classic side dishes for fish are best kept simple. Among the best are steamed parslied rice (page 337), boiled new potatoes (page 320), and pommes frites (page 331).

General Guidelines

These guidelines will get you from the grill to the table in fine form:

"Most people will agree that plain grilled fish, served with wedges of fresh lemon and a little sprinkling of chopped parsley, is special enough. But when the mood or occasion calls for it, a sauce will catapult the meal into the 'extra-special' category."

1) Keep the fish refrigerated until about 30 minutes before grilling. It should be just at room temperature when it goes on the grill.

2) Ignite as many briquets or as much lump charcoal as it takes to make a bed of coals a little larger in size than what the fish will take up on the grill.

3) Fish will stick to a cold grill, so put the cooking grill over the coals and allow it to become good and hot. Once the it is hot, use a wire brush to clean it, if necessary. Next, coat the grate with vegetable oil, using a large basting brush, just before you're ready to put on the fish.

4) Fish should be cooked directly over a hot fire, with the cooking grill 3 to 5 inches above the coals. If you have a covered grill, cook the fish without putting the cover down. One exception to this rule is a large, whole fish (over 4 pounds), which should be cooked using the indirect method with the cover in place (see *Cooking Whole Fish,* page 185) or on a rotisserie (see *Spit Cooking,* page 46).

Small whole fish (less than 4 pounds) can be cooked directly over the coals, just as you would steaks and fillets. If you're cooking fillets, put them on the grill skin side down first. If the fish are tiny, such as herring, make your life easier by grilling them in a hinged wire basket (see page 214).

5) Years ago, the Canadian Department of Fisheries developed a small pamphlet on cooking fish that has since become a classic. In it, they suggest determining the cooking time for any fish (and any cooking method) by simply measuring the fish at its thickest part, and cooking it for 10 minutes per inch of thickness. A 1-inch-thick steak (or fillet, or whatever) would take 10 minutes to cook — 5 minutes per side.

If you're scrupulous about following this timing method, you'll please everyone — even those who say Americans always overcook fish. Those on the cutting edge of cuisine may say this method is too general (and too long), but it's never failed for me, nor have I ever had anyone leave the table in disgust at an overcooked piece of fish.

The Ten Best Wines for Fish

If there's a "Ten Best Grilling Fish" list, there might as well be a "Ten Best Wines for Fish" list, too, because fish and wine go so well together.

The list is divided into three categories: big, medium, and light and flinty dry. The big wines are for fish with distinctive flavors: monkfish, salmon, swordfish, pompano and the like. Medium-bodied wines are particularly good with any freshwater, white-fleshed fish, such as trout and bass, or the mild ocean fish such as sole, mahi-mahi or cod. The light and flinty dry wines are traditionally served very cold, with shellfish of any kind: oysters, scallops, mussels and clams.

Big Wines
1) *California Chardonnays (which seem to be getting better every year)*
2) *Montrachet or Mersault, California Chardonnay's elegant French uncles*
3) *White Zinfandel — why not?*

Medium Wines
4) *Domestic or imported Chablis*
5) *Sauvignon Blanc*

Light and Flinty Dry Wines
6) *Dry Riesling*
7) *Fumé Blanc*
8) *Sancerre*
9) *Entre Deux Mers*
10) *Muscadet (not to be confused with any wine made with muscat grapes — the two wines are at opposite ends of the spectrum)*

6) Turn the fish only once; fish just doesn't put up with being messed with on the grill.

7) Almost all types of fish should be served piping hot, within seconds of coming off the grill, if possible. Serve the fish on a platter that has been heated for 15 minutes in a 250-degree F. oven. Have the rest of your dinner ready to go before putting the fish on the grill, or have someone else finish up in the kitchen while you're tending the entrée.

8) Synchronize your watch with whomever might be helping you in the kitchen. Put the diners on yellow alert: time to wash your hands, mix that last "half one," comb your hair, or whatever else it takes to be presentable and sociable at the table.

9) Sound the 1-minute warning. Have your able assistant bring the hot platter out to the grill. Place the hot fish on the hot platter — and let's eat!

FLANK STEAK

There is only one flank steak per side of beef, and while they may range a bit in size, they are almost always approximately ¾-inch thick. They make excellent eating when marinated and grilled. For more information, see Beef, steak, flank on page 88.

FLOUNDER

Owing to its plenitude and its white, mild flesh, flounder is a very popular fish. The many types of flounder range in size from 1 to 5 pounds, occasionally larger. Small, pan-dressed flounder (gutted, with head, tail and fins removed) can be cooked on the grill, but because flounder is lean, it should be liberally basted with vegetable oil or melted butter before and during the grilling process. Add a generous sprinkling of paprika to both sides of the fish before cooking. Once grilled, top

"Owing to its plenitude and its white, mild flesh, flounder is a very popular fish."

with a little finely chopped parsley, and serve the flounder with several wedges of fresh lemon, or with the elegant beurre blanc (page 300).

My favorite way to cook a mild, lean fish such as flounder is to wrap small portions in grape leaves and grill the little bundles right over the coals. The leaves add a nice tang, and the fish can be seasoned any way you like before wrapping. Handling the leaf-wrapped packets on the grill is infinitely easier than struggling with a lean fillet that wants to stick, no matter what precautions you've taken. For more information, see *Leaf-wrapped Packets* on page 117.

Classic side dishes include boiled new potatoes (page 320), creamed spinach (page 322) and steamed parslied rice (page 337).

For grilling pan-dressed flounder, use the following procedure:

1) About 30 minutes before grilling, take the fish out of the refrigerator.

2) Determine how much space the fish will take up on the grill, and ignite as many briquets or as much lump charcoal as it takes to make a bed of coals that's a little larger. After the fire is lit, put the cooking grill in place and allow it to heat up (fish will stick to a cold grill).

3) Use a wire brush to clean the grill once it's hot. Oil the grill, using a large basting brush and vegetable oil, just before you're ready to grill the fish.

4) Cook the fish directly over a bed of hot coals. If you have a covered grill, don't put the cover down. Baste the flounder with oil or melted butter as needed, to keep it from drying out on the grill.

5) Cook the flounder for 10 minutes per inch of thickness, measured at the thickest part. Turn the fish just once, halfway through the cooking process.

6) After it's cooked, land the fish on a platter that you've heated for 15 minutes in a 250-degree F. oven.

See Fish, page 133, for more information.

"My favorite way to cook a mild, lean fish such as flounder is to wrap small portions in grape leaves then grill the little bundles right over the coals."

FLUKE

By some fluke, flounder is also called fluke. But fluke is really a flounder. If this discussion has made you flounder, see the previous entry, where all will be revealed.

FROG, LEGS

Although Escoffier raised the culinary status of frog legs, they seem more "Huck Finn" than *haute cuisine* to me. Gigging for frogs is fun — right up there with catching crawdads. Favor the smaller legs; they're more delectable and tender than the gargantuan ones you sometimes see.

Plump and refresh the legs by soaking them in ice water for 3 to 4 hours. Dry completely, then toss in a bowl with melted butter. Refrigerate for 20 minutes or so. Meanwhile, ignite the charcoal and position the cooking grate 4 to 5 inches above the fire. Grill the frog legs directly over a moderate fire, turning every 3 to 5 minutes. Total cooking time will be 8 to 12 minutes, depending on the size of the legs.

Serve the frog legs with any rice dish or boiled new potatoes (page 320).

"Although Escoffier raised the culinary status of frog legs, they seem more 'Huck Finn' than haute cuisine to me."

G

GAME HEN

For such little things, Cornish game hens go by a lot of names — game hens, Cornish game hens, Rock Cornish hens, and Rock Cornish game hens. Whatever name you know this poultry by, you'll find it on page 206, under Rock Cornish Game Hen.

GARLIC

There's nothing to grilling garlic, and few things better. Simply put whole heads of garlic on the grill towards the edges of a hot fire. Turn every 10 minutes or so; total cooking time will be 30 to 40 minutes. The garlic will be done when the outside skin is lightly browned (not charred) and the cloves inside are soft. The cooking process removes some of the odoriferous quality of garlic and sweetens its taste.

Elephant garlic can be grilled in the same way. But because elephant garlic lacks regular garlic's pungency, all you're left with when you grill elephant garlic is a smoky quality and a decidedly earthy flavor — savored by some and disliked by others. Total cooking time for elephant garlic will be approximately 50 minutes.

Once cooked, allow the garlic to cool for 5 to 10 minutes, then slice the top ¼ inch or so off the top of the cloves. Toast some thick slices of crusty French bread (page 95) and squeeze a few cloves of roasted garlic on each slice. Spread it with a knife, drizzle with a good-quality olive oil and maybe a grind or two of black pepper. Umm-umm! Serve to stave off hunger pangs before dinner, perhaps with a few shavings of first-rate Parmesan cheese (such as Reggiano) and a little Chianti Classico. Simple fare, and simply delicious.

Grilled French bread, grilled garlic, a little olive oil and thin shavings off a piece of first-rate Parmesan — the makings for a humble and delicious feast.

GOAT

In parts of Italy, Corsica, Saudi Arabia and Greece, roasted young goat (kid or *capretto*) is a popular and special meat. Unless you know someone who raises goats, you will have to special order capretto from your butcher. The meat is very lean and somewhat bland; frequent basting with olive oil and herbs solves both problems. Italians use olive oil flavored with garlic and oregano; Greeks favor olive oil, lemon juice and thyme; and in the Middle East, goat is flavored with coriander, ginger and onion juice. Capretto is best roasted whole on a spit. See *Spit Cooking,* page 46.

GOOSE

Goose is unique in that all of its meat is sweet, succulent and dark. To me, goose seems the perfect game to cook on that first weekend that feels like fall. If you're fortunate enough to be cooking a wild goose, see page 256.

Grilling a goose in a covered kettle grill or on a rotisserie makes one of its major drawbacks — namely the huge quantities of fat that renders from the bird during cooking — a lot easier to deal with. Geese are generally available from 6 to 20 pounds. Younger, smaller birds are considered more toothsome than older, heavier ones. Taking into consideration the weight of the bones and the amount of fat that will cook off, allow at least 1 to 1½ pounds precooked weight per person.

It seems perfectly appropriate to roast a goose over the grill, as it wasn't that long ago that this bird was considered "peasant" fare. I like playing off its humble culinary origins and serve charcoal-grilled goose with such rustic side dishes as whole grilled onions (page 174), grilled apples (page 69), sauerkraut and potato casserole (page 336), a galette of potatoes (page 323) or garlic mashed potatoes (page 324). Regardless of its humble origins, this special meal deserves a good Pinot Noir as accompaniment.

For the following procedure, you will need a covered grill. You can also cook a goose using a rotisserie unit on

Of surprisingly humble culinary origins, grilled goose is delicious when paired with rustic side dishes — grilled apples and onions, and perhaps a nice mound of steaming garlic mashed potatoes alongside.

an uncovered grill (see *Spit Cooking,* page 46).

1) Remove the goose from the refrigerator about 30 minutes before grilling. When you unwrap your grocery-store-bought goose, don't be alarmed by its appearance. The first time I encountered one, I had to do a little investigating to make sure it wasn't a Presto-Log. Store-bought geese are startlingly uniform from end to end and don't look much like other poultry.

2) Ignite 4 to 5 pounds of briquets.

3) Wash and dry a 12- to 14-pound goose. Sprinkle the neck and body cavity with salt and crushed thyme or sage, and rub with half of a cut lemon. Using a sharp fork, prick the skin (without piercing the flesh) of the goose at the base of both wings, the base of the breast on each side, the back sides of the legs, and where the thighs meet the back. Insert a meat thermometer into the thickest portion of the thigh, without touching any bones.

4) When the coals are hot, arrange them in even amounts on opposite sides of the fire grate. Position a large, disposable, aluminum drip pan in the center, between the coals. Put the cooking grill in place and position the goose directly over the drip pan. Put the lid on, leaving both top and bottom vents fully open.

5) The goose will take approximately 2 to 2½ hours to cook. It will be done when the thermometer reaches 180 degrees F. Your goose should be golden brown and perfectly cooked. Allow it to rest for 15 minutes or so before carving.

Note: To make it easier to handle the rendered goose fat, let the drip pan stay inside the grill until it's cool. Once the fat has congealed, it will be much easier to handle, believe me. Goose fat has long been considered about the best fat there is for frying foods, it can be used for relieving dry, chapped hands, and is said to work wonders on cow udders. Just thought you'd want to know…

The Goose That Got Away

Goose, known for its rich flavor, is also known as something of a pain to cook. Domestic geese are so fatty that cooking one in an oven can present some difficulties — like the time a friend of ours cooked one for a special dinner. After the first course, she went into the kitchen, presumably to check on the bird. She didn't return. About five minutes went by before a small voice came from behind the kitchen door: "Honey, can you come here for a minute?" Her husband left the table. He didn't return.

After an awkward period of time, a lovely platter of goose, sauerkraut and braised apples was finally served. It was a delicious meal, but we never found out what the delay was — until a couple of years later.

It seems that when our friend was checking on the goose, the whole pan slipped out of the oven, more or less completely covering the linoleum floor with hot goose fat. Talk about an oil spill! Our friends said the kitchen floor was still slippery when they sold the house years later.

Don't let this happen to you! Far better to roast the goose outdoors in a covered grill or, better yet, on a rotisserie (see page 46).

Round Fish vs. Flat Fish

The fish world is divided between two different body types, typically called round and flat.

Flatfish start out swimming vertically, then later take to swimming horizontally, often close to the bottom. The eye on the lower side of the fish gradually moves up to the top. With both eyes located on the top of its body (not to mention fact that its roving eye leaves a visible trail), the flatfish has a very odd expression. Its backbone runs down the center of the fish, with numerous smaller bones that extend outward.

Unless flatfish are very large, the flesh tends to be quite thin, and can only be cut into fillets. These delicate fillets (such as sole and flounder) can be sautéed to perfection in a frying pan, but are difficult to handle on the grill. The exceptions to this rule are the very large flatfish, such as halibut, which can be cut into steaks.

Round fish, such as salmon, trout, and bass, are, well, more rounded, and their eyes are on opposite sides, looking out. The spine runs down the center of the fish, with small bones extending from both the top and the bottom. The bones on the bottom spread out in an almost "wishbone" shape, and protect the fish's innards.

Because the flesh is thicker, it is possible to cut either steaks or fillets from round fish. Not surprisingly, some of the best fish for grilling are round fish.

GOOSEFISH

Although it's hard to see why, goosefish is one of the names for that incredibly ugly (but very tasty) fish most often sold as angler. For more information, see Angler, page 68.

GROUPER

Grouper is just one of several ocean fish — halibut and sea bass included — favored for their white, mild, lean flesh. Grouper fillets and steaks cook up beautifully on the grill.

Most of the time, a simple brushing of olive oil and a powdering of paprika is all that's called for before grilling. Sprinkle some finely chopped parsley on top of the grilled grouper, and serve with wedges of fresh lemon. If you're in the mood for something more exotic, consider marinating the grouper, for no more than 30 to 40 minutes, in herb marinade (page 291), flavored with your favorite herb.

Classic side dishes include boiled new potatoes (page 320), steamed parslied rice (page 337) and marinated cucumbers (page 327).

1) Remove the steaks or fillets from the refrigerator about 30 minutes before grilling. The fish should be just at room temperature when it goes on the grill.

2) Make a bed of coals (or lump charcoal) that's a little larger in size than what the fish will take up on the grill. Ignite.

3) Put the cooking grill over the coals and let it heat up (fish will stick to a cold grill). Clean the grill with a wire brush, then coat it with vegetable oil, using a large basting brush.

4) If the fillets have the skin intact, place them on the grill skin-side down first. Cook directly over a bed of hot coals, with the grill 3 to 5 inches above the fire. If you have a covered grill, don't use the cover.

5) The fish should cook for 10 minutes per inch of thickness. Turn just once, halfway through the total cooking time.

6) Serve the grouper hot off the grill; have everything else ready to go before cooking the entrée. Help keep the fish piping hot by serving it on a platter that you've heated for 15 minutes in a 250-degree F. oven.

See Fish, page 133, for more information.

GROUSE

As with most upland game birds, the only suitable grouse for grilling are young birds. A good indicator of youth is a pliable breastbone and plump legs. The best method of grilling young grouse is to flatten them (see *Flattening Poultry,* page 111).

Strong-flavored vegetables such as parsnips, turnips, carrots or Brussels sprouts seem particularly appropriate with any wild game. Parsnips and turnips are excellent puréed together; carrots are delicious done right on the grill (see page 99); and Brussels sprouts, steamed until just barely tender, then drizzled with butter (why not dice up a little red pepper into the butter as it melts?) are very tasty with grilled grouse. Either grilled new potatoes (page 196) or wild rice casserole (page 338) are fitting side dishes. Finally, a good Pinot Noir with some age on it would be a nice complement to the young bird.

Cook the grouse on a covered or uncovered grill. If using a covered grill, do not put the lid in place. Count on a total cooking time of approximately 8 to 10 minutes (4 to 5 minutes per side), directly over hot coals with the cooking grate 3 to 5 inches from the fire. Start with the skin side down. Baste frequently on both sides with melted butter that has been seasoned with your favorite herb. Serve the grouse hot off the grill.

As with any wild game, strong-flavored vegetables such as parsnips, turnips, carrots or Brussels sprouts seem particulary appropriate. Parsnips and turnips are excellent puréed together; carrots are delicious done right on the grill.

"Scrod, as small as they are (under two pounds), should be pan-dressed (gutted, and with head, tail and fins removed) before grilling. Your fishmonger will do this for you if asked. If a member of your household brings home some freshly caught scrod, it should be prepared the same way."

H

HADDOCK

When smoked, haddock is finnan haddie; when small, it's scrod; when cooked on the grill, it's great.

A lean, mild fish, haddock should be liberally oiled — or marinated — before grilling. You'll probably see the larger haddock in your fish market cut into steaks or fillets; baby haddock will likely be sold as "baby cod" or scrod. Scrod, as small as they are (under two pounds), should be pan-dressed (gutted, and with head, tail and fins removed) before grilling. Your fishmonger will do this for you if asked. If a member of your household brings home some freshly caught scrod, it should be prepared the same way.

Haddock in any form is good enough by itself to enjoy quite plain, with only a liberally brushing of oil and a healthy sprinkling of paprika on both sides, grilled, and served up with fresh wedges of lemon and some finely chopped parsley scattered on top. Haddock also takes well to the flavors of a number of marinades; try fresh ginger-garlic marinade (page 290), lime-garlic marinade (page 292), or herb marinade (page 291). Marinate for no more than 30 minutes.

One way to keep haddock moist is to wrap it in grape leaves before grilling. Although this is a rather time-consuming project, the results are definitely worth the effort. (See *Leaf-wrapped Packets,* page 117.)

Serve haddock with steamed parslied rice (page 337), grilled new potatoes (page 196) and any fresh vegetable that's currently in season.

1) Keep the fish refrigerated until about 30 minutes before grilling.

2) Put the cooking grill over the coals and allow it to become good and hot; fish will stick to a cold grill. Use

a wire brush to clean the hot grill, if necessary. Oil it just before you're ready to cook the fish, using a large basting brush and vegetable oil.

3) With the cooking grill 3 to 5 inches above the coals, cook the haddock directly over a hot fire. If you're cooking fillets with the skin intact, place the fish skin side down first.

4) Cook for 10 minutes per inch of thickness, turning once, halfway through the cooking process.

5) Fish should be served hot off the grill, so be sure that everything else is ready to go before putting the fish on the grill. Land the grilled haddock on a platter that has been heated for 15 minutes in a 250-degree F. oven.

See Fish, page 133, for more information.

HALIBUT

Most of us will only encounter halibut as uniform steaks, cut up and lying on a bed of ice in the fish market or supermarket display case. But wouldn't it be something to encounter one of these creatures full-grown, at 600 pounds? On second thought, maybe it wouldn't.

Halibut has a texture quite unlike other lean, white-fleshed ocean fish. It's excellent on the grill, and unusual because halibut, along with swordfish, will turn out great even after it has been frozen.

Fresh halibut steaks practically jump out of the display case. No matter what else I might have had in mind for dinner, if I see those gleaming white, fresh halibut steaks, I buy them, rush home and make Halibut Florentine (at right). If you like spinach, give this recipe a try. If not, simply put a little vegetable oil and paprika on both sides of the steaks, cook them on the grill, serve with a few fresh lemon wedges, and get ready for some good eating. This is one of my favorite fish; it's hard to do wrong by it, unless you overcook it.

Classic side dishes for halibut include any rice dish (but especially "baked" basmati rice, page 316), boiled

Halibut Florentine

This dish can be cooked in a single large baking dish, or individually in au gratin dishes. It's almost a meal by itself, needing only some crusty French bread and a glass of white wine as accompaniments.

4 halibut fillets
2 packages frozen, chopped spinach
White sauce (see recipe, page 302)
4 tablespoons Parmesan cheese, grated
Lemon wedges for garnish

1) Cook the spinach according to package directions. Spread the spinach on a dinner plate, top with a matching plate and squeeze the two plates together tightly — over the sink, please! This is the best way I know of to really "drain" spinach.

2) Make the white sauce, using the recipe on page 302. Keep warm.

3) Lightly oil or butter the baking dish or au gratin dishes and arrange cooked spinach in an even layer on the bottom.

4) Grill the halibut steaks according to the instructions at left, but remove them from the grill just prior to being fully cooked — about 8 minutes total cooking time per inch of thickness.

5) Preheat broiler, turned to "high."

6) Set grilled halibut on top of spinach. Spoon white sauce over the fish, enough so some runs onto the spinach as well. Sprinkle with Parmesan cheese. Put the pan or dishes under the broiler just until the cheese melts and sauce starts to bubble. This should only take a minute or two. Garnish with lemon wedges and run it to the table.

new potatoes (page 317), or black-eyed peas (page 318).

1) Let the halibut come to room temperature before putting it on the grill by removing it from a refrigerator about 30 minutes prior to cooking.

2) Ignite as many briquets or as much lump charcoal as it takes to make a bed of coals that's a little larger in size than what the fish will take up on the grill.

3) Fish will stick to a cold grill, so put the cooking grill over the coals and let it heat up. Once it's hot, use your wire brush to clean it. Coat the grill with vegetable oil, using a large basting brush, just before you're ready to cook the fish.

4) Grill the halibut directly over a bed of hot coals, with the cooking grate 3 to 5 inches away from the fire. If you have a covered grill, cook the halibut without putting down the cover.

5) Cook the steaks for 10 minutes per inch of thickness, measured at the thickest part. Plan on turning the fish only once — half the total cooking time on each side.

6) As with most fish, halibut should be served hot off the grill. Land the steaks on a platter that you've heated for 15 minutes in a 250-degree F. oven. Have the rest of your dinner ready to go before cooking the fish, or have someone else finish up in the kitchen while you're minding the grill.

Note: In certain parts of the far west, it is possible to ask your fishmonger for a "chicken halibut" — namely, a small halibut, under 10 pounds. These can be grilled whole on a rotisserie and make for very memorable eating. See *Spit Cooking,* page 46.

See Fish, page 133, for more information.

Wouldn't it be something to encounter a halibut full-grown, at 600 pounds?

HAM, CURED

I have tried cooking whole hams on the grill several times, with and without the benefit of huge quantities of aluminum foil. The results have been okay, but not great. With a whole cured ham, the point is to heat it through, and perhaps add a little additional flavor with a glaze. There's no call for the additional smoky flavor added by charcoal cooking. In short, although it's possible to cook a ham on the grill, a conventional oven is far better suited to this job.

HAM, CURED, STEAK

Somehow, over the last 30 years or so, the humble ham steak seems to have been all but forgotten as being fit for the grill. But there's nothing easier to cook, and all ages seem to relish it. A grilled ham steak makes for great eating, especially when served with complementary side dishes.

The most important step in grilling a ham steak is the first one, namely, selecting the ham steak itself. It should be one to two inches thick. The thickness is important because it allows you to produce a nice, crispy exterior without drying out the interior of the meat. If you have trouble finding a ham steak this thick, ask your butcher to slice one for you.

If you choose to marinate the ham steak, do so at room temperature for about 1 hour before grilling (4 to 6 hours in the refrigerator), or simply baste the ham steak with a marinade while you grill it. Concoct your own custom marinade by picking one ingredient from each of the categories under *Mix and Match Marinade* at right. Some cooks prefer to coat the ham steak with Dijon mustard, or make their own mustard paste from dry English mustard that has been moistened with water, white wine, or vermouth.

As good as it is by itself, there's something about ham that lends itself wonderfully to all sorts of side dishes. (If you're reading this while you're hungry, watch out!) Try cornbread; coleslaw (page 321); hominy "souffle" (page 324); grilled yam wedges (page 260); any

Mix and Match Marinade

To make a custom marinade for ham, choose one ingredient from each of the following categories:

Liquid: Apple juice, pineapple juice, cherry juice, orange juice, grapefruit juice, fruity white wine or dry vermouth.

Flavoring: Lemon or orange peel, dry mustard, Dijon mustard, garlic, honey or real maple syrup.

Oil: A light vegetable oil is best, such as peanut or safflower, or whatever you have on hand.

A typical ham steak won't require much more than a cup of marinade. Start with 1 cup of liquid, flavor it as intensely as you wish, then add 2 tablespoons of oil. Mix the ingredients together and marinate the ham steak for 1 hour, longer if desired. Baste the ham steak with the marinade as it cooks on the grill.

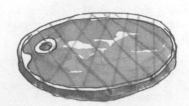

When buying ham steak for the grill, select one that's at least one to two inches thick.

bean dish, such as cowboy beans (page 321), black-eyed peas (page 318) or Italian white bean salad (326); or that great standby, plain 'ol mashed potatoes (page 327). For dessert, give it up for grilled bananas (page 72), served with a little whipped cream and toasted almonds. Hog heaven, indeed! Ice-cold beer is the beverage of choice with this entrée.

1) Before grilling, allow about 30 minutes for the ham steak to come to room temperature.

2) Start approximately 40 to 50 briquets.

3) When coals are covered with light gray ash, push them into a single layer, leaving a little space between the briquets. Cured ham should be cooked over a moderate fire, so wait another 10 minutes before putting on the steak. On open grills, position the cooking grill about 4 inches above the coals.

4) Place ham steaks directly over the coals and cook for about 7 to 10 minutes per side, until the outsides are nicely browned. Baste with leftover marinade. Serve hot off the grill or at room temperature. Cold leftovers are great for that midnight raid on the refrigerator.

HAM, FRESH

The term "fresh ham" is really something of a misnomer that, for some reason, has an appeal for today's cooks. I can only speculate that it has something to do with evoking images of farm cooking, large families, long tables and Sunday suppers. Just for the record, a fresh ham is a leg of pork. It's fresh — that is, not cured, nor smoked, nor air-cured, nor nothing else.

A fresh ham (or leg of pork) is seldom cooked today, which is unfortunate; it ranks right up there with the world's great roasts, and is especially good when cooked over the coals, or even better, on a rotisserie (see *Spit Cooking,* page 46). I may be one of those who likes the name "fresh ham," but you'll find this cut of meat discussed under Pork (fresh ham, page 188).

HEARTS

At first blush, one would think it was possible to cook all hearts in the same way, but this is not true. Depending on the type of heart you wish to grill (beef or chicken) look under that particular heading for specific instructions.

HERRING

Nothing printed on this page is going to make someone like (or even try) herring. Its flavor — like gefilte fish and lutefisk — is something that you almost have to grow up with in order to enjoy. Found in both the Atlantic and the Pacific, herring are quite small, usually in the 2- to 8-ounce category. Its flesh has a distinctive (most would say strong) flavor and is high in those good omega-3 long-chain fatty acids. Herring's high fat content makes it ideal for grilling. It's good when cooked without any seasoning and served with a few wedges of fresh lemon.

Keep the side dishes simple: boiled new potatoes (page 320) or pommes frites (page 331), and maybe a little old-fashioned creamed spinach (page 322). An ice-cold bottle of beer is the thing to drink with herring.

Because herring are so small, they should only be cooked on the grill using a hinged wire basket. For grilling instructions, see *Hinged Wire Baskets*, page 214.

HOT DOGS

Hot dogs are number one with kids, not to mention plenty of adults. In addition to the old standby, which is made from a variety of meats, there are the all-beef hot dogs, turkey dogs and even chicken dogs. Most hot dogs are precooked and only need to be warmed through for about 5 to 10 minutes over a moderate fire. But many people prefer their hot dogs practically black, which is best achieved over a hot fire. As long as you're cooking the dogs, grill up some liberally buttered buns at the same time. It elevates the humble hot dog a notch or two.

A Cross-cultural Phenomenon

In thinking about the way barbecue is eaten in this country, a theory began to develop. It probably doesn't prove the one-time existence of the lost continent of Atlantis, but a very diverse group of cultures all seem to like a very similar type of food.

The food in question is something quite different from the sandwich, which seems fairly Anglo to me. What we're talking about here is the soft bread, spicy meat and even spicier condiment "roll-up."

In America, it's the classic barbecue "sandwich." Traditionally, it's made with one piece of squishy white bread, some barbecued meat, a little coleslaw, some dill pickle slices and extra hot sauce.

In Mexico, it's a burrito: flour tortilla, chopped or shredded spicy meat, beans and spicy sauce.

In China, it's Peking Duck: succulent morsels of duck meat, pieces of crispy duck skin, thin strips of green onion and spicy hoisin sauce, rolled up in a rice flour "pancake."

Even the ubiquitous hot dog can be considered in this category: a soft bun, spiced meat, relish, sauerkraut and a spicy sauce — mustard!

See what I mean?

J

JAPANESE EGGPLANT

Japanese eggplant are long and thin, and excellent for grilling. Generally, they have far fewer seeds than their larger, fatter cousins. They can be cut in cross-sections or cubed and threaded on skewers. See Eggplant, page 127, for more information.

JACK MACKEREL

Technically, Jack Mackerel is a jack, not a mackerel, but it can be grilled in exactly the same way as mackerel. See page 166 for grilling instructions.

JACKSMELT

Some fish need a little public relations work to help them achieve the popularity they deserve. As an all but unknown fish, jacksmelt could certainly use a little fanfare — or maybe just a name change.

Mild-flavored, moderately fat and fairly firm, jacksmelt is usually seen in the display case as a pan-dressed fish (whole, but gutted and with head, tail and fins removed), averaging approximately 1 pound. It is excellent for grilling, either plain or marinated. To grill it plain, first brush with olive or vegetable oil and dust with paprika on both sides. If you want to marinate the fish, by all means do so — but only for 30 minutes to 1 hour. Try garlic, rosemary and rosé marinade (page 290) or herb marinade (page 291).

Serve with boiled new potatoes (page 320), steamed parslied rice (page 337) and grilled whole tomatoes (page

"As an all but unknown fish, jacksmelt could certainly use a little fanfare — or maybe just a name change."

232). A chilled bottle of Sauvignon Blanc would go nicely with this meal.

1) Remove the jacksmelt from the refrigerator about 30 minutes before cooking time.

2) Determine how much space the fish will take up on the grill and ignite a bed of coals (or lump charcoal) that's a little larger in size.

3) Fish will stick to a cold grill, so put the cooking grill in place and let it get hot. Just before grilling the fish, clean the hot grill with a wire brush and coat it with vegetable oil, using a large basting brush.

4) Place the fish directly over the hot coals. If you have an adjustable grill, the cooking grill should be 3 to 5 inches above the coals. Don't use the cover on a covered grill.

5) Cook for 10 minutes per inch of thickness, measured at the thickest part of the fish. Turn only once, halfway through the cooking time.

6) Fish should be served hot off the grill — within seconds, if possible. Heated plates help; slip them into a 250 degree F. oven about 15 minutes before eating time, along with a platter for the fish. Everything else should be ready to go before the fish hits the grill.

See Fish, page 133, for more information.

See Fish, page 133, for more information.

Everything Old Is New Again

"The outdoor terrace has come of age in America. It is now a status symbol of good, exuberant American living, out in the air, and under the sun... .

"The dining room has blossomed out, too. Formerly, the tantalizing aroma of meat broiling over the coals was associated with camping trips in the wilderness or at the shore. In our time the charcoal grill has become a fixture of the outdoor living scene, a step from the living room, or the kitchen, door. The bags of charcoal displayed at the supermarket are evidence enough of the popularity of cooking on the terrace. And dining outdoors is now enjoyed, not just during vacations, but at home, any day that the weather permits."

— Dorothy Childs Hogner, from Gardening & Cooking on Terrace and Patio, published in 1964.

K

KID

No, it's not what you may think — we're talking about baby goat here. Actually, not right here, because you'll find kid (or *capretto,* as they call it in Italy) under Goat, on page 140.

KIDNEYS

Kidneys, like hearts, are delicious when grilled to the rare stage, but toughen if cooked any longer. Beef, veal, lamb and pork kidneys can all be grilled; beef and pork kidneys have the strongest flavor. Lamb kidneys are an essential component of the classic Mixed Grill (page 169).

To prepare the kidneys for grilling, gently pull away the outer layer of fat and the thin membrane that encloses the kidneys. Slice each kidney almost in half, and remove the white core that's inside. (A small pair of sharp scissors will help.) After brushing liberally with melted butter, the kidneys can be grilled as is, but they will be easier to handle if threaded loosely onto two parallel bamboo skewers. Soak the skewers in hot water for about 30 minutes before adding the meat.

Grill the kidneys directly over a moderate fire, with the grill 3 to 5 inches from the coals. Depending on their size, the kidneys will cook to the rare stage in 3 to 5 minutes per side.

An alternate method for preparing kidneys is to cut them into 1-inch pieces and wrap them individually in small pieces of bacon. This will help keep the kidneys moist. Place the wrapped kidneys on skewers and grill them over a moderate fire until the bacon is crisp. Keep your water pistol handy; the bacon grease may cause flare-ups.

Small food is easier to handle on the grill if you string it on two parallel bamboo skewers. Soak the skewers in hot water for 30 minutes or so before putting them over the coals; this will help to keep the ends from burning off.

KING SALMON

The king salmon, which can weigh up to 25 pounds, is considered tops in the salmon department. For more information, see Salmon, page 209.

Everything Old Is New Again II

"Since we first started out,
We've simply run about, unending.
And life's been one long route.
We're always opening plays,
or closing cabarets.
It seems our ways need mending.

Let's let the dressy dames,
with hyphenated names,
in search of faster games,
fly by…

Content with staying home,
we'll never let them know,
the nicest place to go
is bye-bye.

Why don't we try not to roam?
What if we threw
a party for two,
and invited only you and me?

I long to see by the fireside
my girl and me sitting by her side.
Wouldn't that be nice?
We've tried everything else twice.
So why don't we try staying home?

Let us begin to cut
the folks who merely strut
and talk of nothing but their incomes.
Let's have no further use
for going on the loose
the moment the orange juice
and gin comes.

Our new love affair
will make us cease to care
how many parties they're giving

We're done with being smart
and so we're going to start
to learn the gentle art of living.

All the home folks we know
pay for it later in Reno.
Just being still,
might give us a brand new thrill.
So why don't we try staying home?"

— *Cole Porter, 1929*

L

LAKE TROUT

All trout are excellent when cooked on the grill. They are also a real treat when smoked. For more information on both methods of cooking, see Trout, freshwater and sea, page 234.

LAMB, BREAST

Lamb breast benefits from long, slow cooking, a process that will render out much of the fat associated with this cut. Here in Kansas City, most barbecue joints offer lamb breast in addition to the more traditional pork and beef.

Classic side dishes include coleslaw (page 321), Italian white bean salad (page 326) and mashed potatoes (page 327).

Lamb breast can be prepared in one of three ways. If you want to try barbecuing lamb breast, choose either the first or third method.

a) Use a dry rub before grilling and serve a sauce with the lamb breast after it has been cooked. Massage the dry rub evenly into the breast, shake off any excess, place it on a platter and allow it to sit at room temperature for 1 hour or so. This method appeals to those who like that old-fashioned, traditional barbecue flavor. Try barbecue-style dry rub (page 309) and serve with your favorite bottled barbecue sauce (or use one of the recipes found on pages 297 to 298).

b) Marinate the lamb breast for 2 to 3 hours and then grill, basting with the leftover marinade. This works only for non-traditional barbecue marinades (any marinade that isn't tomato-red in color). Try garlic, rosemary and

Surprisingly, lamb breast is a frequent subject for tradtional barbecue preparation. Although not as popular as beef brisket, barbecued lamb breast has many enthuiastic supporters.

rosé marinade (page 290), Greek marinade (page 290) or Southwestern marinade (page 294). Each of these produce very flavorful results, but *not* in the barbecue style. Just for the record, if you try to grill any meat that has been marinated in a tomato-based sauce, it's almost impossible to keep the sauce from completely burning during the cooking process.

c) Grill the lamb breast without any seasoning until almost done, then mop with a traditional barbecue sauce during the last 10 minutes or so on the grill. This method produces less intensely spiced meat than the first method, but still with that old-timey flavor. The few minutes the coated lamb breast is on the grill allows the sauce to set and adhere, but avoids the problem of burning. Additional sauce can be heated and poured over cut meat at the table. Use your favorite bottled sauce or one of the recipes given on pages 297 to 298.

Prepare the lamb breast using one of the three procedures just described. The meat is best cooked in a covered grill, either by first searing on both sides and cooking away from the heat for approximately 30 minutes (indirect method), or by using the following traditional slow-cook method:

1) Remove the lamb breast from the refrigerator about 30 minutes before cooking. This will allow it to come to room temperature before it goes on the grill.

2) Ignite 40 to 50 briquets. Once they are covered with a light gray ash, separate the briquets into equal amounts and push to opposite sides of the fire grate. Place a disposable aluminum pan in the center, between the coals, and fill half-full with water. Put the cooking grill in place.

3) Once the coals reach the moderate stage, place the lamb breast directly over the drip pan. Put the cover in place, leaving the bottom vent completely open and the top vent about half open. Turn the meat every 30 minutes. If you're using a non-tomato-based marinade, baste the lamb breast with leftover marinade each time you turn it. Total cooking time will be about 2 hours, at

Lamb Facts

Lamb that is labeled "genuine lamb," "lamb," or "spring lamb" must, according to the U.S.D.A., be less than a year old. Between one and two years old, sheep are classified as "yearlings"; "mutton" is the term used for sheep more than two years old (see Mutton, page 172).

The term "spring lamb" identifies lamb processed between the first Monday in March through the first Monday in October. Years ago, lamb production peaked in the spring; during the rest of the year if you wanted spring lamb, you would have to settle for frozen meat.

The U.S.D.A. grades lamb as prime, choice and good. Most of what is available in supermarkets is either prime or choice. The U.S.D.A. also sponsors a program to encourage sheep producers to raise leaner lamb, using new feeding management and production practices. After being graded by U.S.D.A. inspectors, the lamb is given a red, white and blue sticker proclaiming it as "Certified Fresh American Lamb." Approximately the top third of the lamb produced in America receives this designation.

which point the lamb breast will be well done — the only way this particular cut should be served.

4) To maintain a low but constant temperature, add 10 more lit briquets, 5 on each side, every 30 minutes or so (see *Keeping the Fire Going,* on page 34).

5) When the lamb breast is nicely browned on both sides, remove it from the grill and allow it to rest for 15 minutes or so. Slice at an angle, across the grain, into thin slices.

LAMB, BUTTERFLIED LEG

Butterflied legs of lamb have become very popular grilled fare. In addition to being absolutely delicious, they are easy to grill, easy to carve, and take well to any number of marinades. And there's no waste! If you have a backyard event coming up that includes feeding a crowd of people, by all means consider a butterflied leg of lamb cooked on the grill.

Let the marinade determine the menu. Here are a few sure-bet combinations:

Garlic, rosemary and rosé marinade (page 290): Italian white bean salad (page 326), grilled whole tomatoes (page 232), grilled ratatouille (page 332), plenty of warm, crusty French bread and a cold rosé, such as Bandol.

Indian yogurt marinade (page 291): cold rice and pea salad (page 320), marinated cucumbers (page 327) and warm pita bread. Best served with cold beer.

Greek marinade (page 290): grilled chevre (page 100), roasted peppers (page 91), grilled eggplant (page 127) and warm pita or French bread.

1) Remove the lamb from the refrigerator about 30 minutes prior to grilling. To make certain that the meat is done to your liking, it's a good idea to insert a meat thermometer into the thickest portion of the lamb.

2) Ignite approximately 55 to 65 briquets. Once the coals are covered with a fine gray ash, arrange them in a

A butterflied leg of lamb is perfect for grilling when you're expecting a large crowd. It adapts to any number of marinades, from Middle Eastern-style to those classic flavors of Greece — rosemary, garlic and black peppercorns.

single layer in the center of the fire grate. Put cooking grill in place (5 to 6 inches above the fire if you have an adjustable grill).

3) Place the lamb directly over a hot fire. If you are using a covered grill, put the lid in place, leaving top and bottom vents completely open. Turn every 10 minutes or so. Move meat away from the fire if it begins to char.

4) Total cooking time should be between 40 and 60 minutes. For medium-rare meat, remove the lamb when the thermometer reaches 140 to 150 degrees F. Let it rest on a carving board for10 minutes or so, then slice against the grain. Serve with any juices that accumulate on the board.

LAMB, CHOPS

Lamb chops are one of the true delights to come off the grill — the flavor of lamb and the flavors of the grill just seem to go together. Only recently have Americans embraced the notion of eating their lamb rare or medium-rare; if you haven't given it a try, by all means do. While it may not be an empirical truth, lamb *does* seem to be at its best when it's considerably less than well-done.

The goal, then, is to keep the meat pink on the inside, the outside nicely browned, and the fat practically crisped. An impossible task? Not at all. It simply calls for starting with approximately 1½-inch-thick chops and a bed of coals that has gone from very hot to moderately hot. Once the coals are covered with a fine gray ash, wait about 10 to 12 minutes before putting the chops on the grill. If the chops in the meat case are skinny little things, ring the buzzer and ask the butcher to cut you some thick ones.

There are a number of marinades that enhance rather than mask the flavor of lamb. Try all-purpose marinade (page 289), garlic, rosemary and rosé marinade (page 290) or herb marinade (page 291). Or simply oil and pepper them before grilling and serve with Béarnaise sauce (page 298).

Party Menu

Butterflied, marinated leg of lamb is a great centerpiece for an outdoor menu. Even those who thought they didn't like lamb will come away with a change of mind after they've tried your version.

A 6- or 7-pound leg (weight before boning) will serve eight people. Choose the marinade of your choice from the suggestions given on pages 289 to 295. Here are a few ideas for side dishes: Italian white bean salad — this is better than it may sound. There's something about the combination of white beans and lamb that's just right. For recipe, see page 326.

If it's summer and the tomatoes are ripe, how about a big platterful of thick tomato slices, sprinkled with chopped basil, ground pepper and a little drizzle of vinaigrette? For vinaigrette recipe, see page 71.

Marinated cucumbers and, served nice and cold, would be good. See page 327.

A large piece of feta cheese, swimming in a shallow pool of good-quality olive oil, with oregano and freshly ground black pepper sprinkled on top, is perfect either as an hors d'oeuvre or served with the grilled lamb. A bowl full of black or green olives — good ones from Spain, France, Italy or Greece — are just right for snacking on with the feta cheese.

Pita bread, which is great when briefly heated on the grill, is good for making "pocket" lamb sandwiches. Be sure to have a bowl of plain yogurt to use as a sauce.

Call up some friends. Cook this menu. You'll have a great time!

As far as side dishes go, classic pairings include steamed asparagus or artichokes, galette of potatoes (page 323) or grilled potato wedges (page 196) basted with a simple mix of salt, pepper, rosemary and olive oil. Serve with a Chateauneuf du Pape or one of the other wonderful red Rhones, and get ready to enjoy yourself.

1) Remove the chops from the refrigerator approximately 30 minutes prior to grilling. If you are cooking them plain, rub the chops with olive oil and dust with freshly ground pepper.

2) Ignite 55 to 65 briquets or an equal amount of lump charcoal. If you are cooking a large number of chops, use enough charcoal to create a bed of coals approximately the same size as the area the meat will cover on the grill.

3) Once the coals are covered with light gray ash, arrange them into a solid bed in the center of the fire grate. Put the cooking grill in place (3 to 5 inches above the fire if you have an adjustable model) and wait 10 minutes or so for the fire to burn down a little.

4) Place the chops directly over the coals. On covered grills, put the lid in place and leave both top and bottom vent holes completely open.

5) Turn the chops every 3 to 5 minutes. They should cook to medium-rare in 12 to 14 minutes.

LAMB, GROUND

Lamb "burgers" are particularly good when cooked over charcoal. Grilling renders much of the characteristic fat away from the ground lamb, as opposed to cooking the meat in it, as you would in a skillet. It's the flavor of the fat that many people respond to when they say they "don't like lamb." But grilled ground lamb may convert a few lamb-haters to lamb-lovers.

Start with lean ground lamb, seasoned with a little salt and freshly ground pepper. Shape the meat into patties approximately ¾-inch thick. If you plan on

Well-seasoned lamb patties are just the thing to put into pita bread — along with all the fixings: chopped tomatoes, cucumbers and onions, a little lettuce and a dollop of plain yogurt flavored with cumin and cayenne. Delicious!

inserting the patties into pita bread, shape them into long ovals instead of rounds.

If you're not plagued with trying to please finicky palates, ground lamb takes very well to some fairly exotic seasoning. Pressed garlic and minced onion are relatively safe bets. But why not take it a step further and add a scant amount of chopped mint? Moving up the exotic scale, there's rosemary (or that classic lamb combination of rosemary *and* garlic), or ground cumin and ginger for a Middle Eastern flavor (great in pita bread with slices of cucumber and a dollop of plain yogurt), or in the Indian style with curry powder — again, delicious in pita bread with a little chutney and cucumbers for added crunch. By this time you have left the 11-year-old contingent far behind, but any of these seasonings make very tasty treats for adventurous eaters.

Grill the patties as you would hamburgers, directly over moderate coals, with the cooking grill approximately 3 to 5 inches above the fire. Total cooking time will be around 8 to 10 minutes; turn once, halfway through the total cooking time.

Lamb, leg, bone-in

There's no comparison between a leg of lamb cooked in a covered grill or on a rotisserie (see *Spit Cooking,* page 46) and one cooked in an oven. At least for my own taste, this is *the* way to roast lamb. The following procedure is the essence of simplicity and produces a classic roast leg of lamb.

Note: Between the layer of fat and the meat, there is a thin covering on the leg that's known as "fell." If the fat has been removed, you'll be able to see it clearly. Leave the fell in place; it helps preserve the meat's succulence.

Using the tip of a small, sharp knife, make six to twelve incisions around the leg (depending on your preference for the taste of garlic), and push pieces of peeled and quartered fresh garlic into each incision. Rub the exterior of the leg lightly with a little olive or vegetable oil; dust heavily with freshly ground black pepper and about a teaspoonful of crushed rosemary.

Great side dishes for a traditional roast lamb include

There's just no comparison between a leg of lamb cooked in a covered grill and one cooked in the oven. Once you've tried it, you may never cook lamb indoors again. Choose the smaller sirloin half (left) or the more traditional shank end (right).

grilled potato wedges (page 196), grilled new potatoes (page 196), grilled whole tomatoes (page 232), Italian white bean salad (page 326) and any fresh vegetable.

The following predure requires a covered kettle grill. You may also cook a leg of lamb using a rotisserie unit on an uncovered grill (see *Spit Cooking*, page 46).

1) Remove the leg of lamb from the refrigerator 30 minutes before cooking. Insert a meat thermometer into the thickest part of the roast; avoid hitting any of the the bones.

2) Ignite approximately 55 to 65 briquets or an equal amount of lump charcoal.

3) Once the coals are covered with a fine gray ash, separate them into two equal amounts and push to either side of the fire grate, leaving the center free of fire. Place the drip pan in the middle of the fire grate, between the coals. Put the cooking grill in place, and position the lamb so it's right over the drip pan. Put the cover on the grill, leaving both the top and bottom vents completely open.

4) A leg of lamb will take approximately 15 to 20 minutes per pound to reach the medium-rare stage — about 150 degrees F. on your meat thermometer. Start checking the thermometer after about 1 hour, remembering that the internal temperature rises much more quickly towards the end of the cooking time than at the beginning. If you want the leg medium-rare, take it off the grill when the thermometer reaches 145 degrees F., and allow to rest indoors on a platter, loosely covered with foil, for 10 minutes or so. Slice and serve with the juices that accumulate on the platter or Béarnaise sauce (page 298).

LAMB, RACK

If I were limited to just one choice of meat for cooking on the grill, it would probably be a rack of lamb. Racks come in various sizes (from four to eight ribs), depend-

One great side dish for a charcoal-roasted leg of lamb is grilled potato wedges (page 196). The potatoes can be cooked on the grill as the same time as the lamb.

ing, I think, on the whim of the butcher. At any rate, count on three to four ribs per person. Two ribs is usually too few, except for the daintiest appetites, and four is usually too many, but it at least provides the possibility of having some leftovers to gnaw on the next day.

Although it's not absolutely necessary, ask the butcher to make a cut along the length of the rack, between the meat and the rib bones — but not all the way through to the other side. This not only makes carving easier, it also gives you the opportunity of inserting a little garlic, ground pepper and rosemary down there before you put the rack on the grill. (My mouth is watering just at the thought of this.)

I'm sure there are many other things to serve with a rack of lamb, but I'm completely stuck on fresh, fat asparagus and galette of potatoes (page 323) — that, with a bottle of Cote Rotie, and I count myself among the truly fortunate.

If you're looking for an appetizer to serve before this meal, you couldn't possibly go wrong with a few thick slices of French bread toasted on the grill (page 95), spread with a little chevre, also warmed on the grill (page 100). I think I'd better stop here (unless someone wanted to make a rhubarb pie for dessert, *please,* with just a dollop of vanilla ice cream on top), because as far as I'm concerned, this is as good as food gets.

But back to the rack of lamb. If you care to, make incisions in between the rack and insert slivers of garlic into the meat. Lightly rub the outside of the rack with olive oil and dust the entire outside surface with freshly ground black pepper. Insert a meat thermometer into the center of the rack, with the face pointing out from the cut end. Now, it's ready for grilling. The following instructions apply to either a covered or uncovered grill.

1) Let the lamb sit at room temperature for 30 minutes before cooking.

2) Ignite approximately 25 to 35 briquets or an equal amount of lump charcoal (more if you're cooking more than two racks).

3) When the coals are covered with a fine gray ash, arrange them into a solid bed, a single layer thick, in the

Lamb and Nutrition

Compared to other meats, lamb contains very little marbling (internal fat running through the meat). Because most of the fat is on the outside edges of the meat, it is easily trimmed — which means fewer calories.

A three-ounce serving of lamb has approximately 176 calories and contains only 78 milligrams of cholesterol, or approximately 26 percent of the American Heart Association's recommended 300 milligrams per day.

center of the fire grate. Allow the fire to burn down for 5 or 10 minutes.

4) Place the rack of lamb on the grill, fat side down, directly over the coals, with the cooking grate 3 to 5 inches above the fire (if it's adjustable). If you're using a covered grill, put the top in place, with both top and bottom vents completely open. Grill the rack in this position for approximately 5 to 7 minutes, until the surface is nicely browned.

5) Turn the rack every 5 to 7 minutes. (If you're using a covered grill, it may not be necessary to turn the rack more than once, unless you feel it's becoming too brown.) Total cooking time will be 35 to 50 minutes, depending on the size of the rack. Watch the thermometer carefully; remove lamb from the grill when the thermometer reaches 135 degrees F. for rare; 150 to 155 degrees F. for medium-rare to medium. Slice between the bones with a sharp knife, creating individual chops. Serve with any juices that accumulate on the board.

Just one last thing: If it happens to be spring, someone should buy somebody a big bouquet of fresh lilacs. Put them in a prominent location where they can be enjoyed while you're eating this extraordinary meal; by candlelight, they will have a lovely, intoxicating effect.

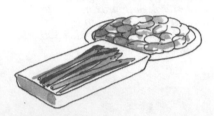

"I'm sure there are many other things to serve with a rack of lamb, but I'm completely stuck on fresh, fat asparagus and galette of potatoes."

LAMB, SHISH KABOB

Traditionally cut from a boned leg, marinated lamb shish kabob is pretty hard to beat. Marinate for 4 to 6 hours or overnight in all-purpose marinade (page 289), garlic, rosemary and rosé marinade (page 290), Greek marinade (page 290), Indian yogurt marinade (page 291) or red wine marinade (page 294).

For more information on this classic grilled fare, see *Skewer Cooking,* page 56.

LINGCOD

This fish, which is not a cod at all, is sadly underutilized. Some people are put off by the slight greenish tinge of the raw flesh, but rest assured, once cooked, it turns pure white. Lingcod is lean and mild, and the fillets are excellent for grilling.

Grill lingcod fillets plain, with just a brushing of oil and a dusting of paprika on both sides. Serve with boiled new potatoes (page 320), steamed parslied rice (page 337) and grilled whole tomatoes (page 232). A chilled bottle of Sauvignon Blanc would go nicely with this meal.

1) About 30 minutes before cooking, take the lingcod out of the refrigerator.

2) Ignite as many briquets or as much lump charcoal as it takes to make a bed of coals a little larger in size than what the fish will take up on the grill. Put the cooking grill in place and let it heat up.

3) Once the cooking grill is hot, clean it with a wire brush. Just before you're ready to put the fish over the coals, oil the grill, using a large basting brush and vegetable oil.

4) If the fillets have the skin intact, place them on the grill skin side down. Grill the fillets directly over a bed of hot coals.

5) Cook the lingcod 10 minutes per inch of thickness, measured at the thickest part. If, for example, the lingcod fillet is 1 inch thick, it will take 10 minutes to cook — 5 minutes per side. Turn the fish only once. Don't use the cover on covered grills.

6) The fish should be served hot off the grill, on a platter that has been heated for 15 minutes in a 250-degree F. oven.

See Fish, page 133, for more information.

Paprika and Fish

There is a special affinity between fresh fish and paprika, one that may transcend mere taste. Some contend that there is a chemical reaction between the paprika and the fish that prevents the skin of the fish from becoming tough and hard during the grilling process. Whether that's actually true or not I've had trouble confirming.

I do know, however, that all the old-time fish restaurants in San Francisco follow this practice, and always have. Some of these places were started by immigrants from the coast of Dalmatia and many had cooks from that region, one that has now been incorporated into Yugoslavia (for the moment, at any rate). The tradition of combining fish and paprika immigrated with them, and although most of the Dalmatian chefs are now long gone, the paprika is not.

Every day, it seems, another bit of folk wisdom is confirmed by modern science. Paprika's effect on fish may or may not be one of those old tales proved true. Meanwhile, I continue to enjoy the combination of flavors, especially the good, hot paprika imported from Hungary.

LIVER

You're not going to be able to sell this dish to everyone, but for those who love liver (count me in), charcoal grilling is hard to beat. Also hard to beat is Helen Evens Brown's and James Beard's recipe for it, which appeared in *The Complete Book of Outdoor Cookery,* first published in 1955 and fortunately reissued in 1989 by Perennial Library. The book is a classic; so is the following:

"Thick liver steaks, grilled over charcoal until they are crisply brown on the outside and juicily pink in the middle, are epicurean treats. Have the liver — calf or beef — sliced about 1½ inches thick, butter the steaks well, and grill as you do a steak, testing them by making an incision with a small, sharp knife — you will be able to see when it is done to your liking. Serve with Béarnaise sauce [page 298] and with grilled tomato and bacon, or a great bowlful of french fried onions. Liver steak is also good served with butter and lemon wedges, and accompanied by spinach flavored with tarragon. A bottle of chilled California rosé wine or some beer seems particularly fitting."

Enough said.

LOBSTER

I hope everyone has a chance, at least once, to grill just-caught lobster on the beach, over a driftwood fire. There's nothing quite like it.

Lacking a beach (not to mention ocean), a boat pulling up to the dock with fresh lobster and a load of driftwood, make do with your backyard grill and the freshest lobster you can find. There seem to be a couple of good grocery stores, even in the most landlocked of cities, that carry live lobsters in those bubbling tanks. (I say *live,* but I don't think carrying on in such cramped quarters with an intolerable number of cell-mates and rubber bands on your claws is any lobster's idea of a good time.) Too much time in the tank can make for a less than vital lobster. Before you buy one, ask to feel the heft of a few and buy the heaviest.

As with all shellfish, the most important thing is not

There's nothing quite like grilling just-caught lobster on the beach over a driftwood fire.

to overcook the lobster. With prolonged cooking, the delicate texture, flavor and aroma of shellfish goes through a transformation and becomes something less than appetizing. With such a splendid and savory creature, there's no need to add any additional flavors with marinades or basting sauces; let the lobster be the star of the show. Serve with drawn butter, mayonnaise and wedges of lemon. Lots of warm, crusty French bread is practically essential. A tossed salad, corn on the cob, coleslaw (page 321)? Only if you want. Beer, I think, is the beverage of choice; lacking that, a nice Chardonnay will do.

1) Ignite 55 to 65 briquets or an equal amount of lump charcoal. You'll want a hot fire to cook the lobster quickly.

2) Once the charcoal is covered with a light gray ash, arrange into a single layer in the center of the fire grate. Put the cooking grill in place (approximately 3 to 5 inches above the fire if it's adjustable).

3) Kill the lobster by stabbing the tip of a sharp knife right behind the top of its head at the cross-shaped mark. (Have a beer first, and see *Murder in the Kitchen*, at right.) Split them down the middle, lengthwise; discard the intestinal canal, *et al.* (Have another beer.)

Note: The tail meat will cook in 8 to 10 minutes; the claws and legs will take 10 to 14 minutes. There are two ways to handle this: Either remove the legs and claws before putting the body on the grill, and put them on first; or put the whole lobster on the grill, cook until the tail meat is done, remove from the grill, take off the legs and claws and cook a couple of minutes longer.

4) Place the lobsters on the grill, cut side down, directly over the coals. Turn in 4 to 5 minutes. Cook an additional 4 to 5 minutes. Take the bodies off the grill as soon as the tail meat turns an opaque white. Grill the legs and claws a couple of minutes longer. Heap onto a platter and serve them up.

Murder in the Kitchen

"The first victim was a lively carp brought into the kitchen in a covered basket from which nothing could escape. The fish man who sold me the carp said he had no time to kill, scale or clean it, nor would he tell me with which of these horrible necessities one began. It wasn't difficult to know which was the most repellent. So quickly to the murder and have it over with. On the docks of Puget Sound I had seen fishermen grasp the tail of a huge salmon and lifting it high bring it down on the dock with enough force to kill it. Obviously I was not a fisherman nor was the kitchen table a dock. Should I not dispatch my first victim with a blow on the head from a heavy mallet? After an appraising glance at the lively fish it was evident he would escape attempts aimed at his head. A heavy sharp knife came to my mind as the classic, the perfect choice, so grasping, with my left hand well covered with a dishcloth, for the teeth might be sharp, the lower jaw of the carp, and the knife in my right, I carefully, deliberately found the base of its vertebral column and plunged the knife in. I let go my grasp and looked to see what had happened. Horror of horrors. The carp was dead, killed, assassinated, murdered in the first, second and third degree. Limp, I fell into a chair, with my hands still unwashed reached for a cigarette, lighted it, and waited for the police to come and take me into custody. After a second cigarette my courage returned and I went to prepare poor Mr. Carp for the table."

From the wonderfully entertaining book, The Alice B. Toklas Cook Book, by Alice B. Toklas.

Smoked Fish

This is a book about grilling, not smoking, but there are two types of fish that are so easily smoked in a regular covered kettle grill that they deserve mention here, namely trout and mackerel. Both make an excellent and special appetizer; you don't need to tell anyone how easy it was to do.

You will need a whole fish, of course (with head and tail left on, if desired), in the ½- to 2-pound size range (if your trout are from the store, they will almost always be farm-raised and almost exactly 8 ounces); a covered grill; about 15 to 30 briquets (depending on the number of fish you are smoking) or an equal amount of lump charcoal; some "smoking" chips (any will do, but the flavor imparted by apple and alder chips are both particularly good with fish); vegetable oil; and a little soy or teriyaki sauce (optional).

Soak 3 or 4 good handfuls of smoking chips in water for 30 minutes. Ignite the charcoal. Remove the fish from refrigerator and paint it with soy or teriyaki sauce (recommended, but not necessary). Allow to sit at room temperature while the coals ignite.

Once the coals are covered in a fine gray ash, push them to one side of the fire grate.

...continued on page 167

M

MACKEREL

For people who enjoy a full-flavored fish, mackerel makes fine eating. There are several species of mackerel, most ranging in size from one to four pounds, with oily flesh that varies in color from white to red. Buy the freshest mackerel possible, which is most often available as fillets or as small whole fish.

Because of its oily flesh, mackerel holds up very well on the grill. (It's also delicious when smoked; see *Smoked Fish* at left.) The mackerel's distinctive taste also combines well with many strong-flavored marinades. Try fresh ginger-garlic marinade (page 290) or lemon-white wine marinade (page 292). If you marinate the fish, do so for only 30 minutes to 1 hour.

Classic side dishes include steamed rice (page 337), marinated cucumbers (page 327) and grilled potato wedges (page 196).

1) Take the mackerel out of the refrigerator 30 minutes before grilling.

2) Determine how much space the fish will take up on the grill, and make a bed of coals that's a little larger in size. Ignite the briquets (or lump charcoal).

3) Put the cooking grill in place and allow it to heat up before putting on the fish; it will stick to a cold grill. After the grill is hot, use a wire brush to clean it, if necessary, then coat it with vegetable oil.

4) If you have an adjustable grill, position the cooking grate 3 to 5 inches above the coals. On covered grills, cook without the lid in place.

5) Small whole fish (less than 4 pounds) can be cooked

directly over the coals, uncovered, just like steaks and fillets. If you're cooking fillets, put them on the grate skin side down first. Cook the fish for 10 minutes per inch of thickness. Turn the fish just once, halfway through the cooking time.

6)   Serve the fish while it's piping hot, on a platter that has been heated for 15 minutes in a 250-degree F. oven.

See Fish, page 133, for more information.

Mahi-mahi

In most books you'll find this listed as "dolphin," but that moniker has caused so much confusion with consumers, there's now a movement afoot to call dolphin by its Hawaiian name — mahi-mahi. Mahi-mahi is not a mammal, but a beautifully colored, tropical fish, ranging in color from blue-green to chartreuse. The flesh of mahi-mahi is firm with a delightfully mild, fresh flavor. This fish ranges in size from 15 to 35 pounds and is very popular in the Islands. At one time, mahi-mahi rarely showed up in mainland fish markets, but it's now becoming more readily available. Because it has such a good, natural flavor, mahi-mahi should be prepared simply, with just a brushing of vegetable oil before cooking and a few wedges of fresh lemon on the table. In Hawaii, they sprinkle it with chopped macadamia nuts.

Keep side dishes equally simple: steamed rice (page 337) or grilled new potatoes (page 196). Good vegetables include sautéed Swiss chard or Chinese cabbage, sprinkled with Japanese rice wine vinegar.

1)   Take the fish out of the refrigerator 30 minutes before grilling time. It should be at room temperature when it goes on the grill.

2)   Ignite a bed of charcoal that's a little larger in area than what the fish will take up on the grill. Put the cooking grate in position (3 to 5 inches above the coals if you're using an adjustable model) and allow it to become good and hot.

...continued from page 166

Place the wet smoking chips on top of the hot coals. Put the cooking grill in position. Liberally oil the fish on both sides with vegetable oil (it's easiest to do with your hands). Place the fish on the cooking grill, opposite the fire. Put the lid on, keeping both top and bottom vents completely open, with the top vents positioned over the fish, opposite the fire. (This has the effect of pulling the smoke up around the fish.)

Total smoking time for an 8-ounce fish will be about 30 to 40 minutes (lengthen the smoking time accordingly for larger fish); turn once after 10 or 15 minutes, adding more wet smoking chips if necessary. After it's smoked, gently remove the whole fish with a spatula. Place on a platter and allow to cool.

You'll find that the skin comes off easily if you simply start lifting it with the tip of a sharp knife either at the head or tail end. Serve proudly with crackers, a little mayonnaise (flavored with a clove or two of pressed fresh garlic) and wedges of fresh lemon. One of the ultimate hors d'oeuvres!

This is a dolphin. It is a mammal.

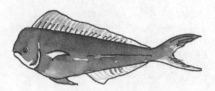

This is a mahi-mahi, sometimes sold as dolphin or dolphinfish. It is no relation whatsoever to dolphin, and definitely not a mammal.

3) Use a wire brush to clean the hot grill, if necessary. Just before you're ready to grill, coat both the fish and the cooking grill with a mild vegetable oil, using a large basting brush.

4) Cook the fish directly over a bed of hot coals. If you have a covered grill, cook the fish without putting the cover down.

5) Cook the mahi-mahi 10 minutes per inch of thickness. For example, a 1-inch fillet would take 10 minutes to cook — 5 minutes per side. Plan on turning the fish only once — half the total cooking time on each side.

6) Fish should be served hot off the grill — within seconds, if possible — so have the rest of your meal ready to go before putting the fish on the grill. Heated plates help keep the fish piping hot, so slip the plates into a 250 degree F. oven about 15 minutes before eating time, along with a platter on which to land the fish immediately after grilling.

See Fish, page 133, for more information.

MARSHMALLOWS

It's debatable whether or not these airy little confections are grilled or toasted over the coals — not that it really makes any difference, just as long as you don't put them directly on the grill! Marshmallows have been and always will be the highlight of an outdoor meal for the junior set.

Although skewers and coat hangers can be put into service, a nice straight branch with a pointed end — one that hasn't been sprayed with pesticides — is just what you need. Wait until the coals are low, remove the cooking grill (put it in a safe, out-of-the-way place; it will be hot) and let the kids have at it, twisting, twirling, and toasting to their hearts' delight.

MELON

Grilled melon may sound a little strange, but it's actually very good, especially with pork. Cantaloupe is my favorite, but casaba, Crenshaw, honeydew and Persian melons can all be successfully grilled. The point is simply to heat it through, and have it pick up a little of the smoky flavors of the grill. To do this, slice the melon into approximately 1-inch-thick (at the widest part) wedges or rounds, or, if you're skewer-cooking, into cubes. It's not necessary, but you may prefer to peel the melon before grilling.

Brush with a little melted butter on all sides and grill over a moderate fire for a total of 3 to 5 minutes, turning frequently. If you have children, they'll think you've gone 'round the bend; if you serve it to guests, they'll have something to talk about on the way home. I say, if it tastes good, serve it up anyway.

MIXED GRILL

Generally agreed as having originated in Britain, today the term "mixed grill" has come to mean many things. In England, traditional mixed grill still means a combination of lamb or mutton chop, lamb kidney, bacon and sausage, usually threaded on a skewer and usually overcooked. The truth of the matter is that cooking so many different items on a single skewer is difficult. Not to mention the fact that there aren't as many takers for "variety meats" (such as kidneys) as there once were.

In this country, the term has come to mean almost any combination of meats (usually including sausage or bacon) cooked on the same skewer. Mixed grilled can be cooked, more or less successfully, if you take the time to make sure all the pieces are roughly the same size. But I can't say that I recommend it.

This may be one of those historic dishes that are best left in history — or for that trip to England, where the ambiance and the ale will more than make up for the less-than-perfect morsels on your plate.

"Grilled melon may sound a little strange, but it's actually very good, especially with pork."

Every type of mushroom has its own personality and taste. We are indeed living in fortunate times to have such a large selection of mushrooms so widely available. Not that long ago, the unusual types were for the exclusive enjoyment of those who actually got out there and hunted wild mushrooms.

The following mushrooms are particularly well-suited to the grill. All should be cooked until just tender and served as is (wonderful as a sidedish to any grilled meat or as a vegetarian main course), with just a drizzle of very good olive oil, a pinch of salt and maybe a sprinkling of finely chopped fresh parsley. Alternatively, they can be used to flavor a luscious sauce, wonderful on grilled veal chops or beef steaks (see Rustic Mushroom Sauce at right).

Button mushrooms: *These are the standard white to light tan small mushrooms. While their flavor is very mild, grilling intensifies what is there, and adds some of the smoky quality associated with wild mushrooms.*

Crimini: *Looks like a larger version of the standard button mushroom, only darker brown in color and meatier in texture. Excellent grilled.*

Matsutake: *If you can find these Japanese mushrooms, grown on pine logs, by all means try them. Very meaty texture holds up well on the grill. Try them cooked whole, and then thinly sliced, served up on pieces of grilled French bread. Don't forget the juices!*

Oyster mushrooms: *These are so delicate they must be handled with extreme care on the grill. Not as meaty nor as strongly flavored as some of the others, but excellent nonetheless. A nice choice for the cream sauce described at right.*

Shiitake: *A Japanese mushroom that grows principally on oak. Large, somewhat floppy, and probably the meatiest and most intensely flavored mushroom currently available commercially. Excellent for grilling.*

MONKFISH

Monkfish is just one of the many names for the fish most commonly sold as Angler, an excellent choice for grilling. For more information, see Angler, page 68.

MUSHROOMS

Where once there were just plain white mushrooms, all of sudden the produce department is filled with all manner of fungi. Oyster mushrooms, shiitaki, brown Criminis and a host of others. This is true progress for people who really like to eat! Not that there's anything wrong with those white mushrooms we've seen for so long, except by comparison, they're a little bland.

The earthy flavor of any mushroom combines perfectly with the rustic, slightly smoky flavor of the grill — one of those charmed combinations, I think. The point in cooking mushrooms on the grill is not really to grill them, but to warm them through, pick up a little of the smoky flavor, and have them sweat a bit.

White mushrooms and brown Criminis are sturdy enough to stand up to skewering, which makes them very easy to handle on the grill. Baste them with olive oil while they cook. They're ready to eat when they can be easily pierced to the center with the point of a sharp knife.

The floppier, more delicate varieties should be handled with care. Coat them with a little olive oil as gently as you can. Instead of skewering, put them right on the grill, towards the edges of the fire or on top of whatever else you might be cooking. (This works especially well in a covered grill with the top in place.) Ten minutes or so in this inferno will wilt these delicate beauties until they are just tender.

Serve grilled mushrooms plain, as the very exotic garnish they are, or use them to make this very special sauce:

Rustic Mushroom Sauce

Slice the grilled mushrooms and toss them into a moderately hot frying pan with a little melted butter. Sauté gently, add a tablespoon or two of dry sherry (or some Madeira, if you have some, m'dear), juices from whatever meat you've just carved, a little beef or chicken stock and a tablespoon or so of heavy cream. Heat, but don't boil. Before serving, stir in a few drops of fresh lemon juice. This extraordinary sauce is delicious and somehow fitting during the first cold snap in fall.

Mussels

Mussels may be the most overlooked shellfish of all, but they rank right near the top with me. A bucketful of steamed mussels Bordelaise and a couple of Bloody Marys will fix you up faster than you can say, "I didn't really say that last night, did I?"

Be that as it may, mussels are also easily grilled, right in their shells, politely opening when they are ready to eat. This is special-event food, so be sure to have the right sort of participants around before you get started.

Buy a lot of mussels. Maybe a dozen per person, even if you're only serving them as appetizers. Once you convince someone to eat a mussel, they'll be right back for another — and another. When it comes time to purchase the mussels, favor the smaller ones — those that are under 3 inches in length. Not only are the smaller mussels more tender, they're less intimidating for the uninitiated.

If the mussels haven't already been debearded (the "beard" is that little bunch of fibers that sticks out between the shells), do this by pulling the fibers off with a twist and a yank. Wash the mussel shells under cold running water, using some kind of abrasive pad or brush (not one with soap in it). Once that's done, grilling them is a snap.

While the fire is still good and hot, simply arrange the mussels on the grill (positioned 3 inches from the coals if the grill is adjustable), directly over the coals. They should pop open in about 2 to 3 minutes.

Have everyone standing around the grill because you're going to take them off as soon as they open (otherwise they toughen up). Wearing a fireproof mitt, take the mussels off one by one, twist off the top shell, and pass them out.

If you want to look like an old pro, use an empty set of mussel shells as a pair of tongs for removing the mussel meat from the shell.

Serve with wedges of lemon, Tabasco Sauce sauce, melted butter or perhaps some mignonette sauce (page 302) close at hand for dipping. If any of the mussels don't open, toss them out.

This is an animated, delicious way to start a meal. And because the mussels cook so quickly, there will still be plenty of life in the coals for cooking the main course.

MUTTON

Interestingly, mutton has all but disappeared in this country; most of what we raise is exported to countries that do not have a cultural bias against two-year-old sheep. There are a handful of restaurants around the country who pride themselves in still offering mutton to their patrons. Generally speaking, it is handled in the same way as lamb (see Lamb, pages 154-162), with the exception that extra care is taken to trim it of its rather strong-flavored fat.

If you don't know someone who raises sheep, it is unlikely that you will ever encounter mutton — unless you happen into Jack's Restaurant in San Francisco some night. As one of the oldest restaurants in San Francisco (opened in 1867 and still operating in its original Sacramento Street location), Jack's menu offers mutton chops to a very discriminating clientele. If you get the chance, give it a try.

O

OCTOPUS

"Nature's toothbrush," I believe, is how the Chinese refer to octopus. Does this give you any clues? Chewier than its much smaller cousin, the squid, octopus will need some tenderizing before grilling. And be forewarned, while its relatively mild flavor will win some votes, its texture won't.

It's unlikely that you will encounter a whole octopus on your next trip to the fish counter; far more likely that it will be cut into manageable pieces. You can ask the fishmonger to get the butcher to tenderize it for you, or bring it home and pound the heck out of it.

Simply brush the octopus with oil before grilling or marinate it. Try fresh ginger-garlic marinade (page 290), lemon-white wine marinade (292) or Southeast Asian-style marinade (294).

Octopus is good served hot, at room temperature, or cold (thinly sliced on an exotic seafood salad). It's also good as a little appetizer, cooked up before the main course — conversation pieces, as it were.

1) Look at the octopus and determine how much space it will take up on the grill. Make a bed of coals that's a little larger in size and ignite them.

2) Octopus will stick to a cold grill, so put the cooking grill over the coals and let it heat up. Just before putting on the octopus, clean the hot grill with a wire brush and oil it, using a large basting brush and vegetable oil.

3) Grill the octopus directly over the fire, with the cooking grate about 3 to 5 inches over the coals (if it's adjustable). If you're using a covered grill, cook without putting the cover down. And don't leave the grill! Octopus cooks quickly.

Be forewarned, while the relatively mild flavor of octopus will win some votes, its texture won't.

4) Cook just until the octopus turns an opaque white (a matter of only a few minutes) and no longer, or it will toughen beyond the point of enjoyment.

ONION

Yellow, white and red dry onions are all excellent on the grill. Just for the record, they are termed *dry* because of their dry skins.

Onions can be cut into ½-inch-thick rounds, quarters, or in half, brushed with vegetable oil, melted butter, or any marinade with oil in it, and successfully grilled. If you're cooking onion halves, leave the skins on while you cook them, with the thought that it's better to char the skins than the insides. Remove the skins before serving.

The rounds will cook quickly — approximately 2 minutes per side, and can be grilled directly over the coals. Quartered or halved onions will take longer. To cook them without burning, position them at the edge of the fire or wait until the fire is at the moderate stage and grill directly over the coals. Quartered or halved onions may take from 12 to 20 minutes to become tender enough to eat. It's a real delight to eat grilled onions that still have a little crunch to them, so don't grill them to the point where they are limp.

The small white boiling onions, when you can find them, are also excellent grilled. Simply cut off the tops and bottoms, leaving the skins intact, and string on bamboo skewers that have been soaked for 30 minutes or so in hot water. Roll the onions around on the grill until you can easily pierce the flesh with the tip of a sharp knife. Remove the skins before eating and, if desired, toss lightly with a little balsamic vinegar, salt and freshly ground pepper.

Sliced onions are proverbial favorites on grilled hamburgers and liver; the little boiling onions are wonderful served as an accompaniment to any roast — whether chicken, beef, pork or lamb. Good, hearty winter fare.

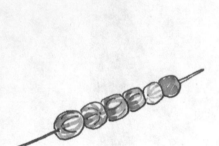

Small white boiling onions, when you can find them, are excellent for grilling. Simply cut off the tops and bottoms and string them on small bamboo skewers.

Ono

Ono is the Hawaiian name for wahoo. What name this fish is marketed under is currently something of a toss-up. Perhaps the two names should be combined and hyphenated — wahoo-ono? At any rate, this relative of the mackerel is outstanding cooked on the grill. For the time being, you'll find more information on this delectable fish listed under Wahoo, page 253.

Oysters

Have you ever invited an assemblage of guests for dinner that you weren't quite sure would get along? In situations like these, it's a good idea to provide a little action to relieve some of the social strain. There's no better way to do this than by grilling up some oysters as appetizers — right in their shells. These are, to my mind, one of the best things a grill can produce.

Let's say you're having eight people over. Half of them, maybe, will love oysters. The other half wouldn't think of putting one of those things in their mouths. Right away, everyone has something to talk about, while you're busy starting a good hot fire in the grill.

Before your guests arrive, start by washing the oysters under running water, using a good stiff scrub brush. If they're available, a backyard and a garden hose are great for this job. Keep the oysters cool and damp until you're ready to grill them.

While the fire is still good and hot, simply arrange the oysters on the grill, directly over the coals. The best thing about oysters is that they tell you when they're ready to come off the grill by opening up their shells, so all you have to do is stand there, wearing your fireproof mitt, and take the oysters off one by one, pull off the top shell (a small screwdriver or oyster knife will come in handy), and pass them out.

Use whatever powers you have to convince those who have never tried oysters to throw caution to the wind. Have wedges of lemon already cut, Tabasco Sauce, melted butter, the pepper grinder and perhaps some mignonette sauce (page 302) close at hand for dipping,

Oyster Lore

Oysters are one of the most controversial of all foods. People either love them or hate them, and it seems the older one gets, the more difficult it is to be converted into an oyster-lover.

Once upon a time, oysters were universally scorned, being viewed as "poor people's food." It was only after they became scarce that oysters were valued as gastronomic gems. When the pilgrims arrived in America, the bays were teaming with oysters. Even though these early settlers had been existing on very lean provisions during their voyage, they ignored the oysters, regarding them as unfit to eat. My guess is that this reaction may have had something to do with lingering seasickness, but who knows?

If you like oysters, try to make your way to a good oyster bar, one that offers a wide selection of American and European varieties. Sample all of them. The subtle (and sometimes not so subtle) differences are quite remarkable. This is the only way I know of to determine your personal favorites.

Oysters spawn during the summer months (the months without "Rs" in them). Aficionados will tell you that oysters are less desirable during the R-less months, a period when they become somewhat flaccid and fatty. Far preferable are the oysters harvested during the late fall and winter, when colder water temperatures keep them firm and delectable.

Here's Brave New World author Aldous Huxley's rather bizarre observation on oysters: "I suppose that when the sapid and slippery morsel — which is gone like a flash of gustatory summer lightning — glides along the palate, few people imagine that they are swallowing a piece of machinery (and going machinery too) greatly more complicated than a watch." Few, indeed.

dripping, grinding and squeezing. If any of the oysters don't open, toss them out.

From this point on, your dinner party will probably be a big success. The oysters cook quickly, so there will still be plenty of life in the coals for cooking the main course. Try the whole grilled Salmon on page 209. You and the renowned hostess Perla Mesta will go down in history.

"Let's say you're having eight people over. Half of them, maybe, will love oysters. The other half wouldn't think of putting one of those things in their mouths. Right away, everyone has something to talk about, while you're busy starting a good hot fire in the grill."

P

Parsnips

The number of people who are actually going to grill parsnips is even less than the number of people who like parsnips, so I'm probably talking to a very small group here. But, like carrots, the earthy flavor of any vegetable that is grown underground is particularly well-suited to the rustic, slightly smoky flavors imparted by charcoal grilling. Parsnips definitely fall into this category, and I, for one, far prefer grilled parsnips to the same vegetable boiled or steamed.

According to Rosalind Creasy, this country's leading authority on vegetables, when it came to parsnips and the early colonists, they wanted them *big*. Instead of being harvested in the summer or fall, they were often left in the ground to "sweeten" during the cold winter months, to be eaten in late winter and early spring when precious few fresh vegetables were available. While boiling the bejesus out of them was probably the most common way of preparing parsnips back then, they were also roasted over an open fire, basted with drippings from a roast.

Take a clue from our early forebears, and look for those big fat parsnips in the market. Forget peeling them; simply use a plastic scouring pad to scrub them briskly under cold water. Dry thoroughly and rub with vegetable oil or brush with melted butter. Depending on how hefty they are, the parsnips will take at least 20 to 30 minutes to cook; longer if they are particularly large. Place them directly on the grill, at the edges of the fire. Baste with butter or vegetable oil during the cooking process, turning every 5 to 7 minutes. They will be done when the tip of a sharp knife easily pierces through to the middle of the parsnip. Serve hot off the grill, cut up into pieces, with melted butter, salt and pepper. Pretty darn good with a roast "joint" of beef.

"…the earthy flavor of any vegetable that is grown underground is particularly well-suited to the rustic, slightly smoky flavors imparted by charcoal grilling."

There are more than 7,000 varieties of peppers grown throughout the world. All of them belong to the genus Capsicum and the majority of them are hot. As you can see from the listing below, the familiar, blocky "bell" pepper is not.

What makes a pepper hot is its amount of capsaicin — a volatile oil found in the flesh of the pepper, but concentrated in its interior ribs. The ability to measure the relative hotness of peppers is a rather recent breakthrough. The hotness is measured in Scoville units, which reflect the number of uniform units of water it takes to neutralize the capsaicin (the heat-causing property of the pepper).

Hot peppers are invaluable as an ingredient in sauces and marinades, figuring prominently in many Asian, Southeast Asian, Caribbean and Latin American recipes. As good as hot peppers are in sauces and marinades, the plain old bell pepper (in any of its beautiful colors) is the best for grilling. Let the following list guide your choice of peppers for marinades and sauces:

…continued on page 179

If you're from New England and want to read about what you call partridge, you'll find it under Grouse, on page 143. If, on the other hand, you hail from the South, and really want to read about quail, you'll find that entry on page 199. The true partridge is what we're considering here.

The distinctive flavor of partridge stands up well to equally distinctive side dishes. Try wild rice casserole (page 338); grilled new potatoes (page 196), with a simple mix of olive oil, salt, pepper and rosemary; grilled carrots (page 99); or steamed Brussels sprouts. And how about that fine Bordeaux you've had secreted away? What are you waiting for?

Although not native to America, farm-raised partridge can be special-ordered from butchers in most parts of the country. Be sure to specify a young partridge in the 1- to 1½-pound range. Older birds should be cooked using a moist heat method to counteract their tendency to dry out. Although partridge can be grilled on a rotisserie, it's better to cook them as quickly as possible, directly on the grill. To do this, split and flatten the birds (see *Flattening Poultry,* page 111).

1) Let the partridge sit out at room temperature for 30 minutes before grilling.

2) Ignite enough charcoal to form a bed a little larger in area than what the partridge will cover on the grill. Once the coals are covered with a fine gray ash, arrange them in a single layer, sides just touching, and allow them to burn for about 10 minutes; partridge is better cooked over a less-than-hot fire. If it's adjustable, position the cooking grill 3 to 5 inches from the fire.

3) Baste the flattened partridge with butter and put it on the grill, directly over the coals, skin side up. Total cooking time will be approximately 15 to 20 minutes. Turn the partridge several times, basting the birds each time with liberal quantities of melted butter.

4) After about 15 minutes on the grill, wiggle a leg to test for doneness; the joint will easily move up and down when the bird is done. Serve hot off the grill.

PASTRAMI

This is surely an oddity, but a tasty one. Years ago, I arrived at a friend's house for dinner. He was outside at the grill, surrounded by a group of expectant people, grilling, of all things, slices of pastrami! One of those little loaves of thinly sliced pumpernickel and a pot of hot mustard were at the ready. My friend grilled the pastrami quickly, passed the slices out, and everyone made their own miniature pastrami sandwich appetizers and smacked their lips a lot.

If you'd like to give this a try, simply slice the pastrami thicker than you would for a mile-high sandwich. Each slice should be a little less than ¼-inch thick. Grill the slices directly over the coals while the fire is still good and hot. The pastrami will cook in just a couple of minutes, so keep a close eye on the grill and have your long-handled tongs ready to pull the slices off the second they're heated through and sizzling at the edges.

PEPPERS

It seems as if there are more new peppers to explore every year. The family includes everything from the familiar green "bell" pepper, and its colorful cousins, to the hot pepper clan, diverse in both size, shape and intensity of fiery flavor. While the hot peppers are outstanding used fresh in any number of sauces or salsas, it is the milder bell peppers that really come to life on the grill. See Bell Peppers, page 91.

PETRALE

Old-timers in San Francisco almost always refer to sole as "petrale." Of the several types of Pacific sole, petrale is considered the finest. Technically, the Pacific soles are flounder, but they have been marketed under the name of sole for so long that it would be pointless to change it. It doesn't really make any difference what you call it, as long as you know how to cook this delicious fish. For more information, see Sole, page 221.

...continued from page 178

Pepper	Scoville Units
Bell pepper	0
Pimento	0
Sweet Banana	0
Cherry	100-500
Mexican Bell	100-500
Big Jim	500-1,000
Anaheim	500-1,000
New Mexican #6	500-1,000
Ancho	1,000-1,500
Pasilla	1,000-1,500
Poblano	1,000-1,500
Cascabel	1,500-2,500
Rocotillo	1,500-2,500
Jalapeño	2,500-5,000
Serrano	5,000-15,000
De Arbol	15,000-30,000
Piquin	30,000-50,000
Cayenne	30,000-50,000
Tabasco	30,000-50,000
Aji	50,000-100,000
Chiltepin	50,000-100,000
Thai	50,000-100,000
Habañero, or Scotch Bonnet	150,000-300,000

Pig, whole roast

There are two ways to go about roasting a whole pig. The method you choose depends more upon what you're celebrating than anything else.

A suckling pig is three to eight weeks old and weighs between 6 and 20 pounds. Very impressive when presented, suckling pig is definitely special-occasion food. A 12- to 15-pound suckling pig will feed 10 to 12 people and should be cooked on a rotisserie.

From a suckling pig, we move on to an older, larger animal, one that can weigh as much as 100 pounds or more. (A spectacle reserved for grand events like coronations or the announcement of your candidacy for the U.S. Senate; a 100-pound pig will serve approximately 100 of your closest friends or supporters.)

Generally, a pig that's under 40 pounds or so is best cooked on a rotisserie (see *Spit Cooking,* page 46). Those of a more gargantuan size are usually better off cooked in a pit.

Cooking an older, larger pig — say, around 100 pounds — is a spectacle reserved for grand events like coronations or the announcement of your candidacy for the U.S. Senate.

Pigeon

Given a protective layer of fat to keep them from drying out (see *Fattening Lean Meats,* page 123), pigeon, and their close relative, squab, can be cooked on a rotisserie (see *Spit Cooking,* page 46). Perhaps easier, and just as delicious, is to flatten them (see *Flattening Poultry,* page 111) and grill them directly over the coals. Expect some of the small bones to break in the process; this will not affect the quality of the grilled bird.

Squab is a special breed of pigeon, raised for the table. At 28 days old, they are very succulent birds that taste as close to duck as you can get, without rolling out of bed at 4 o'clock in the morning and going out into the marshes. In case you were wondering, those are squab pictured on the cover of this book.

Pigeons or squab don't need much flavor enhancement. Before grilling, simply brush the birds with melted butter or a mild vegetable oil and dust with salt and pepper, along with a sprinkling of your favorite herbs (rosemary and oregano are excellent).

Serve with grilled polenta (page 183) or wild rice

casserole (page 338). Any sautéed greens, such as spinach, are a nice accompaniment, especially if sprinkled with a little balsamic vinegar before serving.

1) Ignite 40 to 50 briquets or an equal amount of lump charcoal — enough to create a bed of coals, a single layer deep, slightly larger than the area the birds will cover on the grill.

2) Once the coals are covered with a fine gray ash, arrange them in an even layer, with the sides just touching. The pigeon will cook in a total of just 6 to 8 minutes, so the fire will have to be hot to produce nicely browned birds.

3) On adjustable grills, position the cooking grate 3 to 5 inches above the coals; on covered grills, cook without the lid. Place the birds directly over the fire, skin side up.

4) Cook for 3 to 4 minutes. Turn the pigeons and cook for an additional 3 to 4 minutes, being careful not to let them burn. Serve hot off the grill.

PIKE

The Great Lakes contain one-sixth of the world's fresh water. They also contain some great sports fish, like the pike. These are among the longest-lived of any freshwater fish and sometimes weigh up to 30 pounds. One biologist described pike as "mere machines for the assimilation of other organisms," referring to their ability to dart in and out of weedy water, ambushing any passing prey with great agility.

The flesh of pike is lean, fairly firm and quite mild. Marinating is the favorite (and easiest) method to ensure a moist fish. Try fresh ginger-garlic marinade (page 290), herb marinade (page 291) or lemon-white wine marinade (page 292).

Another proven method for keeping lean fish moist is to wrap it in grape leaves. Although it is a somewhat time-consuming project, the results are definitely worth the effort. See *Leaf-wrapped Packets,* page 117.

Durable Pleasures

Cooking, fishing and gardening are what I call the three great "durable pleasures." If you are successful at fishing and gardening (provided you raise some food crops), there's the additional gratification of eating the results of a pleasurable pastime. And as much as I enjoy the act of cooking, I think I enjoy sharing a meal with others just as much.

These durable pleasures need to be preserved, and the best way to do so is to introduce them to a youngster. Ask any good cook, or anyone who enjoys fishing or gardening, how they got started and inevitably the answer is "my grandfather...my aunt...an old neighbor of mine..." or something like that. Interestingly, it is rarely a parent who introduces a child to these pleasures; parents may condition a child to be receptive to the allure of these pastimes, but it seems a mentor relationship is what works in the durable pleasure department.

If you enjoy any of these activities, ensure that someone else will too. It may be the biggest gift you can give someone you're fond of.

"The only pineapple worth grilling is a fresh, fully ripe one. Hold the fruit up to your nose; it should have a luscious, sweet aroma. Tug on a leaf at the top of the pineapple; if it's ripe, the leaf will pull out easily."

Good side dishes included boiled new potatoes (page 320) or steamed parslied rice (page 337) and any fresh vegetable.

1) Keep the fish refrigerated until about 30 minutes before grilling. It should be just at room temperature when it goes over the coals.

2) Ignite enough charcoal to make a bed of coals directly under the fish. Put the cooking grate in place and let it get hot. Clean the grate, using a wire brush, and oil it, using a large basting brush and vegetable oil.

3) Small whole fish (less than 4 pounds) can be cooked directly over the coals, without the lid, just as steaks and fillets. Large, whole fish (over 4 pounds) should be cooked using the indirect method with the cover in place, or on a rotisserie (see *Spit Cooking,* page 46).

4) Coat the fish with oil before putting it on the grill. Cook it 10 minutes per inch of thickness. For example, a 1-inch thick steak (or fillet, or whole fish) will take 10 minutes to cook — 5 minutes per side. Turn the fish once, halfway through the total cooking time.

5) To help keep the fish hot, serve it on a platter that has been heated for 15 minutes in a 250-degree F. oven.

See Fish, page 133 for more information.

PINEAPPLE

I admit to having a prejudice against pineapple served any way but fresh. It seems to me that when I was a kid, a lot of very bad food got served up in the name of Hawaiian exoticism, and the common denominator was always chunks of canned pineapple.

Luckily, nowadays some of the syrupy quality of pineapple has been left behind and what's taken it's place is a fresher approach influenced by Caribbean cuisine. Without all that syrup and cornstarch, the characteristic flavor and acidic sweetness of pineapple comes through, and is a great addition to many grilled dishes, especially grilled ham steak (page 147).

The only pineapple worth grilling is a fresh, fully ripe one. Hold the fruit up to your nose; it should have a luscious, sweet aroma. Tug on a leaf at the top of the pineapple; if it's ripe, the leaf will pull out easily.

Using a very sharp butcher knife, cut off the top of the pineapple and the prickly skin. If small "eyes" of the skin are left in the flesh, cut them out with the end of a potato peeler or the tip of small sharp knife. Quarter the pineapple lengthwise. Cut away most of the tough core (slice this into thin strips for a chewy treat), and cut the quarters into long wedges about 1 inch thick.

The pineapple wedges can be grilled as is, 3 to 4 minutes per side over a moderately hot fire. If you are serving the pineapple with a main dish that has been marinated, brush the pieces with a little of the leftover marinade. The saltiness of most marinades heightens the flavor of grilled pineapple. In fact, most natives of Hawaii sprinkle a little salt on fresh pineapple as a matter of course, just to increase the flavor. Try it, it's good.

PLANTAINS

Plantains are a close relative of the banana and an important starch in much of the Southern Hemisphere. They can be grilled whole, in their skins, or split lengthwise and grilled on both sides. Choose green or yellow plantains for grilling; green ones have a flavor similar to potatoes; yellow ones, a little like a winter squash.

Grill the plantains directly over a moderate to hot fire until the flesh is tender — not more than 3 to 5 minutes per side. Serve with a squeeze of fresh lime juice and chopped fresh cilantro. An excellent side dish to any tropical meal.

POLENTA

There doesn't seem to be much middle ground with polenta. Serve it to some people and they'll say, "Why, this isn't anything but cornmeal mush!" To which I'd

"There doesn't seem to be much middle ground with polenta. Serve it to some people and they'll say, 'Why, this isn't anything but cornmeal mush!'"

say, "What's wrong with cornmeal mush — especially when there's been plenty of freshly grated Parmesan cheese and a few dollops of butter added to it?"

To grill polenta, start by making a fresh batch (see recipe on page 330), pour it onto an oiled platter and allow it to cool in the refrigerator until firm. It's best to do this the night before you want to grill it. Cut the cold polenta into ¾- to 1-inch-thick slices.

To grill, liberally brush both sides of each slice of polenta with olive oil. Place directly over moderate to hot coals and cook for 6 to 8 minutes, turning once with a sharp-edged, oiled spatula. This process is a lot like toasting bread; the object is not to char the polenta, just to crisp it a little on the outside. A wonderful accompaniment to grilled Italian sausages.

POLLOCK

With its firm, white flesh, pollock is often compared to cod. It cooks up nicely on the grill and takes well to many marinades. Good choices include Dijon marinade (page 289) or herb marinade (291). As with any comparatively mild fish, do not marinate pollock for more than 30 to 60 minutes; the taste of the marinade will overwhelm the flavor of the fish. Serve pollock with boiled new potatoes (page 320) or steamed parslied rice (page 337) and any fresh vegetable.

1) About 30 minutes before cooking time, remove the fish from the refrigerator.

2) Determine how much space the fish will take up on the grill, and ignite as many briquets or lump charcoal as it takes to make a bed of coals a little larger in size. Put the cooking grate in place (3 to 5 inches away from the coals if it's adjustable) and let it get hot.

3) Once the cooking grate is hot, clean it with a wire brush. Oil the grill just before you're ready to cook the fish, using a large basting brush and vegetable oil.

4) Grill the fish directly over a bed of hot coals. Don't

Pollock is one of the many lean, firm, mild-tasting fish that takes well to the flavors of a marinade and grilling over the coals.

use the lid on covered grills. Cook for 10 minutes per inch of thickness. Turn the fish only once — half the total cooking time on each side.

5) Virtually all fish tastes best when it's served hot off the grill. Have the rest of your dinner ready to go before putting the fish over the coals.

See Fish, page 133 for more information.

POMPANO, FLORIDA

Florida pompano is one of the world's great eating fish. Its firm texture, moderate fat content and distinctive flavor make Florida pompano a perennial favorite with gourmets. The so-called "California pompano" or the "Pacific pompano" bear no relation to the Florida pompano, and the two should not be confused.

Ranging in weight from ½ to 3½ pounds, Florida pompano is usually sold pan-dressed (gutted, but with head and tail intact). Whole fish are fairly easy to handle on the grill (see *Cooking a Whole Fish*, at right); just make sure to oil both the fish and the grill before cooking, and have a large spatula or two handy for turning the fish.

With Florida pompano's prized natural flavor, all that's needed prior to grilling is a liberal brushing of olive or vegetable oil and a sprinkling of paprika on both sides. Serve *au naturel* with wedges of fresh lemon and enjoy. Good side dishes include "baked" basmati rice (page 316), steamed parslied rice (page 337) or boiled new potatoes (page 320).

1) The fish should be just at room temperature when it goes on the grill.

2) Put the cooking grill over the coals and allow it to become good and hot before putting on the fish; it will stick to a cold grill. Clean the hot grill with a wire brush and coat it with vegetable oil, using a large basting brush.

3) If you're cooking grill is adjustable, position it 3 to 5 inches over the coals. Don't use the lid on covered grills.

Cooking a Whole Fish

Cooking a whole fish takes more nerve than skill. In many respects, they are easier to handle on the grill than fish steaks or fillets. Here's how:
You can marinate whole fish, but most often all they require is a liberal coating of vegetable oil and a sprinkling of salt and paprika, on both sides and in the cavity as well.

If you're cooking a large fish (over 4 pounds), it's hard to resist the temptation to fill the cavity with things like lemon slices, sprigs of fresh dill, thin slices of onion and cracked black pepper. Whether or not this measurably adds to the finished product, I've never really been able to determine, but it does add to the fun of preparing it. If you decide to do so, you'll need to do a little remedial suturing to hold the aromatic stuffing in place: use the method described in To Truss or Not to Truss on page 243. Rest assured, the crudest stitching will suffice.

Once the fish has been well-coated with oil and seasoning, place it directly over the coals and cook for the requisite time (10 minutes per inch of thickness, measured at the thickest part). The only time the process of cooking a whole fish becomes worrisome is when it comes time to flip it. That's when you need to summon your nerve and just do it.

Using one or two thin-bladed, well-oiled spatulas (depending on how large the fish is), slip them under the fish and just roll it over, and then gently push it back over the coals. Flipping the fish may require some fairly odd contortions, but as long as no one is looking, and the fish turns out great, what difference does it make? To make things easier on yourself, plan on turning the fish only once.

4) Grill the fish directly over a bed of hot coals. Cook it 10 minutes per inch of thickness. For example, a 1-inch pompano, measured at its thickest point, would take 10 minutes to cook — 5 minutes per side. Plan on turning the fish only once, halfway through the cooking time.

5) Have everything else ready to go before putting the fish on the grill; once it's cooked, the fish should be served immediately on a heated platter or plates.

See Fish, page 133 for more information.

PORGY

Porgy, with its moderately firm, flaky flesh, is great for grilling. You'll usually see porgy sold pan-dressed (gutted, but head and tail intact), weighing anywhere from ½ to 3½ pounds, perfect for cooking over the coals.

To ensure easy handling, oil both the fish and the cooking grill before putting the porgy over the coals, and have a large spatula (or two) handy for turning the fish. (See *Cooking a Whole Fish* on page 185 for more information.)

With porgy's fine flavor, all that's really needed prior to grilling is a liberal brushing of olive or vegetable oil and a sprinkling of paprika on both sides. Serve with wedges of fresh lemon. Good side dishes include "baked" basmati rice (page 316), steamed parslied rice (page 337), or boiled new potatoes (page 320).

1) Keep the fish refrigerated until about 30 minutes before grilling. It should be just at room temperature when it goes on the grill.

2) Ignite enough briquets (or as much lump charcoal) to make a bed of coals that's a little larger in size than what the fish will take up on the grill.

3) Put the cooking grill in place (3 to 5 inches from the coals, if it's adjustable) and let it heat up. Clean the grill, using a wire brush. Just before cooking time, oil both the grill and the fish.

If you are one of those people who enjoy the flavor of fresh fish simply prepared, a sauce or marinade may be viewed as gilding the lily. All that's really necessary is a quantity of fresh lemon wedges, a sprinkling of chopped parsley for color, and a taste for some of the finer pleasures of the table.

4) Grill the fish directly over the fire, with the cooking grate positioned 4 to 6 inches above the coals. Don't use the cover on covered grills.

5) Cook it 10 minutes per inch of thickness, measured at the thickest part.

6) Serve the porgy piping hot on a platter that's been heated for 15 minutes in a 250-degree F. oven.

See Fish, page 133 for more information.

PORK, CHOPS

Pork is the most popular meat in the world. Not surprisingly, it takes well to the flavors of a great many cultures. That said, grilled pork chops and steaks are pretty darn tasty all by themselves, served up with simplest of side dishes like warm applesauce and mashed potatoes (see page 327).

If your tastebuds want something a little more exotic, try marinating the chops and steaks (for at least four hours, or overnight) in Chinese-style marinade (page 289), fresh ginger-garlic marinade (page 290), Mexican-style marinade (page 293) or Jamaican Jerk (page 195). Once you try jerked pork, you may never cook it any other way. An excellent and flavorful alternative to marinating is to coat the chops or steaks with a dry rub before grilling (see pages 309 to 310).

Pork chops and steaks have a much better chance of turning out moist and succulent on the grill than they do cooked on the stove or in the oven. Thick chops (1 inch or slightly more) are more succulent than thinner cuts and don't require split-second timing to avoid overcooking. Another hedge against overcooking is to grill the chops and steaks over a moderate rather than hot fire.

1) Remove the pork from the refrigerator approximately 30 minutes before grilling.

2) Ignite 30 to 40 briquets or an equal amount of lump charcoal. If you're cooking a large number of chops or

The "T" Word

The fear of trichinosis has caused people to overcook pork for countless generations. Count yourself lucky to be living in a time when no less an authority than the U.S.D.A. now recommends cooking pork to an internal temperature of 160 degrees F. — that's "medium" rather than very well done.

Just so you know, the Food Safety and Inspection Service (a division of the U.S.D.A.) considers 137 degrees F. as the temperature at which Trichinella spiralis is destroyed instantly. Trichinella spiralis, the parasite that causes trichinosis, is thought to be present in only one-tenth of one percent of all pork in this country.

The fact that there are 23 degrees' difference between the point at which the parasites are killed and the official temperature recommendation gives cooks an added margin of error. By all means, try cooking pork to medium done, a stage at which the meat still retains its succulence.

steaks, use enough charcoal to create a bed of coals, a single layer thick, slightly larger in surface area than what the meat will require on the grill.

3) Once the coals are covered with a fine gray ash, arrange them in a single layer in the center of the fire grate, with their sides not quite touching. Put the cooking grill in place (3 to 5 inches from the coals if you're using an adjustable model). Allow the coals to burn down for approximately 10 minutes.

4) Put the chops directly over the moderate coals. If you're using a covered grill, put the top in place, leaving the top and bottom vents completely open. Turn meat once or twice while cooking. Pork chops cooked in a covered grill will take slightly less time to cook than indicated in the following general guidelines, which apply to open grills: ¾-inch-thick chops and steaks, 8 to 10 minutes; 1-inch-thick chops and steaks, 10 to 14 minutes; 1½-inch-thick chops and steaks, 15 to 20 minutes.

PORK, FRESH HAM

This is one of the great roasts, made even better by roasting in a covered grill. It's also wonderful cooked on a rotisserie (see *Spit Cooking,* page 46). A whole fresh ham (the hind leg of the pig) will run upwards of 15 pounds. It consists of two sections, the butt and the shank. Most butchers will be happy to cut the sections apart and sell you one or the other. Which section is preferable is a matter of personal taste: the butt end is meatier and the shank is bonier — both are delicious.

You can also ask the butcher to bone and tie the roast which, makes it easier to carve. Old-timers will tell you, though, that the bone adds flavor to the meat, so it's a difficult call. You can marinate a fresh ham or, if it's boneless, remove the strings, lay in a good quantity of your favorite herbs, then re-tie and roast it. Again, both ways produce delicious results. If you want to marinate the roast, try marsala marinade (page 292) or all-purpose marinade (page 289), letting it soak overnight.

Pork chops and steaks have a much better chance of turning out moist and succulent on the grill than they do cooked on the stove or in the oven.

If you want to add herbs to the inside of a rolled roast, almost any combination will do. A classic Italian mix includes chopped fresh parsley, chopped fresh basil, a little thyme and plenty of minced garlic and freshly cracked pepper. If you choose this method, just make sure to invite me over!

Depending on the style you choose to flavor the roast, suitable side dishes include risotto (page 333), steamed parslied rice (page 337), garlic mashed potatoes (page 324), hominy "soufflé" (page 324), grilled apples (page 69), grilled pineapple (page 182) or grilled sweet potatoes (page 226).

The following procedure is for cooking a fresh ham in a covered grill. If you're using a rotisserie on an uncovered grill, see *Spit Cooking*, page 46.

1) Allow the roast to come to room temperature by removing it from the refrigerator approximately 30 minutes before grilling. Insert a meat thermometer into the center of the roast without touching any bones.

2) Ignite 55 to 65 briquets or an equal amount of lump charcoal.

3) Once the charcoal is covered with a fine gray ash, divide the coals in half and push to opposite sides of the fire grate, leaving the center free of coals. Place a disposable aluminum drip pan in the middle of the fire grate.

4) Position the roast directly over the drip pan. Put the lid in place, leaving both top and bottom vents completely open.

5) Total cooking time will be between 15 and 20 minutes per pound of meat. The roast will not need to be turned. After the first 90 minutes or so, start checking the thermometer. The roast will be done (but not overdone) when the temperature reaches 155 to 160 degrees F. Remember that the temperature rises much faster towards the end of the cooking process than at the beginning, so watch carefully. Remove the roast from the grill when the thermometer reads 5 degrees shy of the desired temperature; it will continue to cook while it rests on the cutting board.

Another "T" Word

I don't remember ever attending a Tupperware party, but somehow I wound up with one of the best containers in which to marinate, and it has the Tupperware name on it. This is how it's described in their catalog:

"Season-Serve Container — Marinate meat, poultry, kabobs and vegetables quickly and easily by turning the container over several times. High-domed seal and grids in the base let marinade completely surround food."

I don't know what kind of mental image that conjures up for you, but the "Season-Serve Container" is essentially two rectangular, deep plastic trays that lock together. It comes in a handy size, and is sturdier than all-get-out. But the best thing about the Season-Serve Container is its watertight seal, which allows you to flip the whole container over and completely coat whatever is inside with the marinade. Try that trick with a regular plastic-wrapped dish!

I highly recommend the Tupperware Season-Serve container. The catalog copy for this product — along with its name — does not do it justice. If you're interested in ordering one, call Tupperware, toll-free, at 1-800-858-7221.

6) Loosely tent the roast in aluminum foil, and let it rest for 15 to 20 minutes. Serve with any juices that accumulate on the carving board.

PORK, GROUND

Lean ground pork, fashioned into patties or sausage shapes, is excellent cooked on the grill. Ground pork can be cooked plain, or seasoned as strongly as you like it. Here are a few recommendations:

Italian style: Garlic (finely chopped or pressed), fennel seed, red pepper flakes, Italian seasoning. Serve on crusty French rolls with tomato slices and shredded lettuce moistened with a little vinaigrette.

Indian style: Curry powder, powdered ginger, finely chopped onions. Serve in warm pita bread with plain yogurt, chopped fresh cilantro, chopped cucumbers and chutney.

Chinese style: Finely chopped green onions, grated fresh ginger (or powdered dry ginger), pressed or finely chopped garlic, soy sauce. Serve with rice or rolled up in warm flour tortillas with a little hoisin sauce and chopped fresh cilantro.

Mexican style: Chili powder, cumin, oregano. Serve on warmed flour tortillas with chopped tomato, onions, shredded lettuce and confetti salsa (page 301).

Pat the ground pork into the shape you want, keeping it about ¾-inch thick. Grill directly over moderate coals (approximately 4 to 6 inches above the fire if you're using an adjustable grill) for 12 to 14 minutes. Serve on pita bread, buns or tortillas with appropriate condiments. These are a good change of pace from hamburgers!

PORK, LEG ROAST

A pork leg roast is often sold as a "fresh ham," which although something of a misnomer, is a name that persists. For more information on this wonderful roast, see Pork, fresh ham, page 188.

Because of the international popularity of pork, there are a wide variety of marinades and sauces to choose from: Mexican, Italian, French, Indonesian — name a country, and there's probably an outstanding marinade to try.

PORK, LEG STEAK

Occasionally, butchers will offer pork "steaks" cut from the leg of pork. They are handled essentially the same way as pork chops. For more information, see Pork, chops, page 187.

PORK, LOIN ROAST (BONE-IN)

This is a cut of pork that deserves greater popularity. Because a loin roast still has the bones intact, you have a better chance of producing a succulent, flavorful piece of meat. An average-sized, 4-pound pork loin roast will serve six people.

Cook the roast as is (perhaps with a half dozen or so cut cloves of garlic inserted into incisions here and there), or marinate overnight. Good marinade choices include marsala marinade (page 292), herb marinade (page 291), and garlic, rosemary and rosé marinade (page 290).

Depending on how you flavor the roast, excellent side dishes include risotto (page 333), garlic mashed potatoes (page 324), baked potatoes (page 317), grilled apples (page 69) or grilled pineapple (page 182).

To grill a bone-in loin roast, a covered grill is almost a necessity. It can also be cooked on an uncovered grill using a rotisserie attachment (see *Spit Cooking*, page 46).

1) Allow the roast to come to room temperature by removing it from the refrigerator approximately 30 minutes before grilling. Insert a meat thermometer into the center of the roast, with the dial facing out from either of the cut ends.

2) Ignite 55 to 65 briquets or an equal amount of lump charcoal.

3) Once the coals are covered with a fine gray ash, divide equally and push them to opposite sides of the fire grate, leaving the center free of coals. Place a disposable aluminum drip pan in the middle of the fire grate.

4) Position the roast directly over the drip pan. Put lid in

Brine for Pork Loin

An unusual and good way to prepare a boneless pork loin roast is to soak it in a brine for two or three days before grilling. The brine not only flavors the roast but firms the texture of the meat. The basic brine solution is composed of:

> *8 cups water*
> *½ cup sugar*
> *¼ cup kosher salt*

To the basic brine, you can add whatever flavoring you fancy. Three or four bay leaves and two tablespoons of whole black peppercorns are excellent, as is a combination of a half dozen or so skinned and crushed cloves of garlic, two tablespoons of whole black peppercorns and two tablespoons of crushed whole cumin seeds. Feel free to experiment with flavoring the brine; it's difficult to go wrong with this.

Once you've added the flavoring to the basic brine, bring it to a boil for a few minutes, dissolving the sugar and salt. Allow to cool. Place the pork roast in the brine, either in a large covered plastic or glass container or in a plastic bag set inside any type of pan. Tie the top of the bag. Refrigerate for two to three days, occasionally turning the roast in the brine.

Before grilling, remove the roast from the brine and blot it dry. Grill according to the instructions given at left, and prepare yourself for some mighty fine fare.

place, leaving both top and bottom vents completely open.

5) Total cooking time will be between 15 and 20 minutes per pound of meat. The roast will not need to be turned. After the first hour, start checking the thermometer. The roast will be done (but not overdone) when the temperature reaches 155 to 160 degrees F.

6) Closely monitor the temperature, remembering that it rises much faster towards the end of the cooking process. Remove the roast from the grill when it is 5 degrees shy of the desired temperature; the roast will continue to cook while it rests on the cutting board.

7) Tent the roast loosely in aluminum foil while it rests for 10 minutes or so. Carve straight down, between the rib bones, into individual chops. Serve with any juices that accumulate on the cutting board.

Pork, loin roast (boneless)

A boneless pork loin roast, which averages around four pounds, will serve approximately eight people with absolutely no waste. Because it can be grilled ahead of time and carved at room temperature, this roast makes good buffet party food — excellent when thinly sliced and served on small, crunchy rolls.

A boneless pork loin roast can be prepared exactly as a bone-in pork roast (see previous entry), except it won't take quite as long to cook — approximately 12 to 15 minutes per pound of meat. For an interesting way to serve this roast, see *Brine For Pork Loin* on page 191.

Pork, ribs

"Barbecued" pork ribs have long been a staple of the outdoor cook. They are almost always tasty, but frequently burned. The following information is provided in an effort to produce the tastiest possible ribs without

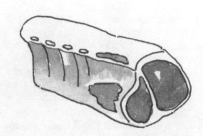

Because a loin roast still has the bones intact, you have an even better chance of producing a succulent, flavorful piece of meat.

burning the heck out of them. Because barbecue is an intensely regional (some would say *personal)* issue, it's difficult say *anything* about it without getting into trouble with someone, somewhere. That said, let's stick to the facts. First, a few words about the ribs.

Spareribs come from the underbelly, or lower rib cage, if you will, of the pig. A full slab contains 13 ribs and weighs 3 pounds or less. These are the favorite of most barbecue enthusiasts.

Babyback or loin ribs come from the upper end of the rib cage, where the expensive cuts of pork are located. They do not come from a baby pig, as I thought before moving to Kansas City. They are, however, smaller than spareribs and can be cooked in a shorter period of time.

Country-style ribs are also from the upper side of the rib cage, but from the fatty end of the loin. (The other end of the loin produces the lean pork tenderloin.) Compared to a loin chop, country-style ribs contain a smaller section of loin meat.

No matter which style of ribs you're grilling, excellent side dishes include grilled sweet potatoes (page 226), hominy "soufflé" (page 324), sauerkraut and potato casserole (page 336) and grilled potato wedges (page 196).

There are three basic methods for barbecuing ribs, and myriad variations. To develop your own variation, use the following methods as a starting point:

1) Apply a dry rub before grilling and serve your favorite sauce with the ribs *after* they have been cooked. This method appeals to those who like that old-fashioned, traditional barbecue flavor. Try any of the dry rubs suggested on pages 309 to 310. Concoct your own sauce, buy it from the store, or use one of the recipes found on pages 297 to 298.

2) Grill the ribs without any seasoning until almost done, and then mop with a traditional barbecue sauce during the last 5 to 10 minutes on the grill. This method produces less intensely spiced ribs than the first method, but still with that old-timey flavor. The few minutes the ribs are on the grill, coated with sauce, allows the sauce to set and adhere, but avoids the problem of charred sauce. Additional sauce can be heated and poured over

Pig Facts

Pork, it is generally agreed, was the first wild animal to be domesticated by man, and remains the most popular meat in the world today. Pork's popularity is due not only to its taste, but to the fact that pigs are comparatively easy to raise, are satisfied with a wide variety of diets, and are prolific, bearing two litters a year — with an average of eleven piglets per litter!

The pigs of old were massive creatures and very fatty, partially because there were so many important uses for the fat. Today's health-conscious consumer has caused changes in pig breeding, resulting in a much leaner animal, far lower in calories than in previous times. An average serving of pork contains only 250 calories.

Unlike beef, which is graded with the designations "Prime," "Choice," etc., pork is graded on a numerical system, from #1 to #3, with #1, not surprisingly, being the best. Most specialty butchers and quality supermarkets sell only #1 grade pork. At its best, pork should be pale pinkish-gray with very white fat, and not too much of it.

Pigs are also classified by age. Suckling pigs are about three weeks old, weigh only 10 to 18 pounds, and have fed only on mother's milk. The term "pig" is reserved for animals up to four months old, which generally weigh about 120 pounds. Hogs, on the other hand, are usually less than six months old and weigh in at about 210 pounds on the cloven hoof.

A traveling salesman's car broke down out in the middle of the country, directly across from a farmhouse. As he walked through the front yard, he was startled to see a pig with a wooden leg run down the driveway. The salesman knocked at the door, was greeted by the farmer, and asked whether he could use the telephone to call for a repair truck. This accomplished, he returned to the front porch where the farmer was sitting.

"Say," said the salesman, "I couldn't help but notice that pig of yours. What's the deal with its…" The farmer broke in and said, "Yeah, that's some pig all right. Last summer my youngest daughter got out of the yard and was playing in the middle of the road. A big truck was barreling along and just about to hit her when that pig raced across the road and got little Mary out of harm's way." "That's really something," agreed the salesman, "but what about the…"

The farmer interrupted him once more, continuing on about the pig: "And then there was the time our stove caught fire in the middle of the night and that pig ran into the house, ran up the stairs, and started squealing and running up and down the hall until he woke everyone up. By that time we could smell smoke, and, well, I guess he saved the whole family!"

Not being able to stand it any longer, the salesman finally blurted out, "That's an incredible story, but what's the deal with the pig's wooden leg?" "Heck," said the farmer, "you wouldn't want to eat a great pig like that all at one time, would you?"

the ribs at the table. Use your favorite bottled sauce or one of the recipes given on pages 297 to 298.

3) Marinate the ribs ahead of time for 2 to 3 hours and then grill, basting with the leftover marinade. This works only for non-traditional barbecue marinades (that is, any marinade that isn't tomato-based, or which doesn't have much sugar, Karo syrup, maple syrup or molasses in it). This will produce very flavorful results, but not in the traditional barbecue style. If you try to grill ribs (or any other meat) that have been marinated in a tomato-based or similar sweet sauce, it's almost impossible to keep the sauce from completely burning during the cooking process.

The following procedure requires a covered grill. You may also cook ribs using a rotisserie attachment on an uncovered grill; see *Spit Cooking,* page 46.

1) At least 30 minutes prior to starting your fire, soak your favorite smoking chips in water. Hickory chips are the most popular (see *Smoking Chips,* page 34).

2) Start approximately 40 to 50 briquets or an equal amount of lump charcoal.

3) Once the charcoal is covered with a fine gray ash, move it all to one side of the cooking grate. Put a couple of handfuls of wet chips on top of the coals. (Some folks swear by adding water — about 1 inch deep — inside the drip pan. Others don't. I don't think the added moisture hurts any, and it just might help. You decide.)

4) Put the drip pan, with or without water, on the fire grate and put the cooking grill in place.

5) Place the ribs of your choice on the grill, on the opposite side of the coals, directly over the drip pan. Put the cover on the grill, leaving the bottom vents completely open and the top vents about half open.

6) Add another couple of handfuls of smoking chips every 30 to 40 minutes, depending on how smoky-tasting you want the end product to be. You may have to add additional charcoal (8 to 10 briquets or an equal

amount of lump charcoal) to the fire (see *Keeping the Fire Going,* page 34). The point is to keep the temperature more or less constant at around 200 degrees F. If you add more smoking chips thoughout the cooking process, alternate them with the additional coals; if you add the wet chips and unlit coals at the same time, you may put the fire completely out.

7) The ribs will be done when the meat starts to pull away from the bone — a process that takes 1½ hours or more.

PORK, TENDERLOIN

A tenderloin of pork is right up there with the chicken breast when it comes to versatility. Either can be enhanced to take on the flavors of almost any culture. New breeding efforts on the part of hog farmers have resulted in meat that is now as lean or leaner than beef. This is especially true of the tenderloin, a naturally lean cut of pork. Here in the Midwest, at least, we have pork of such high quality, it could easily be mistaken for veal.

Tenderloins are available in varying sizes, generally around 12 to 16 ounces. They make excellent eating without a bit of waste. As with other boneless cuts of meat, plan on about ⅓ to ½ pound of meat per person. Tenderloin is also excellent for cutting up in strips, lengthwise, and threading onto skewers (see *Skewer Cooking,* page 56).

Pork is used far more in other cultures than it is here in America. Because of its international popularity, there are a wide variety of marinades and sauces to choose from: Mexican, Italian, French, Indonesian — name a country, and there's probably an outstanding marinade to try. For the best flavor, count on marinating the loin for at least 4 to 6 hours, or overnight in the refrigerator. Some of the best choices include fresh ginger-garlic marinade (page 290), lime-garlic marinade (page 292), Southwestern marinade (page 294) or Jamaican jerk (page 195). Any manner of rice or beans (or both) makes an outstanding side dish.

The covered, indirect method of grilling is the best way to turn out a succulent roast, but it may also be

Jamaican Jerk

The perfect antidote to jaded tastebuds, Jamaican jerk seasoning is an intense experience. I think it may also be addictive. I have yet to discover a recipe for making jerk seasoning at home that comes anywhere close to the product bottled under the label of "Walkerswood," out of St. Ann, Jamaica. It can be ordered from Le Saucier, Faneuil Hall Marketplace, Boston, MA 02109, (617) 227-9649.

Jerk seasoning is unlike anything you have ever tasted, unless you happen to be from Jamaica, or have visited there. It's excellent on any meat or poultry, but clearly outstanding on pork. Don't serve it to your Scandinavian aunts from Minneapolis, however — you'll have them going around the room backwards. Serve it to lovers of hot and spicy cuisine, especially those who think they've tasted everything. They'll be back for more.

Grilled Potato Wedges

Choose medium-sized, brown-skinned baking potatoes to make these "jumbo French fries." Scrub the potatoes under cold water, but do not peel. Cut each into 4 or 6 wedges. Liberally oil them immediately, and sprinkle with salt and rosemary, if desired. Place them on the grill, towards the edges of the fire. Turn them every 7 to 10 minutes, edging them closer to being directly over the coals each time. Depending on how thick they are, they will be grilled tender in 20 to 40 minutes. Check with the tip of a sharp knife; when it pierces all the way through the potato wedge easily, they're ready. Serve hot off the grill. Some would say a sprinkling of vinegar (preferably malt vinegar) is a necessity.

Grilled New Potatoes

Small new potatoes can be skewered (favor metal skewers, which help speed up the cooking time) and grilled to perfection. Wash and dry the potatoes, rub them with a little olive or vegetable oil, and put them on skewers. Place the skewered potatoes towards the edges of the fire, gradually rolling them so they are directly over the coals towards the end of their cooking time. Depending on their size, they should be ready in 20 to 40 minutes. They will be slightly crisp on the outside and creamy on the inside, just the way they should be! Serve with plenty of butter and chopped chives or fresh dill.

cooked on an open grill (with the coals 4 to 5 inches from the grill). Check every 10 minutes or so to make sure the meat isn't burning, and keep your eye on that thermometer! There's no reason to serve dried-out, overly cooked pork anymore (see *The "T" Word,* page 187).

1) Remove the tenderloin from the refrigerator 30 minutes before grilling. It should be at room temperature when it goes over the coals.

2) Ignite about 40 to 50 briquets.

3) Use a meat thermometer with tenderloins and other roasts; it is the only sure way of knowing exactly what your results will be. Place the thermometer horizontally through the meat, with the tip at about the center of the loin.

4) After the coals are completely covered with a gray ash, push them to one side of the grate. Place the loin on the middle of the grill, about 4 inches away from the edge of the coals. Put the lid on the grill, leaving both the top and bottom vents completely open.

5) Turn the tenderloin after 15 minutes.

6) After an additional 15 minutes have passed, turn the roast again, pushing it a little closer to the coals — about 1 inch or so away from the fire — to help brown the outside.

7) Turn the roast again in 5 minutes, and one last time for about 5 minutes longer, at which time the internal temperature should be around 155 degrees F. Each time you turn the roast, edge it a little closer to the coals. Take the meat off when it is about 5 to 10 degrees shy of the desired internal temperature.

8) Allow the tenderloin to sit on the carving board, loosely tented with a piece of foil, for 10 minutes or so before carving. Carve into thick or thin slices, across the grain, depending on how you and your guests like it. Pour any juices which have accumulated on the carving board over meat before serving.

POTATOES

Potatoes offer many possibilities on the grill. There are large, brown, baking potatoes to roast whole in the coals, quartered on the grill (like big, non-oily French fries), or for crunchy grilled potato skins; small, red, new potatoes just right for skewering; and those potatoes of a different color, sweet potatoes (see page 226).

By way of introduction, I should say that I'm totally against partially cooking any vegetable, particularly potatoes, before putting them on the grill. Lots of people recommend precooking as a way of cutting down on the cooking time. I say it's not worth saving time if the results are inferior. Potatoes cooked exclusively on the grill develop a wonderfully crisp exterior and the fluffy, moist insides potato-lovers crave. While it's not realistic to try to "bake" large, whole potatoes on the grill, you can roast them directly in the coals.

There are two ways to go about charcaol-roasting whole potatoes. Both begin by washing the potatoes and pricking them here and there with a fork or knife. The first method is simply to stick the naked potato down there, right in the coals. In approximately 45 minutes, the outside of the potato will be completely black and the insides steamy hot and tender. Alternatively, you can wrap each potato in a double thickness of aluminum foil and nestle the packets in the coals, thereby preserving what many feel is the best part of the potato — the skin.

Consult the sidebars on these two pages for how to make grilled potato wedges, grilled new potatoes, grilled potato skins, and grilled and filled potato skins. You won't go wrong with any of them.

POUSSIN

In the old days, before everything French became chic, poussin were known as "spring chickens." They are small (under one pound) and young (six weeks old). They make for delicious, tender and succulent dining. Count on a half to a whole bird per person, depending on the appetites. Poussin can be marinated any way that chicken can (see *Marinating Chickens,* page 106).

Grilled Potato Skins

Start by baking large potatoes in a 350 degree F. oven (or foil-wrapped in the coals) for at least 1 hour. Split the hot potatoes in half and scoop out almost all of the insides, leaving about ¼-inch attached to the skins. Reserve the insides for making Grilled and Filled Potato Skins (see below), if desired. Do not oil the skins. Place them directly over the coals and grill on both sides just until the edges start to brown and the skins are crisp. These little potato skin boats are delicious eaten with nothing more than butter, salt and pepper. Or, go whole hog and add sour cream and chives.

Grilled & Filled Potato Skins

Follow the procedure for Grilled Potato Skins (above). While the skins are grilling, put the insides of the potato in a bowl, add a little butter, some chopped chives or tops of green onion, freshly ground black pepper and some grated cheddar cheese, if you want. Mix well with a fork. Wrap the filling in a foil pouch and place in a warm (250 degree F.) oven or on the grill. Once the skins are done, spoon some of the filling into each. This is a great way to get kids to eat all of their potatoes.

Serve with a big fresh salad, grilled polenta (page 183) or some grilled bread (page 95) drizzled with olive oil and rubbed with cut garlic, grilled whole tomatoes (page 232), or grilled zucchini (page 263). A good, very cold Chablis would round this meal out nicely.

The easiest way to grill poussin is to split and flatten them (see *Flattening Poultry,* page 111), then cook them quickly, directly over the coals. Total cooking time will be approximately 15 to 20 minutes, with the grill 3 to 5 inches from the coals. Turn every 5 minutes or so; do not let the outside char.

Prawns

Virtually every market in America labels shrimp that are comparatively large in size as "prawns." But technically speaking, the term prawn refers to a few, very specific varieties of *freshwater* shellfish, which are highly regarded in the few locales where they exist. While the distinction is worth preserving, it may be unnecessarily confusing. To simplify the matter, you'll find grilling instructions for prawns listed under Shrimp, on page 218.

The term "prawn" refers to a few, very specific varieties of freshwater shellfish.

Q

QUAIL

In case you're not a hunter, most good-sized communities have at least one store that specializes in poultry. Give them a call and see if they normally carry quail, or if they can special order the quail for you. Here in Kansas City, we have an outstanding farmer's market, not unlike the kind prevalent throughout Europe. Each stall seems to specialize in a couple of items, from herbs to fresh eggs. One fine summer morning, I came across a woman who, in addition to selling the produce from the farm, had a couple of Styrofoam coolers filled with quail, perfectly fresh and dressed. Later that day, after the quail had been marinated for a while, grilled, and served on a bed of hot polenta, a few of us thought we had died and gone to heaven.

You can grill quail whole, if you like, but they are a lot easier to handle if you flatten them first. Split them up the backbone, using a knife or a pair of poultry shears. After splitting them, set the quail skin side up on a cutting board and flatten them, using the heel of your hand. Expect some of the small bones to break in the process. For more information, see *Flattening Poultry,* page 111.

Marinate in olive oil, a little lemon juice and thyme, or try red wine marinade (page 294) or garlic, rosemary and rosé marinade (page 290). Quail don't need much flavor enhancement, so the simpler the better. Serve with polenta (page 330), putting the grilled birds right on top of it so the juices can mingle; or wild rice casserole (page 338). Sautéed greens, such as spinach, go well with quail, especially if sprinkled with a little balsamic vinegar before serving.

Note: Quail taste just as good at room temperature as they do hot off the grill, so don't be afraid to cook them ahead of time and wrap them in foil. Plan on 5 or 6 quail

We're fortunate in having a great farmer's market in our town, where during the summer, it's possible to find everything from fresh herbs to live chickens, an incredible array of just-picked fruits and vegetables, and every once in a while, quail.

per person, depending on the size of the birds and the size of your diners' appetites.

1) Remove the quail from the refrigerator about 30 minutes before cooking. They should be at room temperature when they go on the grill.

2) Ignite 55 to 65 briquets or an equal amount of lump charcoal, depending on the number of quail you are grilling. There should be enough to make a bed of coals a little larger in size than what the quail will cover on the grill.

3) Once the charcoal is covered with a fine gray ash, arrange it in an even layer, with the sides touching. The quail cook in a total of just 7 to 10 minutes, depending on their size, so you'll want a hot fire to produce a crispy skin in a hurry.

4) On adjustable grills, position the cooking grill 3 to 5 inches above the coals; on covered grills, cook without the lid on. Place the birds directly over the fire, skin side up. Cook for about 3 to 4 minutes. Turn quail and cook for an additional 4 or 5 minutes, being careful not to let them burn. Serve them hot off the grill or at room temperature.

A traditional, Italian-inspired combination is grilled quail served on a bed of hot polenta. Once you've tried it, you'll know why it's become a classic.

R

RABBIT

Not that many people eat rabbit, and fewer grill it, which is a shame. Domestic rabbit has a finer texture than chicken, but tastes quite similar. It has a tendency to dry out quickly on the grill, so take precautions by either basting often with a marinade, larding the rabbit before putting it on the grill (see *Larding vs. Barding,* page 129), or wrapping it in thin strips of bacon.

Good marinades include all-purpose marinade (page 289), herb marinade (page 291) and garlic, rosemary and rosé marinade (page 290). Side dishes to consider are polenta (page 330), galette of potatoes (page 323) or grilled potato wedges (page 196). Almost any vegetable in season will complement this meal, or try whole roasted tomatoes (page 232), even when they're not in season.

If you're grilling a wild rabbit, see page 257.

1) Approximately 30 minutes before cooking time, remove the rabbit from your refrigerator and allow it to come to room temperature.

2) Ignite 40 to 50 briquets or an equal amount of lump charcoal.

3) Once the coals are covered with a fine gray ash, divide in half and push to opposite sides of the fire grate. On adjustable grills, position the cooking grate 3 to 5 inches above the fire.

4) On covered grills, position the rabbit pieces in the middle of the cooking grill, away from the fire. Put top in place, leaving both top and bottom vents completely open. On open grills, place the rabbit directly over the coals.

Chicken Imposters

"Well, you know, it tastes like chicken." Rabbit, like frog legs, rattlesnake and a number of other culinary items, seems to receive this description quite frequently. Frankly, I don't think it's complimentary to what's being described, and it's even less of a compliment to chicken. That today's mass-produced chickens don't have much taste is not news. If they did, only chickens would be described as "tasting like chicken."

This fact was brought home one time when we were staying in some out-of-the-way corner of Kauai. There was only one little mom-and-pop grocery store nearby, with a pretty meager selection of comestibles. Somewhat reluctantly, I finally settled on what looked like the skinniest little chicken ever to scratch, along with some rough-looking celery and onions. There was little doubt that all three items were homegrown.

My goal was to poach the chicken and make a few cups of chicken stock in the process. With such scrawny ingredients I didn't hold out much hope for success. As it happens, it turned out there was more "chicken flavor" in that one measly little bird than there was in a whole flock of those plump, factory-made chickens I had become so used to back home. And as impoverished as the celery and onions looked, they were intensely flavored, as if struggling for life increased their essence. Once again, I was reminded of that old kitchen saying: "Seeing is deceiving. Tasting is believing."

If you're tired of tasteless chickens, why not raise a few of your own? That ought to set the neighbors to clucking. Or seek out free-range chickens; they're worth looking for. See Meet Rocky Sr. and Jr. on page 109.

5) Total cooking time will be about 30 minutes. Turn every 7 to 10 minutes, basting each time with leftover marinade. If you've wrapped the rabbit in bacon strips, no basting will be necessary, but watch carefully on open grills to prevent flare-ups, moving the pieces to the side as necessary.

RADICCHIO

As common as radicchio is throughout most of Europe, this brilliant, violet-red "green" is still a bit unusual in this country. Most of the time, radicchio turns up in salads, where it is usually confused with purple cabbage, its rather common cousin. Cooked on the grill, radicchio would have to be considered an "oddment," but if you're a fan of its slightly bitter taste, it's worth trying. All you really are after is wilting the radicchio a bit and letting it pick up a little of the smoky aroma from the coals. By all means, don't char it!

Quarter the small heads, rinse, pat dry and toss in some olive oil. Cook the radicchio away from the direct heat, turn a couple of times and remove it when it starts to become limp. Serve with a dash of balsamic vinegar, a little good-quality olive oil, and some crumbled bacon or, if you're feeling particularly continental, crumbled pancetta. Unusual, yes, but also very tasty with almost any roast meat.

RADISH

We're talking about the long white "icicle" radishes here. And while I don't expect you to run out to the store just to try them on the grill, you should know that they are interesting and delicious. Something about the grilling process quite changes their character. Wash and pat dry; roll them in olive oil, then dust with salt and pepper. Grill the radishes directly over the coals, rolling them around until they just begin to soften. Particularly good with grilled fish, roast chicken or any other fowl. Serve them and see if your guests can figure out what they are.

"Not a word against the radish. Still, it may be lawful to record that it is not of much use in cookery, whatever it may be in eating. May I also venture to say that it is a mistake in a salad — an intrusion; and that the only way to eat it is to nibble it by itself while waiting for the feast, or in any convenient interlude. Be it added that there are few combinations of colour so beautiful and rich as the red and white of radishes against the green of their leaves. In glass dishes upon a dinner-table they are an ornament which may vie with the finest flowers."

From Kettner's Book of the Table, written by E. S. Dallas, originally published in 1877. Probably one of the most original, knowledgeable and enjoyable books ever published on the subject of food and eating.

RAINBOW TROUT

Virtually all of the trout available at grocery stores are farm-raised rainbow trout. They are of very uniform size, usually around 8 ounces, just right for the single diner. The rainbow trout's sweet flesh is favored even by non-fish lovers. For grilling instructions, see Trout, freshwater and sea, page 234.

REDFISH

With the rise in popularity of cajun cuisine, redfish, formerly a specialty of the deep south, has become available in many more markets beyond Mason-Dixon line. So popular, in fact, that this species has come close to being overfished.

Redfish stands up well to a strong-flavored marinade or any of the compound butters found on pages 305 to 306. For marinades, try fresh ginger-garlic marinade (page 290), herb marinade (page 291) any of the commercially available cajun seasonings or a similar dry rub of your own devise (see page 309).

Classic side dishes include steamed parslied rice (page 337), "baked" basmati rice (page 316) or grilled new potatoes (page 196). Grilled whole tomatoes (page 232) or any steamed fresh vegetable would also be appropriate.

1) Keep the fish refrigerated until about 30 minutes before cooking.

2) Put the cooking grill over the coals. Clean the hot grill, if necessary, using a wire brush, and coat it with vegetable oil before putting on the fish.

3) Grill the fish directly over a bed of hot coals. If you have a covered grill, cook the fish without putting the cover in place.

4) Cook the fish for 10 minutes per inch of thickness. Turn the fish just once, halfway through the total cooking time.

Old Country New Potatoes

Throughout most of northern Europe, boiled new potatoes are a standard side dish, particularly relished with fish. Anyone with even the barest plot of land grows their own new potatoes. It's not at all unusual for the cook to go into the garden just before dinner and dig up a couple of servings' worth of potatoes, in the same way as the average American would grab a few potatoes from the pantry.

Most often, new potatoes are boiled in salted water until just tender and served quite plain, with only butter and perhaps a sprinkling of fresh chopped dill. As a staple, potatoes are taken seriously — just how seriously was illustrated to me on a trip to Finland several years ago.

A Scandinavian cousin of mine took what was apparently a long and meal-less train trip from Sweden to Finland to meet me for the first time. Upon arriving at my uncle's farm, the first words out of her mouth were "Quick, boil me some potatoes. I'm feeling weak."

Potatoes are very easy to grow. They are also attractive plants with dark green, leathery leaves and pretty white and gold flowers. Plucking eggs from a hen's nest is the only other activity that's as satisfying as digging up a batch of new potatoes from the moist, dark earth. If you have the room, give them a try.

Any potato variety will produce "new" potatoes; they are merely potatoes that are harvested at an immature stage.

5) Redfish should be served piping hot, on a platter that has been warmed in the oven.

See Fish, page 133, for more information.

RED SNAPPER

Red snapper is regarded by gourmets as one of the best fish to come from the sea. The flesh of true red snapper is lean, succulent and delicately flavored. Red snapper is caught in the Gulf of Mexico; do not confuse the genuine item with rockfish, which is sold as red snapper in many areas. The skin of true red snapper is, in fact, very red. If the fish is sold whole, you can use its color to verify authenticity; if the red snapper is cut into steaks or fillets, you'll have to trust your fishmonger's integrity. If small whole fish (4 pounds and under) are available, grill them whole (see *Cooking a Whole Fish,* page 185).

As valued as it is for its natural flavor, red snapper doesn't need much in the way of advance preparation. Personally, I think marinating red snapper is something of a sin. Simply brush the fish with olive oil and dust with paprika on both sides.

Serve with "baked" basmati rice casserole (page 316), steamed parslied rice (page 337) or boiled new potatoes (page 320); grilled corn on the cob (page 118) or any grilled summer squash (page 223).

1) Take the snapper out of the refrigerator about 30 minutes before grilling.

2) Ignite enough charcoal to create a bed of coals about the same size as what the fish will take up on the grill. Put the cooking grill in place (3 to 5 inches from the fire if the grill is adjustable) and let it get hot. Clean the grate with a wire brush, and coat it with vegetable oil, using a large basting brush.

3) Brush the fish (even whole fish) with a light vegetable oil and sprinkle with paprika. Grill the steaks, fillets or small whole fish (4 pounds or less) directly over a hot fire.

"…do not confuse the genuine item with rockfish, which is sold as red snapper in many areas. The skin of true red snapper is, in fact, very red."

If you have a covered grill, cook the fish without putting the cover down.

4) Cook for 10 minutes per inch of thickness. Plan on turning the fish only once — half the total cooking time on each side.

5) Serve the fish hot off the grill on a platter that has been heated for 15 minutes in a 250-degree F. oven. Have the rest of your dinner ready to serve before putting the fish on the grill.

See Fish, page 133, for more information.

Rex sole

Charcoal-grilling any of the members of the sole group takes some finesse. But successful results are well worth the effort. Rex sole is almost always available only in whole (pan-dressed) form. For grilling instructions, see Sole, page 221.

Ribs

Ribs, grilled or barbecued, are an all-time American favorite. Both pork and beef ribs can be used, but many barbecue enthusiasts insist that only pork spareribs are the "real thing." For more information, see either Beef, ribs, page 79, or Pork, ribs, page 192.

Rock cod

Rock cod is not a true cod, but a member of the plentiful rockfish family found in Pacific waters. For more information, see Rockfish, page 207.

Aficionados of sole, of which there are surprisingly many, claim that they can tell the quality of the sole by inspecting the color of the fish's underside. It seems that this flatfish, which swims horizontal to the ocean floor, takes on the color of the bottom surface. Just so you know, the whiter the bottom the better.

Served cold, grilled Rock Cornish game hens are very good picnic fare. Grill them up the night before and keep in the refrigerator until you're ready to go. If they've been well-marinated or injected with flavoring, these little birds will rival that old-fashioned picnic favorite, fried chicken.

ROCK CORNISH GAME HENS

These little birds are a cross between Cornish gamecocks and Plymouth Rock hens, hence the long-winded name. They weigh in at about 1¼ to 1½ pounds, and are usually found whole in the frozen food case. In the early '60s, when the "gourmet revolution" was just taking off, Cornish game hens were considered elegant fare. Quite frankly, I never thought that much of them, until recently. What was described as a "delicate" flavor, I thought was simply a lack of flavor. And trying to get those little hens to accept the flavors of a marinade was seemingly impossible. Impossible, that is, until I received this demon bulb-baster with an injector needle as a Father's Day gift.

If you want to marinate Cornish game hens using the traditional soak method, just be sure to start early — like two days early. No kidding. Almost any of the marinades found on pages 289 to 295 will work fine; wild game marinade (page 295), red wine marinade (page 294) and marsala marinade (page 292) are tried-and-true favorites. Marinate in the refrigerator and remove birds about 30 minutes prior to grilling.

Far preferable, and much faster, is to mix up your favorite marinade and inject it into the flesh of the bird. You will need a bulb-baster with an injector needle for this process. The results are so outstanding, I think you'll agree that the bulb baster is a kitchen tool definitely worth having. For more information on this utensil, see *Demon Bulb Baster,* page 207. Once injected with the marinade, the game hens will have all the flavor they need to make for good eating — immediately.

Good side dishes include galette of potatoes (page 323), garlic mashed potatoes (page 324) and grilled polenta (page 183).

Cooked whole on the grill, Cornish game hens will turn out delicious, but they are far easier to handle if you flatten them first, even before you marinate them (see *Flattening Poultry,* page 111). If you're lucky enough to have a rotisserie, game hens are also easily cooked on a spit (see *Spit Cooking,* page 46).

Plan on 30 to 35 minutes total grilling time for flattened game hens; 40 to 45 minutes for whole birds. For stuffed birds, increase cooking time by 15 minutes.

1) If you're going to marinate the game hens, start 2 days before you plan on cooking them.

2) Remove the birds from the refrigerator about 30 minutes before grilling, allowing them to come to room temperature before they go on the grill.

3) For 3 or 4 game hens, ignite approximately 55 to 65 briquets, more or less depending on the number of birds you plan to cook.

4) If you are using a covered kettle grill, arrange the hot coals in the center of the fire grate, sides touching. Position the game hens in a ring around, rather than directly over, the fire. Regardless of whether the birds are flattened or whole, start grilling with breast or skin side down. Put the top on the grill, leaving both top and bottom vents completely open.

  If you are using an adjustable or open grill, position the cooking grill 3 to 5 inches above the coals. Place the game hens directly over the fire. Watch carefully for flare-ups, moving hens away from the coals if the flames become intense.

5) After the first 10 minutes, turn the hens. On covered grills, move them directly over the coals. Cook flattened hens, bone side down, for an additional 15 minutes, finishing with a final 5 minutes, skin side down, directly over the coals. Whole birds should be turned on all sides, directly over the coals, every 7 to 10 minutes, for a total cooking time of 40 to 45 minutes.

ROCKFISH

Rockfish is something of a catchall name for many species of the *Sebastes* family. It is often sold as red snapper, which it is not (see page 204). Some rockfish, such as bolina and yelloweye, are excellent for the grill; others are merely adequate.

  Because it is lean and mild, the rockfish is an excellent fish for grilling in grape leaf-wrapped packets.

Demon Bulb Baster

Although almost universally scorned as being a somehow "improper" kitchen utensil, an aluminum bulb baster with a stainless-steel injection needle is okay in my book. I'm sure it's possible to get carried away and inject flavors into all types of foods where they don't belong, but if for no other reason than what the baster can do for poultry, I'll stand by it. Modern methods of commercial poultry production have resulted in some very bland birds. Marinating to add flavor works to a degree, but poultry's naturally fatty skin makes it very difficult for those flavors to sink in.

Enter the demon bulb baster.

I say demon, because the thing looks positively diabolical. (I keep mine hidden in the back of a drawer.) But it works like a charm on Rock Cornish game hens, chicken and turkey. Simply mix up about a cup or so of what is essentially a marinade. Make sure the mixture includes a fat (such as oil or melted butter) along with the other liquids, or else you'll wind up with steamed rather than grilled poultry.

A combination of dry vermouth, pressed garlic, finely ground black pepper, lemon juice, Dijon mustard and olive oil (or melted butter) is wonderful, flavored with whatever herb you prefer. Rosemary, oregano, tarragon or basil are all good choices. With whole birds, inject a couple of tablespoonfuls into each breast, the legs and thighs. If you are using melted butter, the mixture will congeal (making it difficult to inject) unless it is still warm. Inject marinade into individual pieces of cut-up poultry. Use any remaining marinade for basting the poultry during grilling.

Keeping a Log

I used to think such things were bordering on the obsessive, but keeping a record of what was served to whom and when seems like a better idea with each passing year.

This change of heart occurred when two very good friends, who had been to our house for supper repeatedly over the course of a couple of years, casually mentioned that I must really enjoy salmon, because I had served it to them every time they were guests. I went out the next morning and bought a logbook and have used it religiously ever since.

In addition to being of practical assistance — with names and vintages of good wines, notes on what to do differently next time, who attended, who never responded to the invitation (scratch them off the list) and, of course, what was served — over time, this "entertaining logbook" becomes a kind of uniquely personal combination cookbook/scrapbook. Just make sure to keep it in one specific spot, so you can find it when you need it. After all, what good is something that's supposed to help you with your memory if you can't remember where you put it?

The leaves add a nice tang, and the fish can be seasoned in any way that you like before wrapping in the leaves. Handling the leaf-wrapped packets on the grill is much easier than struggling with a lean fillet that wants to stick to the cooking grate (see *Leaf-wrapped Packets,* page 117). If you don't choose this option, the rockfish should be marinated in an oil-based marinade (try herb marinade, page 291) or liberally oiled before grilling.

Good side dishes include boiled new potatoes (page 320), "baked" basmati rice (page 316) or grilled potato wedges (page 196). Tasty vegetables include grilled whole tomatoes (page 232) and any summer squash (page 223); or, if it's in season, steamed asparagus.

1) Take the fish out of the refrigerator about 30 minutes before grilling.

2) Determine how much space the rockfish will take up on the grill, and make a bed of coals that's a little larger on all sides. Ignite the charcoal.

3) Put the cooking grill in place, approximately 3 to 5 inches above the coals on adjustable grills. On covered grills, cook without the lid in place.

4) Once the cooking grill is hot, clean it with a wire brush and coat it with vegetable oil. If not marinated, brush both the sides of the rockfish liberally with vegetable oil and dust with paprika. Place the fish directly over the hot coals.

5) Cook the fish for 10 minutes per inch of thickness, measured at the thickest part. For example, a 1-inch-thick steak or fillet would take 10 minutes to cook — 5 minutes per side. Plan on turning the fish only once.

6) As with most fish, rockfish should be served piping hot. Have the rest of your meal ready before putting the fish over the coals.

See Fish, page 133, for more information.

S

SALMON

It's hard to beat the flavor of fresh salmon grilled over a charcoal fire. Fortunately, with its high fat content, salmon is also among the easiest of all fish to grill, staying moist even if it is slightly overcooked. Salmon is usually sold whole and dressed or in chunk, steak or fillet form.

There are many species of salmon, some native to the Pacific and others to the Atlantic. While many people consider the King salmon to be, well, *king,* I'll grill and enjoy any fresh salmon I can find. Even in inland cities, it is often found fresh in supermarkets, either as steaks, fillets or whole fish.

Most people enjoy the natural flavor of salmon so much that they never consider marinating it, but its distinctive flavor stands up very well to a variety of marinades. If you're in the mood for something different, try fresh ginger-garlic marinade (page 290), Dijon marinade (page 289) or pesto marinade (page 293). Mariante for just 30 to 45 minutes.

If you're cooking the salmon plain, a liberal brushing of olive or vegetable oil and a sprinkling of paprika on both sides is all that's needed prior to cooking. This holds true for whole fish, as well as steaks and fillets.

Good side dishes include boiled new potatoes (page 320), "baked" basmati rice (page 316) or grilled potato wedges (page 196). Tasty vegetables include grilled whole tomatoes (page 232), any summer squash (page 223) or, if it's in season, steamed asparagus. A big Chardonnay is just right with a grilled salmon dinner.

1) Keep the fish refrigerated until about 30 minutes before grilling.

2) Ignite enough charcoal to create a bed of coals a little larger than the space the fish will cover on the grill.

A Crippled Kettle Grill

I received a letter from a friend the other day. In it, she related what could have been a sad tale about a crippled kettle grill. Necessity is the mother of invention, not to mention ingenuity. Because of both, this tale has a happy ending:

"My trusty Weber Jr. lost one of its legs last summer. I continued using it with the game leg just propped against the kettle. Last week I was putting the lid on over some gorgeous salmon steaks when a second leg gave way and the whole thing went belly-up. As there wasn't any time to be lost, I broke the third leg off and set the kettle on top of a terra cotta strawberry jar, which has some nice river rocks in its bottom for ballast. The holes in the jar provide plenty of draft for the fire, and the whole thing looks quite elegant and somewhat Japonesque.

Also, while I sit and tend my meal, I can watch the coals fall down among the rocks, the fire lighting up the strawberry jar's interior. As a matter of fact, I had gone out the very next day and bought a new grill, but I'm going to return it as unnecessary and gauche.

By the way, I did salvage the salmon and the fire — just scraped up the coals and put them back in. And despite the ash coating, the fish was wonderful — Saumon en Cendrilles."

Bravo!

3) Once the coals are covered with a light gray ash, arrange them in an even layer, sides touching, in the middle of the fire grate.

4) Put the cooking grill over the coals and allow it to become good and hot before putting on the salmon. Use a wire brush to clean the grill, if necessary, and a large basting brush to coat it with vegetable oil.

5) Grill salmon steaks, fillets or small whole fish (under 4 pounds) directly over a bed of hot coals on an uncovered grill. Large, whole fish — if you can fit one on your grill — should be cooked according to the directions on page 185, under *Cooking a Whole Fish,* or on a rotisserie (see *Spit Cooking,* page 46).

6) Cook the salmon 10 minutes per inch of thickness, measured at the thickest part. For example, a 1-inch-thick steak (or fillet) would take 10 minutes to cook — 5 minutes per side. If the fillets have the skin intact, put them on the grill skin side first. Turn the fish just once, halfway through the total cooking time.

7) Fish should be served hot off the grill. Heated plates help keep the fish piping hot; slip them into a 250-degree F. oven 15 minutes before eating time, along with a platter on which to land the fish after grilling.

See Fish, page 133, for more information.

SAND DAB

Sand dabs are relatively small fish — generally in the 12-ounce to 12-pound range — and a favorite for generations with habitués of San Francisco's traditional fish grills. Sand dab is usually available as fillets or whole, dressed fish, being too thin to be cut into steaks. With its lean, delicate flesh, sand dab demands a little extra care and attention on the grill. The mild distinctive flavor of sand dab needs no embellishment, other than a liberal brushing of vegetable oil and a dusting of paprika before cooking. Serve with wedges of fresh lemon and a sprin-

"While many people consider the King salmon to be, well, king, I'll grill and enjoy any fresh salmon I can find."

kling of chopped parsley. Traditional side dishes are boiled new potatoes (page 320) or pommes frites (page 331) and creamed spinach (page 322). Great eating!

1) About 30 minutes prior to grilling time, remove the fish from the refrigerator and let it come to room temperature.

2) Ignite as many briquets or as much lump charcoal as it takes to make a bed of coals a little larger than what the fish will take up on the grill. Once the coals are covered with a fine gray ash, arrange them in a single layer, sides touching, in the center of the fire grate.

3) Put the cooking grill in place (3 to 5 inches from the coals if it's adjustable). Once the cooking grate is hot, clean it with a wire brush. Coat both the grate and the fish with vegetable oil, using a large basting brush.

4) Grill the fillets or small whole sand dab directly over the fire. If you have a covered grill, cook the fish without putting the cover down.

5) Total cooking time will be 10 minutes per inch of thickness, measured at the thickest part. For example, a ½-inch-thick fillet or whole fish would take 5 minutes to cook — 2½ minutes per side.

6) Serve the sand dab hot off the grill on a platter that has been heated for 15 minutes in a 250-degree F. oven.

See Fish, page 133, for more information.

SAUSAGE

You could spend the entire summer grilling sausages and never eat the same type twice. Sausages originate from around the world and make use of every herb and spice imaginable. They are made not only with meat, but fruits, nuts, grains and vegetables. They come smoked, cooked, cured or fresh; mild or spicy, and in a variety of shapes and sizes.

Italian Sausage "Jerky"

Over the years, we've developed a very unconventional way of grilling those notoriously fatty, but very flavorful, Italian sausages. The process renders almost all the fat away, leaving the sausages very dry — almost like jerky. This obviously won't appeal to everyone, but we like them. And, just like jerky, they make a great backpack snack.

The process works best in a covered kettle grill, but can also be accomplished on an open unit. Here's how to do it:

Ignite 25 to 35 charcoal briquets or an equal amount of lump charcoal. Once the coals are covered with a fine gray ash, arrange them on one side of the fire grate. Put the cooking grill in place.

Before putting the sausages on the grill, prick them all over with the tip of a sharp knife (this is one instance when you're actually trying to rid the sausages of all their moisture). Put the sausage on the side of the grill away from the fire. Grill for at least 30 to 40 minutes; turn every 7 to 10 minutes.

Each time you turn the sausages, continue to prick them and move them a little closer to the section of the grill over the coals. Towards the end, they should be directly over the coals, at which point they will be shrunken and very brown. Like I said, they're not for everyone, but they are tasty. Serve with Polenta (see page 330) and a generous portion of spinach doused with a little balsamic vinegar. A good casual dinner.

SAUSAGE CHART

The chart on these pages provides a small sample of the flavor possibilities offered by sausages. Exact spice blends used in each type vary according to the style and origin of the sausage. Various types may contain upwards of 25 different herbs and spices. Germans favor garlic, paprika, clove and mace. Mexican sausages feature oregano, cumin and peppers. Italian sausages, of course, contain oregano, thyme and garlic, but also fennel and anise. Sage is a main ingredient in many pork sausages.

The chart lists the main flavor ingredient in each type of sausage for general reference. It was put together from sausages available from a variety of sausage shops, but expect recipes to vary from one locale to another. If there's a maker or brand name you particularly like, mark the name right on the chart. Quality meat markets and specialty shops are the best places to find fresh sausage.

Note: If you're wondering about that ubiquitous sausage, the hot dog, you'll find it on page 149.

Name	Meat Used
Adoville (smoked)	Pork, chitlins
Bangers, British-style (fresh)	Veal, pork, bread crumbs
Beerwurst (smoked)	Pork, beef
Bockwurst (cooked)	Veal, pork
Bockwurst, farmer (fresh)	Veal, pork
Bockwurst, Swiss (cooked)	Veal, pork
Boudin Blanc (cooked)	Chicken or pork
Boudin Noir (cooked)	Pork, beef, blood
Bratwurst, Scheitzer (cooked)	Veal, pork
Bratwurst (Thuringer) (fresh or smoked)	Pork, veal
Chorizo (fresh or smoked)	Beef or pork
Garlic Sausage (Knockwurst) (smoked)	Beef, pork, veal
Italian Sausage (fresh or cured)	Pork
Kielbasa/Polish (fresh or smoked)	Pork, veal, beef
Knackwurst (smoked)	Beef, pork
Lamb, Armenian (fresh)	Lamb
Linguica (smoked)	Beef, pork
Louisiana Hots (smoked)	Beef, pork
Lyonaisse (fresh)	Pork, beef, ham
Schinkenwurst (smoked)	Ham, veal, pork
Wiesswurst (cooked)	Veal, pork

Spices	Comments
Louisiana spice mix	Spicy
Nutmeg, lemon zest, herbs, spices	Moderately spicy
Garlic	Mild
Milk, egg, parsley, onion	Mild
Egg, parsley, onion	Mild
Egg, milk	Mild
Egg white, onion	Mild
Onion	Mild
Milk, egg, spices	Moderately spicy
Spices, onion, egg	Moderately spicy
Peppers, Mexican spices	Very hot and spicy
Garlic	Spicy
Fennel, red pepper, garlic, Italian spices	Can be very spicy
Onion, garlic	Spicy
Garlic	Mild
Armenian spices, peppers	Spicy
Vinegar, peppers, spices	Spicy
Onion, garlic, hot spices	Hot and spicy
Garlic, pistachio nuts	Spicy
Pistachio nuts	Mild
Chives or leeks, parsley	Mild

Sausages are made not only with meat, but fruits, nuts, grains and vegetables. They come smoked, cooked, cured or fresh; mild or spicy, and in a variety of shapes and sizes.

Hinged Wire Baskets

A hinged wire basket is a definite advantage anytime you're cooking a lot of small items, such as sausages, fish or cut up chicken. The sliding ring around the handles ensures a tight grip on whatever sized food you have between the hinges.

The only drawback is that it's long handle precludes use on a covered grill — provided you want the cover completely closed. Most folks agree, however, that's a small price to pay for the convenience of flipping a multitude of morsels in one fell swoop.

As good as they are cooked on top of a stove, sausages taste even better when they've been cooked over the coals. Cooking times vary, depending on what the sausages are made of and whether or not they have been precooked or smoked. Precooked or smoked sausage needs only to be warmed — 5 to 10 minutes depending on thickness. Uncooked pork sausage should be cooked for 15 to 20 minutes, depending on thickness, until the insides are no longer pink.

Cook any sausage directly over low to moderate coals. Sausages split when cooked over a fire that is too hot. Some cooks recommend pricking or making diagonal slices in the casing before cooking the sausages to prevent splitting, a procedure that will cost you valuable juices. The best solution is to cook the sausages at lower temperatures. Precooking fresh sausages in water before grilling is not recommended.

Hinged baskets are a convenient tool when grilling a mess of sausages at the same time; you turn one, you turn them all. (See *Hinged Wire Baskets,* at left.)

For more information on sausages, see the Sausage Chart found on the previous page.

SCALLIONS

Grilled scallions make an interesting side dish to any number of grilled meats; they are especially tasty with grilled lamb.

To grill scallions, simply cut away the root end and any damaged outside layers and trim so about 3 inches of green remains on the top. Brush with olive oil and place directly over moderate to hot coals (perpendicular to the way the grill bars run, please). Cook for 2 to 3 minutes per side. Serve with a sprinkling of salt and a dash of balsamic vinegar. Grilled scallions provide a pungent, earthy high note to any meal featuring other strong-flavored foods.

SCALLOPS, BAY AND SEA

Bay and sea scallops are two different species of shellfish: Bay scallops are *Pecten irradians* and sea scallops are *P. magellicanus.* They differ dramatically in size. To give you an idea, there are approximately 15 to 40 sea scallops to a pound, and between 90 to 100 bay scallops to a pound. The smaller bay scallops are considered more delicate, and quite frankly are so small that they are probably better off sautéed. The larger sea scallops are, to my mind, every bit as delectable and elegant and, much to their credit, well-suited to skewer cooking on the grill. But, and this is an important *but,* they require some special handling and circumstances to do both them and you justice.

As far as handling is concerned, scallops, like all shellfish, require a minimum amount of time on the grill. The trick is to cook them over a very hot fire, watch them like a hawk, and serve just as they reach perfection. Which brings us to the second requirement: timing

I have never been able to figure out how to get more than two servings of skewered scallops off the grill without having them turn lukewarm and, quite frankly, less than delectable. The only solution I've found to this problem is to reserve scallops for those rare but wonderful *tête-à-tête* evenings, maybe when you feel like celebrating at the best place in town — your own home. Here's the lowdown:

If you're celebrating, cover that table for two with a perfectly pressed white linen tablecloth (put it on the kitchen table if it's more comfortable in there), buy a few flowers and light the candles. Set the table with whatever you usually reserve for company, and chill down some extravagant champagne (a fraction of the price at a bottle shop than it would be at a restaurant).

Prepare whatever side dishes you are planning to serve in advance. Everything needs to be ready by the time you put the scallops on the grill. "Baked" basmati rice (page 316) or steamed parslied rice (page 337) would be excellent, as would any fresh vegetable or a simple green salad.

1) Soak small bamboo skewers for about 30 minutes in hot water. Arrange the scallops on the wet skewers,

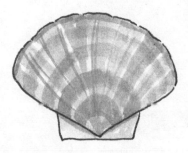

"As far as handling is concerned, scallops, like all shellfish, require a minimum amount of time on the grill. The trick is to cook them over a very hot fire, watch them like a hawk, and serve just as they reach perfection."

"The easiest way to tell if the scallops are done to your liking is to simply take one off a skewer and pop it in your mouth: cook's prerogative!"

alternating each scallop with one-half of a fresh bay leaf. (Dry bay leaves will work, too. Soak them in water first, for about 20 minutes.) Liberally brush the skewered scallops with melted butter just before putting them on the grill.

2) Start the coals, preferably in a small hibachi (see page 23), or in your regular grill. Remember, you want a hot fire, even though the scallops will take only a few minutes to cook.

3) Once the coals are covered with a fine gray ash, arrange them in a single layer. Put the cooking grill in place (about 3 to 5 inches over the coals if it's adjustable) and let it heat up. Put the scallop serving platter and dinner plates in a 250-degree F. oven.

4) While the fire is still good and hot, put the scallops directly over the coals. Do not put the top in place on a covered grill.

5) Cook for 3 to 5 minutes per side, for a total of 6 to 10 minutes. The scallops will be ready when they turn opaque white but are still fairly soft to the touch. The easiest way to tell if the scallops are done to your liking is to simply take one off a skewer and pop it in your mouth: cook's prerogative!

6) While the scallops are cooking, put your side dishes on the table. Have your dinner partner bring you the hot platter, and take the scallops off the grill the moment they are done. Serve with wedges of fresh lemon, if you like. This is a very special and delicious meal. Enjoy!

SCROD

Scrod is baby cod, usually fish under 2 pounds. It can be pan-dressed and cooked on the grill with great success. For more information, see Cod, page 116.

SEA BASS

In some areas of the country, grouper is sold as sea bass, to which it is very similar. For more information, see Grouper, page 142.

SHALLOT

Shallots were a pleasant surprise the first time I tried grilling them; the high heat of the grill sweetens their pungency and turns them into little nuggets of great flavor.

Peel the shallots and roll in a little olive or vegetable oil. Thread them onto small bamboo skewers that have been soaked for 30 minutes in hot water. Cook directly over a moderate to hot fire for a total cooking time of approximately 10 to 14 minutes. It's a treat to find a little mound of these on a platter featuring almost any roast meat. Give them a try!

SHARK

Shark is rapidly gaining in popularity as people discover its excellent flavor and texture (similar to swordfish), and get over their initial squeamishness regarding this legendary group of fish. Shark is usually offered as steaks, fillets, or cut up into chunks, just right for skewers. Grilled shark is moist, meaty and relatively mild — and virtually boneless.

If you notice a faint aroma of ammonia in the fish, it's quite normal and can be removed by soaking the shark in a mild solution of water and vinegar, lemon or lime juice, or milk for 30 minutes or so.

Shark takes to a variety of marinades very nicely. Try lemon-white wine marinade (page 292), Southeast Asian-style marinade (page 294) or fresh ginger-garlic marinade (page 290). Marinate the fish for only 30-45 minutes.

Good side dishes include boiled new potatoes (page 320), "baked" basmati rice (page 316), grilled potato

Once people get over their initial squeamishness regarding this legendary fish, they discover the shark's excellent flavor and texture, one that is quite similar to swordfish.

wedges (page 196), grilled whole tomatoes (page 232) and any summer squash (page 223).

1) Keep the fish refrigerated until about 30 minutes before grilling. It should be just at room temperature when it goes on the grill.

2) Determine how much space the fish will take up on the grill, and ignite as many briquets as it takes to make a bed of coals that's a little larger in size. Put the cooking grill over the coals and let it heat up.

3) On adjustable grills, position the cooking grill 3 to 5 inches above the coals. On covered grills, cook the shark without putting the lid in place.

4) Clean and oil the cooking grate just before putting on the fish. If you're cooking fillets with the skin intact, put them on the grill skin side down first.

5) Cook the shark for 10 minutes per inch of thickness, measured at the thickest part. For example, a 1-inch-thick steak (or fillet, or whatever) will take 10 minutes to cook — 5 minutes per side. Turn the fish halfway through the total cooking time.

6) Serve immediately after grilling on a heated platter (put it in a 250-degree F. oven about 15 minutes before serving time). If you don't have a helpmate in the kitchen, have the rest of your dinner ready to go before putting the fish on the grill.

See Fish, page 133, for more information.

SHRIMP

Shrimp are the most popular seafood in America and, to my mind, there's no better way to prepare them than on the grill. Technically speaking, there's a distinct difference between shrimp and prawns: shrimp are saltwater creatures and prawns, freshwater. Be that as it may, large shrimp are usually sold as "prawns."

"Generally speaking, half the weight of shrimp is in the shell, so if you want a pound of cooked, shelled shrimp, buy two pounds in the shell."

To confuse matters somewhat more, what is sold as "tiger shrimp" in many stores is actually a prawn. They are imported to this country primarily from Malaysia, where they are aquacultured. Their shells are darker and turn a brighter pink when cooked. Although gastronomes may disagree, there's little difference between the taste of tiger shrimp and any other shrimp or prawn you might buy.

All shrimp are classified by weight, that is, how many it takes to make up a pound. The only problem is, different parts of the country seem to give different names to each class; what you know as "large" shrimp may be sold somewhere else as "medium." With that in mind, adapt the following information to your own shrimp situation:

> *Small (also called bay or popcorn shrimp)* — 150 to 200 per pound
> *Medium* — approximately 50 per pound
> *Large* — 30 per pound
> *Jumbo (or Colossal)* — 10 to 12 per pound
> *Extra Colossal* — fewer than 10 per pound

Generally speaking, half the weight of shrimp is in the shell, so if you want a pound of cooked, shelled shrimp, buy two pounds in the shell.

Small bay shrimp are almost always sold cooked, and are too small for cooking on the grill, anyway. Medium and larger shrimp are all excellent candidates for skewering and cooking over the coals. You can devein medium and large shrimp or not, depending on your inclination; jumbo and extra colossal shrimp require deveining. I think all shrimp taste better grilled in their shells, which means deveining after they're grilled. Personally, I find deveining incredibly tedious and avoid it, simply enough, by grilling medium-sized shrimp almost exclusively.

Shrimp are great marinated. Try lime-garlic marinade (page 292), Southeast Asian-style marinade (page 294) or fresh ginger-garlic marinade (page 290).

The most common error in cooking any shrimp is cooking them too long. Once they go on the grill, watch the shrimp like a hawk, pulling them off the moment the meat turns opaque. On both covered and uncovered

Skewering Shrimp

Shrimp, as good as they are on the grill, can be a little difficult to handle unless they are properly skewered. The methods illustrated below will work for any size shrimp.

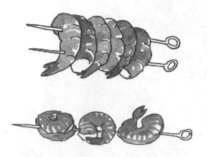

Very large shrimp can be butterflied and skewered, as shown below. If you're using bamboo skewers, it's a good idea to soak the skewers in hot water for 30 minutes or so before putting them on the coals. This will help ensure that there's still something to hold onto when you get ready to take the shrimp from the grill!

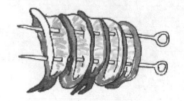

grills, cook shrimp directly over a hot fire, with the grill about 3 to 5 inches above the coals (if it's adjustable). Approximate total cooking times are as follows:

Medium shrimp — 5 to 6 minutes
Large shrimp — 6 to 8 minutes
Jumbo shrimp — 8 to 10 minutes
Extra Colossal shrimp — 10 to 12 minutes

You'll find shrimp easiest to handle if you skewer them on two parallel skewers, as shown on page 219. Shrimp can be served hot off the grill, at room temperature or chilled — they're delicious any way.

SNAPPER, PACIFIC

This is a member of a very large group of fish collectively known as rockfish. For more information, see Rockfish, page 207.

SOFT-SHELLED CRAB

Delectable soft-shelled crabs (as opposed to the many hard-shelled varieties) take very well to the grill, and are the essence of simplicity to prepare. If fresh soft-shelled crabs are available in your area, count yourself lucky and fire up that grill!

Serve with pommes frites (page 331) and coleslaw (page 321).

1) Take the crabs out of the refrigerator about 20 minutes before grilling. They should be close to room temperature when they go on the grill.

2) You'll want to cook the crabs directly over a hot fire, so ignite as much charcoal as it takes to make a bed of coals that's about the same size as the space the crab will take up when placed on the grill. Put the cooking grill in place and let it get hot before cleaning it with a wire brush and coating it with vegetable oil.

"If fresh soft-shelled crabs are available in your area, count yourself lucky and fire up that grill!"

3) Baste the crabs liberally with melted butter and place on the grill directly over the hot coals. Don't use the cover on covered grills.

4) The crabs will take only 6 minutes or so to cook. Turn them just once, halfway through the cooking time.

5) Serve the crabs hot off the grill, with plenty of fresh lemon wedges and your favorite bottled seafood sauce.

Sole

Unless you live on the East Coast, it is unlikely that you will ever encounter the true Dover or Channel sole, except, perhaps, if you holiday in England or Europe. It is the very similar flounders that are sold in Midwestern and Western markets as sole. Be that as it may, they are still exceptionally tasty when cooked over the coals in pan-dressed form (in its fillet form, sole is far better sautéed on top of the stove). Sole is one of the most difficult fish to successfully grill; consider yourself an griller with an advanced degree when it turns out right.

The many types of sole range in size from 1 to 5 pounds, usually around 2 pounds. Small, pan-dressed sole (gutted, with head, tail and fins removed) can be cooked on the grill, but because sole is lean, it should be liberally basted with vegetable oil or melted butter before and during the grilling process. Add a generous sprinkling of paprika to both sides of the fish before cooking. Once grilled, top with a little finely chopped parsley, and serve the sole with several wedges of fresh lemon, or with the elegant *beurre blanc* (page 300).

Another, favored way to cook a mild, lean fish such as sole is to wrap small portions in grape leaves and grill the little bundles right over the coals (see *Leaf-wrapped Packets* on page 117).

Classic side dishes include boiled new potatoes (page 320), creamed spinach (page 322) and steamed parslied rice (page 337).

1) About 30 minutes before grilling, take the fish out of the refrigerator.

"Sole is one of the most difficult fish to successfully grill; consider yourself a griller with an advanced degree when it turns out right."

2) Determine how much space the fish will take up on the grill, and ignite as many briquets or as much lump charcoal as it takes to make a bed of coals that's a little larger. After the fire is lit, put the cooking grill in place and allow it to heat up (fish will stick to a cold grill).

3) Use a wire brush to clean the cooking grill once it's hot. Oil the grill, using a large basting brush and vegetable oil, just before you're ready to grill the fish.

4) Cook the fish directly over a bed of hot coals. Don't use the cover on covered grills. Baste with oil or melted butter as needed to keep it from drying out on the grill.

5) Cook the sole for 10 minutes per inch of thickness, measured at the thickest part. Turn the fish just once, halfway through the cooking process.

6) After it's cooked, land the fish on a platter that you've heated for 15 minutes in a 250-degree F. oven.

See Fish, page 133, for more information.

SPARERIBS

The classic meat for barbecue, spareribs are the breast and rib bones of pork. For more information on this delectable meat, see Pork, ribs, page 192.

SQUAB

A squab is a special breed of pigeon, larger in the breast and ready for the table at 28 days old. As good as they are on the grill, squab could become a replacement for the Rock Cornish game hen. A friend who raises them, advises dunking them into the leftover marinade between each turn on the grill; much better than basting. For grilling instructions, see Pigeon, page 180.

Spareribs...the classic meat for barbecue.

SQUASH, SUMMER

The late Alex D. Hawkes, in his excellent book, *A World of Vegetable Cookery* (unfortunately no longer in print), wrote that "the common nomenclature of the numerous kinds of vegetables known as Squash is almost hilariously confused."

In addition to being a fine cook and writer, Mr. Hawkes was also trained as a botanist — a particularly useful background when it comes to the subject of vegetables. Under the label "summer squash," Dr. Hawkes included not only crookneck, pattypan and scallop types, but also butternut squash, pumpkins and even ornamental gourds!

Quite frankly, you'd have to be out of your gourd to want to grill one. My own practical approach to nomenclature is based on what's commonly found in the grocery store, rather than what's in the garden. Therefore, my version of summer squash includes only the crooknecks, the pattypans and zucchini. These squashes are all great cooked on the grill.

All that's required is to slice the squash crosswise or lengthwise, whichever way you prefer, about ½-inch-thick, brush with a little olive oil, sprinkle with salt and pepper and then grill until just tender — about 8 to 10 minutes.

On a covered grill, I prefer to cook the squash away from the coals for the first 5 minutes or so, and then finish them briefly over the coals for the last few minutes. On an open grill, squash should be kept towards the edges of the fire. Position the cooking grill 3 or 5 inches above the coals if you're using an adjustable grill.

Grilled summer squash of any type is an essential ingredient in grilled ratatouille (see recipe on page 332). Always favor small, firm squash — a stage some would call immature — as these have tender skins, virtually no seed cavities, and a pleasing, fresh flavor. Optimum size for the crooknecks and zucchini is about 4 to 5 inches long; pattypans start to develop tough skins when they are much larger than 4 inches in diameter.

"Quite frankly, you'd have to be out of your gourd to want to grill one."

Cleaning Squid

1. Using a sharp knife, cut off the tentacles. Reserve: some people think these are the best part of the squid. Squeeze to remove the squid's small, bean-like mouth and discard.

2. Inside the squid's body is a small, almost bone-like part; squeeze to remove remove this along with the rest of the squid's internal organs.

3. Remove the skin by simply grasping and pulling. Rinse both body and tenacles in water, then dry. Cut the body into rings. Marinate, if desired, before skewering and grilling.

SQUASH, WINTER

The winter squash category includes many hard-skinned varieties such as acorn, butternut, crookneck, Hubbard and turban. Some, like the Hubbard and crookneck, can reach mammoth proportions, often weighing 40 pounds or more. Others, like the acorn or butternut, are considerably smaller, almost always under five pounds.

Because of their relatively hard skin, all of the winter squash are great "keepers," meaning they will keep for months in the refrigerator or root cellar, should you happen to have one. Their flesh is a little like a cross between a sweet potato and a pumpkin, but generally sweeter and somewhat drier.

The most popular way to cook winter squash is to bake them in an oven and flavor them with butter, brown sugar and/or sherry. The smaller winter squash can be cut in half and grilled on a covered grill, cut side up, with the cavity filled with your favorite flavoring, much as you would in an indoor oven. Because they will take upward of 30 minutes to cook, place the squash slightly away from the direct heat of the coals. Leave both the top and bottom vents completely open.

As an alternative, 1½- to 2-inch chunks of any type of peeled winter squash can be put on skewers, brushed with a little melted butter and grilled on either an open or covered grill. Depending on the size of the chunks, they should cook in 15 to 20 minutes; turn every 5 minutes or so.

SQUID

The rest of the world knows how tasty squid is, but Americans are a bit reluctant to take these odd-looking sea creatures home from the fish market. Squid's unfortunate lack of popularity has resulted in it being one of the least expensive of all seafood. Squid is excellent when marinated and quickly grilled. Try Greek marinade (page 290), lemon-white wine marinade (page 292) or Southeast Asian-style marinade (page 294).

The easiest way to handle squid on the grill is to cage it in a hinged wire basket (see page 214) or string it on small bamboo skewers. For cleaning instructions, see *Cleaning Squid,* page 224.

1) Remove the squid from the refrigerator about 30 minutes before cooking time.

2) To prevent the squid from sticking to the cooking grate, allow the grate to become good and hot, then use your wire brush to clean it. Coat the grate (or the wire basket, if you're using one) with vegetable oil just before you're ready to cook the squid, using a large basting brush.

3) Grill the squid directly over a bed of hot coals. If you have a covered grill, cook the squid without putting the cover down.

4) The squid will be done when the meat turns opaque white — approximately 3 to 5 minutes per side. Do not overcook, or it will become *very* chewy. Serve hot off the grill with plenty of fresh lemon wedges and an ice-cold bottle of good Chablis — delicious!

STEELHEAD

A prized sports fish, steelhead is the name given to rainbow trout as it returns from the sea to freshwater rivers. For more information, see Trout, freshwater and sea, page 234.

STURGEON

Sturgeon is meaty fish, with dense, white flesh. As such, it is perfect for grilling, either as fillets or cut up into cubes and skewered. Sturgeon also takes well to marinades. Try fresh ginger-garlic marinade (page 290), herb marinade (page 291) or lemon-white wine marinade (page 292), but don't overdo it — 30 to 60 minutes in the marinade will be enough to flavor the sturgeon without overwhelming its natural taste.

"It is said that when sturgeon are in season, no less than two-thirds of the females consist of roe. It is certainly odd to think of a fish weighing perhaps 1,000 pounds, being two-thirds made up of eggs. Here is life rushing into reproduction with a vengeance. At such rate of reproduction the world would soon become the abode of sturgeons alone, were it not that the roe is exceedingly good, and the lovers of caviar are more general than Shakespeare knew."

From Kettner's Book of the Table, written by E. S. Dallas in 1877

Keep the side dishes simple. "Baked" basmati rice (page 316), boiled new potatoes (page 320) and steamed parslied rice (page 337) are excellent choices.

1) Take the fish out of the refrigerator about 30 minutes before grilling.

2) Ignite as much charcoal as it takes to make a bed of coals that's a little larger in size than what the fish will take up on the grill. Put the cooking grill in place, 3 to 5 inches above the coals, and let it get hot.

3) After the cooking grill heats up, clean it with a wire brush. Use a large basting brush to coat the grate with vegetable oil.

4) Grill the fish directly over the fire on an uncovered grill. Cook the sturgeon for 10 minutes per inch of thickness, measured at the thickest part. Turn just once, halfway through the total cooking time.

5) Fish should be served immediately after grilling. To keep the fish piping hot between grill and table, slip a platter for the fish into a 250-degree F. oven 15 minutes prior to serving.

See Fish, page 133, for more information.

SWEET POTATOES

If you were referred to this page from "Yams," then you're aware that I am not unbiased when it comes to these tubers. Before continuing, however, it's important to know a little more about yams and sweet potatoes.

Yams, although becoming increasingly available in this country, are different from sweet potatoes, in fact, they are from two different genera. Yams are in the genus *Dioscorea* (which includes at least 250 species); and sweet potatoes are known botanically as *Ipomoea batatas*. Yams are an important staple throughout much of the tropics, but have not been widely grown in, nor often imported

"Then there is the prodigious Giant or White Yam, today widely cultivated in the tropics under a wealth of other names. This is a showy, profuse vine (Dioscorea alata and variants) with underground tubers weighing as much as one hundred pounds, and attaining lengths of more than eight feet! The texture and flavor of most of these forms are inferior to those of their smaller brethren, but they are important food plants, often encountered in native markets from the Antilles to India."

From A World of Vegetable Cookery, probably the best book ever written on the subject, by Alex D. Hawkes

to, America. When you do see true yams in American grocery stores, they will usually be cut into pieces and wrapped in cellophane.

Sweet potatoes, on the other hand, have been grown in this country for a long time. How the common names became confused is not important. The only thing to remember — and this *is* important — is that two types are generally sold in grocery stores: one with yellowish skin and mealy, fairly dry flesh, and one with reddish-orange skin with denser, sweeter flesh. For grilling, it's the drier, yellowish type you want, even though the description "mealy and dry" isn't very appealing.

And now on with the sweet potato saga, which turned out to be one of the real surprises of this project. Believe me, I never would have tried them if it hadn't been for the encyclopedic nature of this book. In an effort to be fair, I bought a bagful and tried them several ways: parboiled and grilled, microwaved and grilled, quartered and put over the coals, and whole, pushed next to the coals, right down there on the fire grate.

The night we tried them was convivial, so I must admit to not paying a great deal of attention to my least favorite vegetable. But when aromatic wafts finally reminded me of my responsibility, we rescued the tubers from the fire. The parboiled and partially cooked (microwaved) sweet potatoes were pedestrian. The quartered pieces cooked directly over the coals were better by half. But the ones stuck next to the coals were the clear favorites of all those attending the "yam bake."

The skins were completely and unappetizingly charred — not a promising beginning. I cut into one, dabbed a couple pats of butter onto what looked to be very fluffy flesh, and decided that a couple of squeezes of fresh lime juice and a healthy sprinkling of chopped fresh cilantro were in order. Man, oh man! It was scrumptious! A total surprise. Instead of adding other sweet ingredients (like maple syrup, marshmallows and raisins), the real treat is in supplying the opposite. The very tart and sour flavor of lime plays off the sweet potato's natural sweetness, and a little butter softens the effect beautifully.

This is a highly recommended vegetable for grilling (see *Cooking in the Coals,* at right). Count on at least 45 minutes to an hour for the sweet potato to cook in the

Cooking in the Coals

Although it may sound a bit rustic, potatoes and sweet potatoes can be cooked in the coals, rather than over them. So can corn, wrapped in its husks or in foil. Kids especially get a kick out of this cooking method, bringing, as it does, a little camp life to the backyard.

Potatoes and sweet potatoes should actually be buried in the coals. Wash the skins first, then push them down into the fire. In approximately 45 to 60 minutes, they will be completely blackened on the outside, but tender and fluffy on the inside.

For corn, pull back the husks and de-silk. Cut one inch off the end of the ear. Soak the corn in cold water for 20 minutes. Tie husk ends together with a thin strip of husk or wet cotton string. Or, de-husk the corn and wrap in two layers of aluminum foil. Lay the corn directly on the coals. Turn frequently. Total cooking time will be approximately 8 minutes.

coals. Take the time to lift off the cooking grill every 15 minutes or so, to give them a quarter turn. Have a small dish at the ready with a few pats of butter and several wedges of lime. And even though you can't eat the peel (as with baking potatoes), the insides of these tubers will be so delightful that you won't mind a bit. Really!

Try serving with any jerked grilled meat (see page 195), goose or ham. We're talking seriously good food here. Remember, it's the yellowish-colored sweet potato you want — and hold those marshmallows.

SWORDFISH

Swordfish is one of the best fish for grilling. An unusual combination of firm but lean flesh helps swordfish hold up well, and it is one of the very few fish that can be frozen, thawed and grilled with little loss of quality.

Most people enjoy the natural flavor of swordfish so much that they never consider marinating it, but it can be quite delicious. If you're in the mood for something different, try Greek marinade (page 290), herb marinade (page 291) or lime-garlic marinade (page 292). Marinate for 30 to 60 minutes.

If you're grilling the swordfish plain, a liberal brushing of olive or vegetable oil and a sprinkling of paprika on both sides is all that's needed prior to cooking. This holds true for cubed swordfish, steaks and fillets.

Good side dishes include boiled new potatoes (page 320), "baked" basmati rice (page 316) or grilled potato wedges (page 196). Tasty vegetables include grilled whole tomatoes (page 232) and any summer squash (page 223) or, if it's in season, steamed asparagus. A big Chardonnay is just right with a grilled swordfish dinner.

1) Take the swordfish out of the refrigerator about 30 minutes before grilling.

2) Determine how much space the fish will take up on the grill, and make a bed of coals that's a little larger in size. Ignite the briquets. Put the cooking grill in place (3 to 5 inches above the coals if it's adjustable).

Swordfish is one of the best-suited of all fish for grilling. Its dense flesh holds up very well on the grill and its flavor is complemented by the rustic aroma of a charcoal fire.

3) Once the cooking grill is hot, clean it with a wire brush and coat it with vegetable oil.

4) Position the fish directly over the hot coals. If you're cooking fillets with the skin intact, put them on the grill skin side down. On covered grills, cook the swordfish without the lid in place.

5) Cook the swordfish for 10 minutes per inch of thickness, measured at the thickest part. Plan on turning the fish only once, halfway through the total cooking time.

6) Serve piping hot, on a platter that has been heated for 15 minutes in a 250-degree F. oven. The rest of your meal should be ready to go before the fish hits the grill.

See Fish, page 133, for more information.

See Fish, page 133, for more information.

San Diego Swordfish Saga

In response to that classic line from a daughter, "Mom, I'm bringing someone home for dinner that I'd like you to meet," my future wife was asked what she would like to have served for dinner. "Let Dad grill some swordfish," she replied.

All went swimmingly, until I had the bad sense to pop the question the moment His Honor slid the swordfish onto the grill. After considerable hemming and hawing, I managed to get the marriage proposal out, but not before completely flustering a seasoned grill chef (not so much because of the proposal but, what with my stammering, it took me so long to get to the point).

The ruling on the swordfish was overcooked in the third degree, but the remainder of the story has turned out rather splendid.

If I didn't apologize at the time for ruining those perfectly fresh, San Diego swordfish steaks, George, allow me to do so here. Thanks for your grace and tact, and for the implicit lesson in timing — not to mention your sage advice: "Kissing don't last; cooking do."

T

TEMPE

Tempe, an Indonesian variation of tofu, is widely available at health food stores. Like tofu, it is a soybean product. Most tempe looks a little like skinless sausages. Because it is denser than tofu and has more texture and flavor, many people prefer tempe. If you've never had it, try it side by side with tofu for a vegetarian version of mixed grill. Marinate and grill in the same way as tofu (page 231).

TILEFISH

Tilefish (also called tile bass) is not often seen in markets, which is unfortunate, as this warm water fish tastes much like lobster. Tilefish is most often sold as fillets or steaks, and occassionally in chunk form for use on skewers.

One way to cook a mild, lean fish such as tilefish is to wrap small portions in grape leaves and grill the little bundles right over the coals. The leaves add a nice tang, and the fish can be seasoned any way you like before wrapping. Handling the leaf-wrapped packets on the grill is much easier than struggling with a lean fish that wants to stick to the cooking grill. For more information, see *Leaf-wrapped Packets,* page 117.

Given its delectable flavor, a marinade isn't needed, although lemon-white wine marinade (page 292) and herb marinade (page 291) are complementary. If you opt to marinate, do so for no more than 30 to 45 minutes. If not, simply brush the fish with a liberal coating of mild vegetable oil and sprinkle both sides with paprika.

Good side dishes for tilefish include "baked" basmati rice (page 316), steamed parslied rice (page 337) or boiled new potatoes (page 320).

"Tilefish is not often seen in markets, which is unfortunate, as this warm water fish tastes much like lobster."

1) Keep the fish refrigerated until about 30 minutes before grilling. It should be just at room temperature when it goes on the grill.

2) Determine how much space the fish will take up on the grill, and make a bed of coals that's a little larger in size. Ignite the charcoal.

3) Fish will stick to a cold grill, so put the cooking grill in place (about 3 to 5 inches over the coals, if you're using an adjustable grill) and let it get hot. Clean the hot grill with a wire brush, and coat it with vegetable oil, using a large basting brush.

4) Grill the fish directly over a bed of hot coals. If you have a covered grill, cook the fish without putting down the cover.

5) Cook for 10 minutes per inch of thickness, measured at the thickest part. For example, if the fish is 1 inch thick, the total cooking time will be 10 minutes — 5 minutes per side. Turn the fish only once, halfway through the cooking process.

6) Tilefish should be served piping hot, so have everything else ready to go before putting the fish on the grill.

See Fish, page 133, for more information.

TOFU

Yes, it's true. Tofu *can* be grilled, and it is delicious. Lest you think that this is some sort of ultimate California weirdness, let me point out that the first time I ever ate grilled tofu (or *heard of it,* for that matter) was in Kansas City.

Alone, tofu doesn't taste like much. But, as with many bland foods, tofu takes well to marinades and other flavorings. The best tofu for grilling is the "hard" type (which is hardly hard, but certainly harder than the soft type). There is also a considerable difference in "hardness" from one brand to another; keep experi-

In Its Favor

It's difficult to mention tofu without eliciting a snigger of contempt or suspicion, which is unfortunate. The back panel of one particular brand of tofu contains the following information:

"One acre of land dedicated to soybean farming produces sixteen times more edible protein than one acre of land used for beef production.

"The same fossil-fuel energy required to produce 15 pounds of soybeans produces only one pound of feedlot beef.

"More than half of all water used in the United States is used for livestock production."

It's been my experience that youngsters are far more willing to try tofu, and like it, than those grown-up kids known as adults. Give it a try.

menting until you find the firmest brand. Slice the tofu about ½-inch thick and marinate it in bottled teriyaki sauce (or make your own, page 295), fresh ginger-garlic marinade (page 290), or Southeast Asian-style marinade (page 294).

"Hard" tofu holds up very well on the grill. Cook directly over the coals for only as long as it takes to heat it through. Turn the tofu once or twice using a spatula rather than a fork. Actually, you can cook it for as long as you want because it's practically impossible to overcook. Not to mention that I've never run into anyone who's requested their grilled tofu rare — yet.

Serve grilled tofu with steamed rice (page 337). As long as you're being esoteric, might as well make it "baked" basmati rice (page 316), or better yet, brown rice. Skewered vegetables, such as bell peppers, onions and cherry tomatoes, make a good accompaniment, as does sautéed Chinese cabbage or bok choy, served with a little rice vinegar sprinkled on top.

Unless you're serving brown rice with your grilled tofu, there's no need to wear a black turtleneck while eating it.

"Unless you're serving brown rice with your grilled tofu, there's no need to wear a black turtleneck while eating it."

TOMATO

Tomatoes really come to life on the grill — even those strange, hard pink things one finds deposited in markets during the off-season. There are several ways to successfully grill tomatoes:

a) slice large ones into thick (about ½ inch) slices;
b) slice off about the top one-quarter of large tomatoes and core them almost through to the other end;
c) skewer cherry tomatoes (using two parallel skewers)
d) marinate and skewer pear-shaped ('Roma') tomatoes.

My favorite method is the second. Slice off the top quarter of large tomatoes, core them using a small, sharp knife; slice a little off their bottoms so they easily sit upright. Arrange them on a platter and fill the cavity with about ½ tablespoon of good olive oil, a little pressed garlic, salt pepper, and a sprinkling of fresh chopped basil (dried is fine, or substitute marjoram, oregano, or rosemary). Do this before you start preparing the rest of the dinner, so the flavors will have a chance to permeate through the tomato. Let the tomatoes sit at room temperature for an hour or so.

When it comes time to cook the tomatoes, place them right side up on the grill, away from the fire. As your main course cooks, gradually slide the tomatoes closer to the fire, but not directly over it. Do not turn. The point here is not to make the tomatoes crispy, but simply to heat them all the way through and absorb a little of that smoky aroma.

Large tomatoes will take 15 to 20 minutes to cook. Leave them on the grill, out toward the edge, even after you've taken the main course off the grill. When you're ready to eat, bring in the tomatoes, hot off the grill, and serve them forth. Talk about good!

Thick slices of large tomatoes are grilled in much the same way as whole tomatoes, but because of the amount of exposed cut area, they are not as juicy — still delicious, mind you, but just not as juicy. Follow the same procedure, marinating the slices in olive oil and whatever flavoring you desire for about 1 hour before grilling. Grill the tomato slices away from direct heat for 2 minutes per side, and then directly over the coals for about 1 minute per side; any longer and you'll run the risk of them falling apart.

Cherry tomatoes, cooked on skewers, are good, but because they are uncut, they will not accept the flavors of a marinade. Again, cook initially away from the direct heat, for about 3 to 5 minutes per side. Finish up for about 1 minute per side over the direct heat. Use two parallel skewers; otherwise, the tomatoes will spin around every time you try to turn them.

Those firm, flavorful paste or "pear" (sometimes sold as 'Roma') tomatoes can be cut in half, marinated, skewered and grilled with great success. Grill for the same amount of time as cherry tomatoes. These are the tomatoes of choice when traditional round tomatoes are out of season.

🍎

Easy, Tasty Tomato "Sauce"

Tomatoes cooked on the grill until soft can be considered a "sauce." In some Middle Eastern countries, grilled whole tomatoes are placed on a plate, smashed with a fork, and the grilled entree placed on top of the cooked, smashed tomato.

Whether it's grilled chicken, lamb, fish or veal, the grilled tomato will make a wonderful "sauce" if you just remember to press it down with a fork first. Great on pasta or polenta, too.

Trout Wrapped in Corn Husks

Trout, in its various forms, holds up quite nicely on the grill. I was intrigued to read in a very old book on outdoor cooking that the small pan-sized trout could be wrapped in corn husks and grilled over the coals. I have a feeling that the inspiration for this didn't spring from necessity, but that it was discovered that a small trout fit neatly into the corn husk with a little extra room for tying at both ends.

Whether or not it's really necessary, husk-wrapped trout is sure to impress onlookers. One of the true advantages of this method is that it allows the cook to season the cavity of the fish with a little herb butter and hold it in place where it can work its magic.

If the husks aren't very green, soak them in water for 30 minutes before use, along with enough to tie the packages at both ends.

TROUT, FRESHWATER AND SEA

Trout fall into three basic categories, based on where the fish reside: freshwater, freshwater but temporarily found in saltwater, and saltwater. All have rather magical names, conjuring up images of rushing mountain streams, where one hopes the fishing is as good as the scenery.

True freshwater trout include rainbow, brown, golden and cut-throat. Very similar in taste and conformation (but not truly trout) are the Dolly Varden, brook and lake or Mackinaw "trout." This group is sometimes lumped together under the name of "char." Rainbow trout *(Salmo gairdneri)* are the ones you see in the market, being widely aquacultured; you have to catch the other beauties for yourself. When the rainbow and cut-throat migrate to the ocean, the rainbows are called steelheads (sometimes referred to as "salmon trout"), and cut-throats are called steelhead cut-throats. Trout that spend their entire life in saltwater include the gray sea trout and the spotted sea trout. Clear as Kafka, right?

Nomenclature aside, most trout have similar mild-flavored, moderately fatty flesh, excellent for grilling and smoking (see *Smoked Fish,* page 166). Trout sold in markets are remarkably uniform, usually around ½-pound each; luck and skill will determine the size of your catch. Farm-raised trout are usually sold dressed (gutted, but with head and tail intact), and are easy to handle on the grill; just make sure to oil both the fish and the grill before cooking, and have a large spatula (or two) handy for turning the fish. (See *Cooking a Whole Fish,* page 185, for more information.)

With trout's prized natural flavor, the only thing needed prior to grilling is a liberal brushing of olive or vegetable oil and a sprinkling of salt and pepper. Some trout aficionados like to place a sprig of rosemary in the cavity of the fish before grilling; others prefer dill, thyme or tarragon. Serve plain with wedges of fresh lemon.

Good side dishes include "baked" basmati rice (page 316), steamed parslied rice (page 337) or boiled new potatoes (page 320).

1) Remove the trout from the refrigerator about 30 minutes before cooking.

2) Ignite as many briquets or as much lump charcoal as it takes to make a bed of coals that's slightly larger than the space the fish will take up on the grill.

3) When the trout go over the coals, the cooking grate should be hot, cleaned and well-oiled. Use a wire brush to clean the grate and a large basting brush to coat it with vegetable oil.

4) Grill the fish directly over a bed of hot coals. On adjustable grills, position the cooking grill 3 to 5 inches above the fire. If you have a covered grill, cook the fish without putting down the cover.

5) Cook the trout for 10 minutes per inch of thickness. For example, a 1-inch thick trout, measured at its thickest point, would take 10 minutes to cook — 5 minutes per side. A small trout, say ¾-inch thick, would take approximately 7½ minutes to cook, a little over 3 minutes per side.

6) Turn the fish only once — halfway through the total cooking time.

7) Serve the trout hot off the grill on a platter that has been heated for 15 minutes in a 250-degree F. oven. Have the rest of your dinner ready to go, or have someone else finish up in the kitchen while you're tending the grill. That's only fair, isn't it?

See Fish, page 133, for more information.

TUNA

The tuna family includes albacore, bluefin, bonito, and yellowfin. With its rich, meaty flavor and firm texture, the various types of tuna are very easy to handle on the grill. Not only that, but of all the methods of preparing tuna, grilling is probably the best. For grilling instructions, see Albacore, page 66.

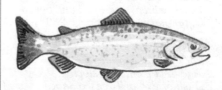

"Rainbow trout are the ones you see in the market, being widely aquacultured; you have to catch the other beauties for yourself."

Grilled Turkey Tonnato

Although this dish is traditionally made with veal, turkey makes an excellent, less expensive substitute, and marinating the turkey makes it far more flavorful. I've also eliminated the customary bed of aspic Vitello Tonnato is served with, replacing it with a bed of lettuce and vegetable garnishes.

As you read through the ingredients needed for the sauce, you may wonder if the word "tuna" is a misprint. It isn't. If you think a sauce made from tuna is odd, just try it — the Italians have been doing it for centuries. This is truly an outstanding dish. Serve at room temperature with grilled French bread (page 95) and nice cold Chardonnay or Sauvignon Blanc. Serves four.

Ingredients needed:
1 turkey breast, skinned and boned
Dijon marinade (see page 289)
1 can tuna, packed in oil
¾ cup mayonnaise
Juice from ½ lemon
¼ to ½ cup chicken stock
Dash or two of Tabasco Sauce
½ to 1 teaspoon oil from a tin of anchovies
½ head lettuce
6 Roma (plum type) tomatoes
2 to 3 tablespoons capers
2 to 3 tablespoons chopped parsley

Optional garnishes:
6 anchovy fillets
4 hard-boiled eggs
½ cucumber, peeled and sliced

…continued on page 237

TURKEY, BREAST, SLICED

Boneless, skinless turkey breast can be thinly sliced (approximately ¼-inch thick) and grilled like scallops of veal. And just like with the veal, turkey scallops require split-second timing to avoid drying out. Slice the breast a little thicker (approximately ⅜- to ½-inch thick), and you have the equivalent of a turkey "steak."

Both ways of slicing produce excellent results on the grill, and both scallops and steaks take well to marinades. A couple of notes on slicing the raw meat: Use a large, *very* sharp butcher knife and, although it isn't necessary, the meat will be much easier to slice if you put it in the freezer for 30 minutes prior to cutting.

Classic marinades for turkey scallops are lemon-white wine marinade (page 292), herb marinade (page 291) or marsala marinade (page 292). Turkey steaks can employ the same marinades or the more robust flavors from Dijon marinade (page 289). If you choose not to marinate the meat, coat the turkey pieces liberally with vegetable oil and a sprinkling of your favorite herb before putting on the grill.

Serve with cold rice and pea salad (page 320), mashed potatoes (page 327) or steamed rice (page 337). If you're interested in trying something a little different for an outdoor summer buffet, try a grilled variation of the classic Italian dish, *Vitello Tonnato* (see recipe on these pages).

Because the cooking time is so brief, both scallops and steaks should be cooked directly over the coals on either a covered or uncovered grill. The cooking grill should be 3 to 5 inches above a bed of hot coals.

Turn either cut only once, using a thin-edged spatula rather than a fork. Total cooking time for the turkey scallops will be approximately 3 to 4 minutes and about 8 minutes for the thicker turkey steaks. Serve hot off the grill.

TURKEY, BREAST, WHOLE

There's not much that can't be done on the grill with a turkey breast. As we have been advised to eat "lighter," this lean, white meat has achieved almost phenomenal popularity over the past few years. The most important caveat with turkey breast is simply to not overcook it, which causes the meat to lose much of its appeal.

Turkey breast can be grilled whole, either with or without the bone and skin; it can be cut into slices (see previous entry) and grilled almost like veal scallops (for which it is frequently mistaken); or it can be cut into chunks and grilled on skewers (see Turkey Brochettes, page 238). Whether whole or cut into pieces, turkey breast takes well to marinades, cooks up relatively quickly and is sure to please both young and old.

For a turkey breast, I strongly recommend leaving the bones and skin intact. This will help ensure a moist, flavorful finished dish. If you're really watching your weight, remove the skin, but leave the bones. Marinate the breast for at least four hours (or overnight); try Dijon marinade (page 289), fresh ginger-garlic marinade (page 290), lemon-white wine marinade (page 292) or herb marinade (page 291). Dry rubs are also effective, especially if you are cooking a skinned breast; try one found on pages 309 to 310.

Because of its irregular shape, the breast will be easiest to marinate in two plastic bags (one placed inside the other) rather than a dish or bowl. Mix up the marinade, put the breast in the double-thick plastic bag, pour the marinade over the breast and tie a knot at the top. Place the bag in a bowl (just in case it leaks) and store in the refrigerator. Turn the bag over a few times during the marinating process. (Or use a special marinating container made by Tupperware; see page 189.)

Serve the turkey breast with risotto (page 333), garlic mashed potatoes (page 324) or "baked" basmati rice (page 316).

You greatly increase your chances of producing moist meat by cooking turkey breast on a covered grill. It can be cooked directly over the coals on an open grill, but you'll have to watch it carefully to avoid overcooking and drying out the meat. The best bet is to use a meat thermometer; remove the breast when the thermometer registers 155 degrees F.

1) Remove from the refrigerator approximately 30 minutes prior to grilling.

...continued from page 236

1) Using a very sharp knife, cut the turkey breast into ⅜-inch slices, cutting against the grain.

2) Mix ingredients for Dijon marinade (page 289). Marinate turkey slices in a shallow dish for 4 to 6 hours.

3) Remove the turkey from the marinade and grill, according to the directions on page 236 (under Turkey, breast, sliced). Place the tomatoes on a couple of skewers and cook, over indirect heat, at the same time as you grill the turkey. The tomatoes will take longer to cook than the turkey — approximately 15 minutes; longer if they are unusually firm.

4) Slice the head lettuce into very thin ribbons (what French cooks refer to as a chiffonnade). Spread evenly on a large platter.

5) When cooked, arrange the turkey slices on top of the bed of lettuce (you want the lettuce to wilt a little). Set aside.

6) Make tonnato sauce by placing the tuna, mayonnaise, lemon juice, anchovy oil and Tabasco Sauce in a blender. Blend until smooth. Use chicken stock to thin the sauce enough that it will easily pour.

7) Pour tonnato sauce over turkey slices. Sprinkle with capers and chopped parsley. Garnish with grilled tomatoes, cut into halves, and cucumber slices, anchovy fillets and hard-boiled egg halves, if desired. A great al fresco lunch or dinner.

2) Ignite 40 to 50 briquets or an equal amount of lump charcoal.

3) When charcoal is covered with gray ash, arrange in an even layer on one side of the fire grate. Put the cooking grill in place (3 to 5 inches away from the coals on adjustable grills).

4) Insert a meat thermometer into the thickest portion of the breast. Position the turkey breast on the cooking grill on the opposite side of the coals, bone side down. Put the lid in place, leaving both the top and bottom vents completely open.

If you're using an uncovered grill, begin by placing the breast skin-side up and turn every 7 to 10 minutes.

5) The breast will take from 45 to 55 minutes to cook to an internal temperature of 155 degrees F. Although it isn't really necessary to turn the breast when using a covered grill, you can brown it a little more completely by turning it once, about 10 minutes before you take it off the grill. At this point, you can position the breast directly over the coals without fear of burning.

6) Remove the breast from the grill. Place it on a cutting board and cover with a loose tent of aluminum foil. Allow to rest for 10 to 15 minutes. If you've left the bones intact, the breast will be easiest to cut if you completely remove the bones before you begin carving.

TURKEY, BROCHETTES

This is one of my favorite ways of serving turkey. When cut into chunks 1 to 1½ inches square, strung onto skewers and quickly grilled, it makes for tender, succulent turkey — better than what's usually served at Thanksgiving! The larger the chunks, the less likely they are to dry out while grilling.

Marinate the chunks of turkey for 4 to 6 hours; try Dijon marinade (page 289), fresh ginger-garlic marinade (page 290), lemon-white wine marinade (page 292) or herb marinade (page 291). Or try wrapping each

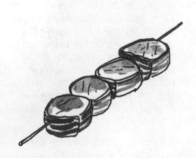

"Try wrapping each chunk of turkey with a small piece of prosciutto before skewering. The prosciutto imparts a pleasant aromatic quality to the turkey and eliminates the need for marinating…"

chunk of turkey with a small piece of prosciutto before skewering. The prosciutto imparts a pleasant aromatic quality to the turkey and eliminates the need for marinating or any other flavoring, save for a little pepper and olive oil (to prevent the brochettes from drying out on the grill). These flavorful morsels are delicious cold, too, should there be any leftovers.

1) Remove the turkey from the refrigerator about 30 minutes before grilling. It should be at room temperature when it goes on the grill.

2) Ignite approximately 40 to 50 briquets or an equal amount of lump charcoal.

3) String chunks of turkey onto skewers, packing them fairly tightly to keep the meat from drying out.

4) On covered grills, wait for the coals to be covered with a light gray ash, then arrange them in a single layer on one side of the fire grate; put the cooking grill in place. Once the cooking grill is hot, brush it with oil and immediately position the skewered turkey on the side away from the coals. Put the lid down, leaving both top and bottom vents completely open.

On open grills, arrange the coals in an even layer and place the cooking grate 3 to 5 inches above the coals. Position the skewers directly over the coals.

5) Total cooking time will be approximately 12 to 15 minutes, a little shorter or longer, depending on the size of the chunks of turkey. Turn two or three times during the grilling process. On covered grills, move the skewers directly over the coals for the last 6 to 8 minutes, turning once in this position.

"A turkey burger on a good, cracked wheat bun, with plenty of mayonnaise and a little cranberry sauce, stands on its own culinary merits."

TURKEY, GROUND

I had my doubts about turkey burgers, so I assembled a panel that included two 11-year-old tasters to help me out. To my surprise, we *all* liked them. A turkey burger on a good, cracked wheat bun, with plenty of mayonnaise and a little cranberry sauce, stands on its own culinary merits.

With the rise in popularity of lean meats, ground turkey is widely available in most supermarket butcher departments. Although it adds fat, incorporating a little heavy cream into the ground turkey makes for a much moister burger and helps hold it together. If there are a bunch of calorie-counters in your household, don't tell them, just do it.

Put the ground turkey meat in a bowl and add approximately 3 or 4 tablespoons of heavy cream per pound of meat. Add salt, ground white pepper and a small amount (about ½ teaspoon) of poultry seasoning. Mix well, using your hands.

Melt a few tablespoons of butter. The ground turkey is quite sticky, so start the patty-making process by rubbing some of the melted butter on your hands; shape the meat in whatever way you want, approximately ½-inch thick. Place on a ceramic plate and brush with the melted butter. Do not place the patties on waxed paper or they will stick — and I do mean stick! Turkey patties are easier to handle on the grill if refrigerated for at least 30 minutes prior to cooking.

Grill directly over moderate to hot coals for approximately 3 or 4 minutes per side. Toast buttered buns on the grill (don't tell the calorie-counters about the butter on the buns, either) while the turkey patties cook. Serve hot. Although it's unlikely that you'll have any leftovers, cold turkey burgers make excellent targets for late-night raids on the refrigerator.

TURKEY, LEGS

One of the best things you can say about turkey legs is that they are economical. Wildly popular at Renaissance Fairs, where people wave them around for theatrical effect, turkey legs are much tamer (and lamer) fare when served at home.

To make up for their rather stringy texture, turkey legs should be well-seasoned with either a dry rub or a marinade. Try any of the dry rubs on pages 309 to 310;

"Wildly popular at Renaissance Fairs, where people wave them around for theatrical effect, turkey legs are much tamer (and lamer) fare when served at home."

or Dijon marinade (page 289). It's difficult for a liquid marinade to successfully penetrate a turkey leg's thick skin, so I recommend using a bulb baster with an injection needle attachment (see *Demon Bulb Baster,* page 207).

Serve the turkey legs with black-eyed peas (page 318), steamed rice (page 337) or coleslaw (page 321).

If you have a covered grill, cook the legs using the indirect method with the lid down and both top and bottom vents completely open. Total cooking time will be approximately 1 hour. Turn every 15 minutes or so, each time moving the turkey legs a little closer over the fire.

On open grills, position the cooking grate approximately 5 inches above the coals and turn the legs more frequently — about every 10 minutes.

Turkey, thighs

Turkey thighs contain succulent dark meat that, compared with turkey legs, is relatively easy for a diner to get at. Just as for turkey legs, thighs can be seasoned with either a dry rub or a marinade. Try any of the dry rubs on pages 309 to 310 or Dijon marinade (page 289).

It's difficult for a marinade to successfully penetrate the thick skin surrounding turkey thighs, no matter how long you let them soak. This is where a bulb baster with an injection needle attachment comes in handy (see *Demon Bulb Baster,* page 207).

If you have a covered grill, cook the thighs using the indirect method (not directly over the coals), with the lid down and both top and bottom vents completely open.

Total cooking time will be approximately 45 to 55 minutes; turn every 15 minutes or so, moving the thighs closer to the direct heat with each turn. On open grills, position the cooking grills approximately 4 inches above the coals and turn the thighs more frequently — about every 10 minutes.

Dealing With Disasters

Unto each griller's career some disasters must fall; I've certainly had my fair share. Once at a multi-generational family gathering, I decided to take a nap after putting two large turkeys on "stereo" Webers. I awoke about an hour later to find the assembled multitude standing around, cocktails in hand, remarking rather acidly that they didn't think the turkeys were cooking at all. Sure enough, both fires had gone out while I was contentedly snoring away.

If this happens to you, there's really nothing to do except order up your own libation, disassemble the grills and remake the fires — in other words, start over. And vow never again to take a nap until you're sure that the fire has really taken off.

If, due to some inexplicable mystery of nature, the fire goes out midway through the cooking process — after an hour or so — you can save time and face by simply putting the partially cooked turkey in the oven at about 325 degrees F. Before sliding the turkey into the oven, stick a meat thermometer in the thickest part of the thigh muscle, without hitting the bone. It will be done when the temperature reaches 175 to 185 degrees F., depending on how well-done you like it. Don't rely on the breast-implanted pop-up thermometer that comes with most turkeys these days; there's something about the high heat of the grill that renders it impotent.

Unconventional Carving

To some degree, all of us seem to labor under certain Norman Rockwellian images of family life. One of the most demanding of these is the head of the household confidently carving a turkey, right there at the table in full view of a dozen pairs of admiring eyes.

In reality, carving is one of those home arts that seems to have been lost over the past generation. The method shown on page 102 is less graceful, and certainly not one you'd want to practice at the table, but it's simple to do and produces attractive slices of light and dark meat for placing on a platter.

If you choose this method, content yourself with parading around with the whole turkey, hot off the grill, in front of your admiring onlookers. Then take the bird in the kitchen, let it rest for 20 minutes or so, dismantle, then serve.

TURKEY, WHOLE ROAST
"Pandora's Turkey"

Of all the procedures and recipes in this book, this is the one I've cooked most often — perhaps a hundred times or more. And it's the only one you'll find in this book that has its own name, "Pandora's Turkey," which refers to the fact that you don't, under any circumstances, take the lid off the grill until the fire goes out. But more on that later.

In our household, grilling is the preferred method for cooking turkey, even for those special, high holiday meals. Pandora's Turkey turns out beautifully brown and crisp on the outside, moist on the inside, and makes the entire neighborhood smell heavenly. The extraordinary part of this procedure is that once I discovered it, I've never had a turkey take more than three hours to cook completely.

At this point a serious warning is called for: Cooking an 18- to 22-pound turkey in three hours or less makes visiting cooks of senior status quake in their aprons. So don't tell Aunt Hattie that the turkey only took three hours to cook until after she's taken her first bite and has pronounced it the moistest, most delicious turkey she ever tasted. Otherwise, she may insist that you put it back in the oven, or wherever you got it from.

If it seems that the procedure given here is overly long, it's only because I've tried to answer all of the questions that have come up over the years. There seems to be something about cooking the main course for a holiday meal that causes a normally confident cook to become cautious. Rest assured, this is the easiest possible way to cook a turkey. The following five steps fully describe the process:

1) Ignite 5 pounds of charcoal briquets in a covered kettle grill (6 pounds if you're stuffing the bird with a bread stuffing).

2) Wash and dry an 18- to 22-pound turkey.

3) Stuff the neck and body cavity with a few handfuls of chopped celery and onions, mixed with a few tablespoons of melted butter and poultry seasoning. Rub the

outside of the bird with vegetable oil or melted butter. Sprinkle with seasoned salt and pepper. Place the turkey in a disposable, aluminum roasting pan. (Disposable, by the way, does not mean that these pans have to be thrown away. If soaked in hot soapy water for a while, they clean up easily.)

4) When the coals are hot, arrange them in even amounts on opposite sides of the fire grate. Put the cooking grill in place, and position turkey (in its pan) directly in the middle. Put the lid on the grill. Leave both top and bottom vents fully open.

5) Do not remove the lid until the fire goes out, approximately 2½ to 3 hours later, at which time your turkey will be perfectly cooked.

That's it! There have been many times that, once the turkey has been put on the grill, I've left the house to do other errands, not giving it another thought until returning home. But like I said, the holidays take their toll on confidence, so here's some additional information.

Look for a bird that is as squat as possible; a high breastbone will prevent the lid of the grill from closing completely. Over the years, I've found that turkeys in the 18- to 22-pound range seem to fit best. If you want a larger bird, it's not a bad idea to do a test before you unwrap the bird. Simply place the turkey on the grill (not lit, of course), and make sure the lid closes.

I roast our turkeys with an aromatic stuffing, one that is *not* meant for eating, as outlined below. If you choose this route and plan on making stock from the turkey carcass afterwards, hang onto the aromatic stuffing; it will improve the taste of the stock.

There will be plenty of juices in the roasting pan. These can be divided up between the gravy pot and for moistening the oven-cooked stuffing. So far there haven't been any complaints in the stuffing department. In fact, no one has ever detected that it wasn't cooked inside the bird.

Last but not least, turkeys cooked in covered kettle grills don't need basting. In fact, if you take the lid off to baste the bird (or even just to peek), you'll blow the whole process. The rapid influx of air causes the coals to

To Truss or Not to Truss?

There's no reason why you should learn how to truss a bird; there are plenty of acceptable alternatives to keep poultry from flopping about while you transport and cook it. But there's something satisfying about being able to expertly truss a bird (even if no one else is watching) that's akin to knowing how to deftly tie a double half-hitch aboard a sailboat or that tie-it-yourself bow tie without thinking twice. Trussing produces a neat, compact bird ready for roasting that somehow looks just right.

If you enjoy mastering this type of esoteric skill, take a look at the illustrations below; there's really not that much to it. This method works for any type of poultry. All you'll need is a butcher's needle and some plain cotton string (nylon or wax-coated string will melt). Butcher's needles are available at cookware specialty shops or restaurant supply houses.

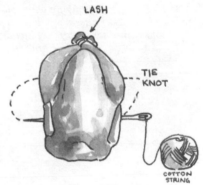

Push a threaded trussing needle through the flesh right next to the "elbow" joint on the wing. Continue pushing until the needle comes out in the same spot on the opposite side of the bird. Next, insert the needle through the thigh and leg joint, at a wide angle so it exits through the fleshy tail. Working your way around the back end, insert the needle through the other leg-thigh joint, this time pushing from an inside angle. In effect, you've circled the bird with string. Close the circle by tying the string in a tight knot. Lash the ends of the two legs together and you're done.

heat up quickly, resulting in an uneven cooking temperature and shortening the life of the coals. At least, that's the only explanation I've ever been able to come up with that makes any sense. At any rate, leave the lid on the grill until the fire goes out. You know what happened to Pandora... .

Ingredients and Equipment Needed

Covered grill

5 pounds charcoal briquets

1 18- to 22-pound turkey (larger, if it will fit on your grill, covered)

2 yellow onions

5 ribs of celery

2 tablespoons poultry seasoning or dried sage

½ cup vegetable oil or melted butter (for rubbing on the outside of the turkey)

Salt, or seasoned salt if you prefer

Pepper

A few metal or bamboo skewers (or needle and cotton thread for trussing)

1) Start with a clean grill, free of old coals. Ignite approximately 5 pounds of briquets. Five pounds may seem like a lot, but this is a special procedure. If you have difficulty determining five pounds, simply buy a 10-pound bag of charcoal and use half.

2) While you're waiting for the coals to catch, prepare the turkey for cooking. Remove the neck and giblets from inside the bird; reserve for making gravy, if desired. Wash the bird thoroughly with cold water. (Don't use soap, like one of my mother's very tidy friends once did!) Pat dry with a towel, absorbing as much moisture, inside and out, as possible. Place the turkey in one of those disposable, heavy-duty aluminum roasting pans, available at supermarkets and variety stores.

3) Coarsely chop the onions and celery. Put in a large bowl and mix with ½ cup melted butter and 1 to 2 tablespoons of poultry seasoning or sage. Place a handful of this aromatic mixture inside the neck cavity. Pull the skin over the cavity and thread it closed, using a small metal or bamboo skewer. Put the rest of the mixture in

Wash the bird thoroughly with cold water, but don't use soap, like one of my mother's very tidy friends once did!

the body cavity and fasten closed with another skewer. Secure the legs to the tail using the metal fastener found on most turkeys, or abandon the skewers and the metal fasteners altogether in favor of trussing the bird using the method shown on page 243.

4) Rub the entire surface of the turkey with about ½ cup of melted butter or vegetable oil. Place the turkey breast side up in the roasting pan and sprinkle liberally with salt and pepper. I prefer finely ground white pepper because it adheres to the surface better than the coarser black pepper. Feel free to used seasoned salt, if desired.

5) Check the fire. The coals are just right when they are completely covered with fine gray ash. Once at that stage, push them to either side of the fire grate in equal quantities, leaving the center free of briquets. Put the cooking grill in place. Position the roasting pan and turkey in the middle of the grill and put the lid on. Leave both the top and bottom vents completely open.

6) Within minutes you will start to hear some action in the roasting pan and smell that delightful aroma. The turkey will be done when the coals have burned out, usually around 2½ hours. You can tell the coals have burned out when the turkey no longer makes any cooking noises inside the grill and smoke has stopped coming out of the vents.

7) Remove the lid — finally — and voilà! A beautifully roasted, mahogany-brown, crisp-on-the-outside, moist-on-the-inside turkey. Carefully move the bird from the roasting pan to the carving board, and let it rest for 15 to 20 minutes before carving (see *Poultry Dismantling,* on page 102). This allows the juices to return to the interior of the meat and makes the turkey much easier to carve. Add any juices that accumulate on the carving board to your gravy, or use for moistening the stuffing.

The Days of Wine and Walnuts

"The turkey should be copped up some time before Christmas. Three days before it is slaughtered, it should have an English walnut forced down its throat three times a day, and a glass of sherry once a day. The meat will be deliciously tender, and have a fine nutty flavor."

From Statesmen's Dishes and How to Cook Them, by Mrs. Stephen J. Field, published in 1890.

(I hope the sherry helps those walnuts go down!)

V

As elegant as they're perceived to be, veal chops are essentially simple bistro food, meant to be enjoyed with gusto. Leave the bone in place, as it adds succulence and allows diners to abandon propriety at the end of the meal, as they pick up the bones and relish those last savory bits.

VEAL, CHOPS

Veal chops are one of the best things you can pull off the grill, as long as you don't overcook them. One hedge against overcooking is to buy thick chops — not less than one inch and not more than two inches thick. Leave the bone in place, as it adds succulence and allows diners to abandon propriety at the end of the meal, as they pick up the bones and relish those last savory bits. That's the way it is with veal chops. As elegant as this meat is perceived to be, the chops are essentially simple bistro food, meant to be enjoyed with gusto.

Veal chops are perfectly delicious cooked plain, with only a liberal coating of olive oil or melted butter, salted and peppered after they come off the grill. They also accept the flavors of any number of marinades: Try Dijon marinade (page 289), herb marinade (page 291), or garlic, rosemary and rosé marinade (page 290).

Side dishes should be kept in the same bistro mode, simple and satisfying. A big basket of hot pommes frites (page 331) or galette of potatoes (page 323) would be just right. Whole grilled tomatoes (page 232), grilled endive (page 130) or a batch of steamed fresh asparagus would round things out nicely, as would a big Chardonnay or a light red Beaujolais or Rhone. This is good eating!

1) Remove chops from the refrigerator about 30 minutes prior to grilling. Make sure they are well-coated with olive or vegetable oil before putting on the grill.

2) Ignite 55 to 65 briquets, or an equal amount of lump charcoal.

3) On both covered and uncovered grills, arrange the coals, once they are covered with a light gray ash, in a single layer, leaving a little space between them. Allow to

burn down for 10 minutes or so. As with any very lean cut of meat, wait until the fire has gone beyond hot to moderate before putting the chops on the grill. A moderate to hot fire will give you a little more latitude in cooking time, and helps avoid the dreaded dry chop syndrome. On adjustable grills, position the cooking grill 2 to 3 inches from the coals.

4) Grill, directly over the fire, for 5 to 7 minutes per side, depending on how thick the chops are and the degree of doneness desired.

5) This is one entrée best served hot off the grill, so make sure everyone is seated and the side dishes are ready to go before you take the chops off the fire. There probably won't be much conversation for the first ten minutes or so after serving — just a lot of smacking and ummming and ahhhing.

VEAL, CROWN ROAST

A crown roast of veal is a rack of rib chops that has been manipulated into an inside-out circle. The characteristic crown shape of this roast is achieved either by tying it with string or actually suturing the ends together. The ends of the rib bones are "Frenched" — that is, they are exposed and given little, white paper frills.

Long considered the *ne plus ultra* of roasts, the center of which is usually filled with a stuffing (with varying degrees of success), crown roasts are most often seen aboard luxury liners and, presumably, at very fancy dinner parties.

As good as the meat may be, the forum this roast takes strikes me as being a bit pretentious — the exact opposite of what grilling is all about. That said, I should hasten to add that if you're compelled to cook one, doing so in a covered kettle grill is probably the best method possible. The type of heat produced by the charcoal will go a long way in ensuring moist, succulent meat — something not always possible in the dry heat of a typical home oven. And another thing, just because the shape of this roast provides an opening doesn't mean you have to

Lapses in attention are probably responsible for the majority of all grilling debacles. With the exception of big roasts, which take a considerable time to cook, the grill chef simply must stand by the grill and watch the food carefully. Running inside for a quick peek at the television is not permitted!

One of the main reasons I think it's important to place the grill in an attractive location and to keep a stool handy (see The Importance of Place, page 21) is simply to keep the chef out there watching the meal, with some degree of comfort and pleasure.

If you are preparing other parts of the meal indoors, try to find someone else to be in charge of that department. It's very easy to become distracted in the kitchen, only to return to the grill to find the main course cooked to a char. The simple fact is that most foods cook up fairly quickly on the grill and they need your complete attention during this period. Once the food is off the grill, you're free to roam wherever you like.

"The characteristic crown shape of this roast is achieved either by tying it with string or actually suturing the ends together. The ends of the rib bones are "Frenched" — that is, they are exposed and given little, white paper frills."

stuff it with something. In other words, forget the stuffing; it always seems to come off as an afterthought, anyway.

The following procedure requires a covered grill:

1) Remove the roast from the refrigerator approximately 30 minutes before grilling. Insert a meat thermometer into the center of the roast without touching any bones.

2) Ignite 55 to 65 briquets or an equal amount of lump charcoal.

3) Once the coals are covered with a fine gray ash, divide equally and push to opposite sides of the fire grate, leaving the center open. Place a disposable aluminum drip pan in the middle of the fire grate.

4) Position the roast directly over the drip pan. Put the lid in place, leaving both top and bottom vents completely open.

5) The roast will not need to be turned. After the first 60 minutes or so, start checking the thermometer. The roast will be done (but not overdone) when the temperature reaches 150 to 155 degrees F. Remember that the temperature rises much faster towards the end of the cooking process than at the beginning, so watch carefully. Remove the roast from the grill when the temperature is 5 degrees shy of the desired doneness; it will continue to cook while it rests on the cutting board. An internal temperature of 165 degrees F. is considered medium-well.

6) Tent the roast loosely in aluminum foil while it rests for 10 minutes or so. Serve with any juices that accumulate on the board.

VEAL, GROUND

As delicate as veal is, it could be argued that ground veal is better suited to stove-top sautéing than to grilling — a decision I'll leave up to individual cooks. Ground veal is very lean; adding a little heavy cream makes for a much moister patty.

Put the ground veal in a bowl and add approximately 3 or 4 tablespoons of heavy cream per pound of meat. Add salt and ground white pepper to taste, and a small amount (about ½ teaspoon) of paprika or herbs (oregano, parsley or rosemary are good).

Melt a few tablespoons of butter. Start the patty-making process by rubbing some of the melted butter on your hands; shape the meat whatever way you want, approximately ½-inch thick.

Place patties on a ceramic plate and brush with the melted butter. They will be easier to handle on the grill if you refrigerate them for at least 30 minutes prior to cooking.

Grill directly over the medium to hot coals for approximately 3 or 4 minutes per side. Serve hot, perhaps with a simple sauce of sour cream thinned with a little chicken stock, flavored with paprika and chopped capers, cooked on top of a stove. Very good with boiled noodles topped with a little butter and parsley.

VEAL, LEG

Perhaps the best way to serve a leg of veal is as a rolled roast. The leg is boned and then tied in a more-or-less uniform shape, perfect for grilling. For additional information, see Veal, rolled roast, on page 250.

"Thick liver steaks are delightful when grilled, served with a heap of sautéed onions and pancetta bacon."

VEAL, LIVER

Veal or calf's liver is considered very fine fare by those who like liver, and is generally preferred to beef liver. Thick liver steaks are delightful when grilled, served with a heap of sautéed onions and pancetta bacon. For more information, see Liver, page 164.

VEAL, ROLLED ROAST

A veal roast almost always is considered "company" food, reserved for special occasions and special guests. I don't think there's any better company, nor more special guests, than one's own family. In the commotion caused by company dinners, the delectability of the food is often compromised; however, on a weeknight, with just you and yours around the table, all are free to enjoy the meal to their hearts' content. Be prepared, however, for some puzzled looks from those same family members as you bring in this beautiful roast. When they ask what the occasion is, just tell them they are.

Although various cuts can be used for a rolled roast, the leg makes one of the tastiest. My favorite method of preparing a rolled veal roast involves untying it once you get home from the butcher, so before you start, make sure you have some cotton string on hand to tie it back up again.

Bring a cube of butter to room temperature and put it in a bowl. Add whatever flavorings you desire. Personal favorites include a combination of three or four pressed cloves of garlic, a healthy dose of freshly cracked pepper, a little rosemary and thyme. (How could you go wrong with that?) Mash the ingredients with a fork and spread the mixture, thickly, on the inside of the rolled-out roast. Re-roll it, tie, and it's ready for the grill.

A rolled roast of veal is best cooked in a covered grill, with the lid in place throughout the cooking process. Any large roast is somewhat difficult to cook over an open grill, but can be managed if you keep all the coals to the back of the fire grate and place a disposable aluminum drip pan directly under the roast. If the only grill you own is an open one, position the roast so it's as close to the fire as it can get without being directly over it, and turn every 10 minutes or so. If the open grill has a rotisserie attachment, by all means use it (see *Spit Cooking*, page 46).

As with any roast, use a meat thermometer to ensure that you cook it to the exact degree you desire. Stick the thermometer into the middle of the roast before you put it on the grill; remove the roast when it is approximately 10 degrees shy of the desired temperature, which for me is "medium," or about 150 degrees F. Set the roast

Be prepared for some puzzled looks from other members of your family when you bring in this beautiful roast. And when they ask what the special occasion is, just tell them they are.

on a platter; it will continue to cook after you take it off the grill.

The best side dish I know of for veal roast is risotto (page 333), but garlic mashed potatoes (page 324) or galette of potatoes (page 323) would also be fine. Add a few grilled whole tomatoes (page 232) to the grill while you're cooking the roast, and you're working on a memorable feast.

The following procedure is for a covered grill:

1) Remove the roast from the refrigerator about 30 minutes before cooking. This will allow it to come to room temperature before it goes on the grill.

2) Ignite approximately 55 to 65 briquets or an equal amount of lump charcoal.

3) Once the coals are covered with a fine gray ash, put the cooking grill in place. While the coals are still very hot, put the roast directly over the fire and quickly sear the entire outside. This won't take long and demands strict attention. By all means, don't leave the roast unattended while it is directly over the coals. Remember, the point here is to brown the outside of the meat, not to char it.

4) Remove the roast from the fire as soon as it has been seared on all sides; place in a roasting pan, preferably one not much larger than the roast itself. Pour about 1 cup of chicken stock, or dry white wine or dry vermouth (or a combination of the two) over the roast. Place the pan and roast aside for a moment.

5) *Back to the grill:* Remove the cooking grate and divide the charcoal into two equal amounts. Push the coals to either side of the fire grate, leaving the center free of fire. Put the cooking grill in place and set the roast (in its pan) smack dab in the middle. Put the lid on the grill, leaving both the top and bottom vents completely open.

6) A 3-pound roast will probably take approximately 1½ hours to reach the "medium" stage — still juicy, but no longer pink. Start checking the thermometer after about 1 hour or so, remembering that the internal temperature

Grilling Garb

Over the years there have been some pretty peculiar outdoor cooking fashion trends. No sociologist I know of has ever done a study on what it all means, and if it does have some significance, I'm not really sure I want to know.

I have several outdoor cookbooks from the 1940s and early '50s, lavishly illustrated with color photographs, which seem to indicate that, while it was acceptable to take off your sportcoat while grilling, taking off your tie or wearing an apron were not. Even more interesting, from a sociologist's point of view, is that women are never pictured grilling. That was quite an era.

About the time Detroit was turning out ever-larger automobiles with ever-larger fins, grilling fashion hit its nadir, with apron ensembles that included matching chef's hats and mits that could be attached to the apron. To make matters much worse, many were adorned with pictures of steers, branding iron logos, or contained succinct messages such as, "Come and git it!" emblazoned across the chest of the apron.

During the late '60s and early '70s, I believe (the memory is a little hazy), it was acceptable to grill without any clothes on at all. The decade of the '80s brought with it a heightened respect for all things professional, including professional grilling garb. From a fashion point of view, I don't think this trend has been all bad. At least it's resulted in the return of the plain white apron and an environment that allows anyone who wants to wear an apron to wear it in the open, and for anyone who wants to grill, to do so with confidence. Sounds like progress to me.

rises much more quickly towards the end of the cooking time than at the beginning. If you want your veal cooked "medium," take it off when the thermometer reaches 155 degrees F., and allow it to rest indoors on a platter, loosely covered with foil, until the thermometer reaches 165 degrees F. Slice and serve with the juices that will have accumulated on the platter.

VENISON

In the last generation or so, the term "venison" seems to have become associated almost exclusively with deer, although it correctly applies to the meat of antelope, caribou and elk, as well. All venison is very lean, with only one-tenth the amount of fat found in beef.

If there are no hunters in your family, you're not entirely out of luck. Deer is becoming readily available in specialty butcher shops. Commercially available venison is raised on preserves, in habitats that very closely approximate the deer's natural domain. Because of this, the deer you buy from the butcher will be almost indistinguishable from what the hunter brings home.

Larger cuts of venison, such as loins, saddles and legs, can be successfully cooked over the coals using a rotisserie (see *Spit Cooking,* page 46). Because of the longer cooking time, it is generally best to marinate the pieces of meat before cooking; this will prevent them from becoming dry.

Because it is so lean, venison requires careful attention on the grill. Steaks and chops can be cooked as you would beef, but over a moderate (rather than hot) bed of coals, and never cooked beyond the medium-rare stage, unless you like tough, dry venison. Be sure to use a meat thermometer. Medium-rare is indicated by a temperature of between 130 to 140 degrees F.

Serve all cuts of venison hot off the grill; they don't take well to standing around. Good accompaniments include grilled new potatoes (page 196) flavored with a simple mix of olive oil, salt, pepper and rosemary; grilled carrots (page 99) and a big red, such as Pinot Noir or a good vintage Cabernet Sauvignon.

"Commercially available venison is raised on preserves, in habitats that very closely approximate the deer's natural domain. Because of this, the deer you buy from the butcher will be almost indistinguishable from what the hunter brings home."

W

WAHOO

If you like swordfish and tuna, you'll like wahoo. It's another of the wonderful fish found around the islands, just now starting to show up in markets outside of Hawaii. With it's dense, moderately fatty flesh, wahoo is tops for the grill. It's great cooked plain, with just a liberal brushing of vegetable oil and a sprinkling of paprika on both sides, served with fresh lemon. But because of its distinctive flavor, wahoo also takes well to marinades and sauces.

If you marinate the fish, 30 minutes to an hour will be enough to flavor it without overwhelming its natural taste. Try fresh ginger-garlic marinade (page 290), herb marinade (page 291), or lemon-white wine marinade (page 292).

Good side dishes include boiled new potatoes (page 320), "baked" basmati rice (page 316) or grilled potato wedges (page 196). Tasty vegetables include grilled whole tomatoes (page 232) and one of the summer squashes (page 223) or, if it's in season, steamed asparagus. A big Chardonnay will accompany this fish nicely; if you've marinated it in something spicy, opt for a couple bottles of cold beer.

1) Keep the fish refrigerated until about 30 minutes before grilling. It should be just at room temperature when it goes on the grill.

2) Determine how much space the fish will take up on the grill, and ignite as many briquets or as much lump charcoal as it takes to make a bed of coals that's slightly larger on all sides.

3) Put the cooking grill over the coals and allow it to become good and hot before putting on the fish, which

Waterfront Grilling

Throughout much of the world, wherever there is water, fishing boats and a dock, there are also grills. If you're interested in everyday sights, it can be great fun to walk along the docks in some foreign port. Aside from seeing almost every type of fish, I've also seen every manner of grill perched on decks — not to mention every manner of cook. One common denominator, however, seems to be the casualness with which these seafaring cooks grill. Granted, most have been grilling fish for a long time, but there's a lesson to be learned from their casual demeanor.

American home cooks have been practically terrorized into thinking that grilling fish should be left to professional chefs. Nonsense! Keep your grill clean, oil both the grill and the fish just before cooking, and cook for 10 minutes per inch of thickness, turning the fish only once. It's as simple as that.

If you're a novice, start with a firm-textured fish, such as swordfish, tuna, halibut or even salmon. As you gain confidence, expand into some of the more delicate varieties.

And if you start to get nervous, just conjure up a wharfside image in Portugal or Greece or wherever, where cooks grill fish at the same time as they're laughing, scratching, usually smoking, kibitzing, conducting business and handling the chores of the boat. Don't take it so seriously. Enjoy yourself!

will stick to a cold grill. After it's hot, use your wire brush to clean the grill. Oil the grill just before you're ready to cook the fish, using a large basting brush and vegetable oil.

4) If you're cooking the wahoo plain, brush both sides liberally with a mild vegetable oil and dust with paprika. If you've marinated the fish, no extra pregrilling preparation will be necessary. Grill the fish directly over a bed of hot coals. If you have a covered grill, cook the fish without putting down the cover.

5) Cook the wahoo 10 minutes per inch of thickness, measured at the thickest part. For example, a 1-inch thick steak or fillet would take 10 minutes to cook — 5 minutes per side. Plan on turning the fish only once.

6) Fish should be served hot off the grill — within seconds, if possible. Heated plates help keep the fish piping hot, so slip the plates into a 250 degree F. oven about 15 minutes before eating time.

See Fish, page 133, for more information.

WEAKFISH

Because of its tender flesh, the sea trout (both spotted sea trout and gray sea trout) are known as weakfish in some markets. For more information, see Trout, freshwater and sea, on page 234).

WHITE SEA BASS

The white sea bass, and its close cousins, the black, giant and striped sea bass, are lean fish with relatively sweet flesh. The best ones for grilling are those under 3 pounds, pan-dressed (entrails removed, but with head and tail intact), and cooked whole. Having the bones and skin intact helps to keep this lean fish from drying out — the one thing you don't want to happen.

Another proven method for keeping lean fish moist is to wrap it in grape leaves. This works well for small (4 ounces and under) pieces of fillets. Although it is a somewhat time-consuming project, the results are definitely worth the effort. See *Leaf-wrapped Packets,* page 117.

With an excellent texture and mild flavor, there's no need for marinating white sea bass. Brush liberally with vegetable oil, dust with paprika, and grill directly over the coals.

Good side dishes include boiled new potatoes (page 320), "baked" basmati rice (page 316), or grilled potato wedges (page 196). Tasty vegetables include grilled whole tomatoes (page 232), grilled corn on the cob (page 118), or any steamed or sautéed vegetable.

1) About 30 minutes before cooking time, remove the fish from the refrigerator.

2) You'll want to cook the fish directly over the fire, so make a bed of coals that's a little larger in size than what the fish will take up on the grill. Ignite the charcoal.

3) Before you put the fish over the coals, the cooking grill should be put in position (3 to 5 inches from the coals on adjustable models), hot, cleaned and well-oiled. Use a wire brush to clean the grate and a large basting brush to coat it with vegetable oil.

4) Cook the fish directly over the fire. Don't use the cover on covered grills.

5) Grill the white sea bass for 10 minutes per inch of thickness. Turn just once, halfway through the cooking process.

6) Serve the fish hot off the grill, on a platter that you've heated in a 250-degree F. oven for 15 minutes.

See Fish, page 133, for more information.

…continued from page 254

6. Borneo, 1896-97. One year in the jungle.

7. Chamorro or Guam Cookery. (Islas Marianas) 1898, six months. "Marooned."

8. French, 1899, 1906.

9. Capri or Near Neapolitan, 1903, six months.

10. Hudson Bay, Upper Ontario, two months, 1915.

11. Seascout Boat Cookery and Boy Scout Camps as Chief Seascout, seventeen years, and still at it. 1911 to 1928.

12. Sahara Desert, six months. Nefta! Hammamet! 1927.

13. In a cocoanut grove on the beach at Waikiki…to try all these stunts to the scorn of the passersby, who thought I was crazy, 1928.

Do these dates overlap? Well, they did. But they represent my DIPLOMA. Now let us start cooking."

You can bet he had a few stories to tell.

"Serve with an outstanding Italian Chianti (you'll have to hunt for it in much the same way as the pheasant — with patience)…"

WILD GOOSE

When it comes to wild goose, it's a young one you want; older wild geese are tougher, and need slower, moister cooking, like stove-top braising, to make them tender. The best indicator of age on a wild goose is the flexibility of its breastbone — the more flexible it is, the younger the bird. Although less fatty than domestic geese, wild geese still have plenty of fat, especially by wild game standards. Follow the directions for grilling domestic geese, on page 140, pricking the skin in all the right places to allow the fat to render easily. As with domestic geese, a wild goose can either be roasted in a covered kettle grill or spitted and cooked on a rotisserie (see *Spit Cooking,* page 46).

WILD PHEASANT

There's something right about grilling a wild pheasant over an open fire. Long an epicurean treat, pheasant often suffers from overcooking, a situation the griller is in the perfect position to avoid.

As with wild goose, the only suitable wild pheasant for grilling are young birds. A good indicator of youth is a pliable breastbone and the very distinctive first wing-tip feather: In a young pheasant it is pointed; in an older bird it is rounded. Save older, tougher pheasant for moist-heat, stove-top cooking.

Best methods of grilling are to flatten pheasant (see *Flattening Poultry,* page 111) or to cook them on a rotisserie (see *Spit Cooking,* page 46).

With any upland game bird, I prefer strong-flavored vegetables such as parsnips, turnips, carrots or Brussels sprouts. Turnips are excellent pureed; carrots and parsnips are delicious cooked right on the grill (see page 99 and 177). Steam Brussels sprouts until just barely tender, and then drizzle with butter, perhaps with a little diced red pepper mixed in. Grilled new potatoes (page 196) or wild rice casserole (page 338) are good side dishes.

Serve with an outstanding Italian Chianti (you'll have to hunt for it in much the same way as the pheasant — with patience) or a good and complex California

Zinfandel (especially those that say they have "wild blackberry and eucalyptus over- or undertones"; whether they do or not, it's a wonderful thought). Savor!

WILD RABBIT

There's not a great deal of difference between a wild rabbit and a domestic one, save for the wild rabbit's slightly stronger flavor and firmer flesh. Unless, of course, the wild rabbit is very old — at which point you're far better off stewing it. With a flavor and texture somewhere between veal and chicken, wild rabbit takes well to marinades. Good choices include fresh ginger-garlic marinade (page 290), marsala marinade (page 292) and red wine marinade (page 294). Although it's totally subjective, I like the way the Italians treat wild rabbits, with grilled polenta (page 183) and some slightly bitter green, like mustard, endive or even spinach, steamed or sautéed. A medium-bodied California Merlot, Zinfandel; or even a fresh Beaujolais will do quite nicely.

WILD TURKEY I

If it hasn't already been broken, crack the government seal and lay the bottle over a moderate fire. When just warm, sit on the back porch and serve with cool branch water, sardines and saltine crackers. Leave some in the bottom of the bottle for tomorrow and stay off the telephone.

WILD TURKEY II

What with the American fascination with white breast meat, it's no surprise that there's quite a difference between a domestic turkey and its wild cousin. Wild turkeys, believe it or not, have more leg meat than breast meat (must be all that running away from the hunters

"Leave some in the bottom of the bottle for tomorrow and stay off the telephone."

that does it), and as much meat on the back as the breast.

Because of turkey's one-time prevalence, Benjamin Franklin wished to see the bird as our national bird instead of the eagle. It's good to note that, due to some very vigilant efforts, the population of wild turkeys is on the increase across America.

Perhaps the best way to grill a wild turkey is to spit-roast it on the rotisserie (see *Spit Cooking*, page 46). But here again, as with almost all wild fowl, don't bother with older birds on the grill. Ideally, you're looking for something in the 6- to 8-pound category. Next best is a bird that's under 10 pounds.

To make up for their lack of fat, wild turkeys should be barded — covered in a thin layer of fat. The most common way of doing this is to blanch bacon or salt pork (by boiling it in water for a couple of minutes), then secure it to the meaty portions of the bird by means of string or skewers. If this seems like too much to do, ask your friendly neighborhood butcher to bard it for you.

Serve with puree of turnips and potatoes, galette of potatoes (page 323), sautéed peas with lettuce (page 336) or grilled whole carrots (page 99). With the meal, drink one of those sandalwood-scented Rhones or, if you bagged the turkey yourself, a Cote Rotie.

WINTER SQUASH

This large and very diverse family of squash are discussed under the heading of Squash, winter, found on page 224.

WOODCOCK

This prized waterfowl, increasingly rare as our marshlands disappear, makes for fine eating. The best way to prepare woodcock is to flatten them (see *Flattening Poultry*, page 111) and grill them directly over a hot fire.

Keep the grill about 3 to 5 inches above the coals and cook for approximately 4 minutes per side. Brush the birds liberally with melted butter during the grilling process; season with salt and pepper after they come off

"Because of turkey's one-time prevalence, Benjamin Franklin wished to see the bird as our national bird instead of the eagle."

the grill. Count on two to three birds per person.

Serve with galette of potatoes (page 323), wild rice casserole (page 338), grilled scallions (page 214) or grilled onions (page 174), or some slightly bitter green (mustard, turnip or beet) sautéed in a little bacon grease, accompanied by a few bottles of not-too-cold ale.

The prized woodcock is becoming increasingly rare as our marshlands disappear.

Y

YAMS

When I was growing up, "Y" stood for yams and yuck, associated with holiday meals eaten too early in the day. The unfathomable addition of raisins, walnuts and miniature marshmallows only made matters worse. Suffice it to say, I had a problem when it came to trying yams on the grill.

I relate this background here, under "yams," because that's what I thought they were — then. I know now that the vast majority of what are sold as yams in this country are actually sweet potatoes. If you want to know how this story ends, see Sweet Potatoes, page 226. I guarantee it has nothing to do with marshmallows.

"Will the real yam please stand up?"

YELLOWEYE

Yelloweye is one of the many common names for the very large family of fish known as rockfish. For more information, see Rockfish, page 207.

YELLOWFIN TUNA

Yellowfin is just one member of the tuna family, which also includes albacore, bonito and bluefin. All types of tuna are ideal for cooking over the coals, either as steaks or cut up into 1-inch cubes and strung on skewers. When grilled, the tuna's dark flesh is transformed to a light, firm texture. For cooking instructions, see Albacore, page 66.

YELLOWTAIL

An ocean fish that prefers the relatively warm waters of the Caribbean, yellowtail is similar to both tuna and wahoo, but is less fatty and somewhat milder in flavor. Yellowtail is excellent cooked over the coals. It's great grilled plain, with just a liberal brushing of vegetable oil and a sprinkling of paprika on both sides, served with fresh lemon.

The yellowtail's mild flavor also holds up well to a variety of marinades. Particularly delicious are herb marinade (page 291) or lemon-white wine marinade (page 292).

Good side dishes include "baked" basmati rice (page 316), or grilled potato wedges (page 196). Tasty vegetables include grilled whole tomatoes (page 232), grilled ratatouille (page 332) or black-eyed peas (page 318). If grilled *au natural*, a big Chardonnay will accompany this fish nicely; if you've marinated it in one of the spicier marinades, opt for a couple bottles of cold beer.

1) Keep the fish refrigerated until about 30 minutes before grilling.

2) Make a bed of coals that's a little larger than the area the fish will take up on the grill, and ignite the charcoal.

3) The cooking grill must be hot, clean and well-oiled when the fish goes on the grill, or the fish will stick (a situation to be avoided at all costs). Put the grill over the coals and let it heat up. Clean it with a wire brush and coat it with vegetable oil. (Use a large basting brush.)

4) If you're cooking the yellowtail plain, brush both sides liberally with a mild vegetable oil and dust with paprika. If you've marinated the fish, no extra preparation will be necessary.

5) Grill the fish directly over a bed of hot coals. If you have a covered grill, cook the fish without putting down the cover. If you have an open grill, position the cooking grill 3 to 5 inches from the coals.

6) Cook the yellowtail 10 minutes per inch of thickness,

A Bay by Any Other Name

If you've never tried combining the flavors of fish and bay leaves, give it a try. There's something very special about the combination, especially when the fish is grilled. The easiest method is to alternate pieces of fish with bay leaves (cut in half, if they are big) on skewers.

If you're lucky enough to have a bay tree in your herb garden, use fresh leaves. If you're not cooking with skewers, you can achieve some of the aromatic quality of bay by throwing a handful of the leaves on the coals as the fish grills. Soak the leaves in water for 30 minutes prior to using this way.

I have been surprised recently to see the leaves of the California bay tree being sold as "bay" leaves for cooking. Don't be deceived. The culinary bay leaf is from the Grecian bay (Laurus nobilis). The California bay (also called California laurel, Oregon myrtle and pepperwood) is Umbellularia californica. While it can be substituted for the Grecian bay, it has a different character and is far more pungent. Stick with the Grecian bay and you'll be much happier with the results.

measured at the thickest part. Plan on turning the fish only once, halfway through the total cooking time.

7) Fish should be served hot off the grill. If you don't have a helpmate in the kitchen, make sure your side dishes are ready to go before putting the fish on the grill. Land the yellowtail on a platter that you've heated for 15 minutes in a 250-degree F. oven.

See Fish, page 133, for more information.

YELLOWTAIL ROCKFISH

You'll find grilling instructions for this member of the plentiful rockfish family on page 207, under Rockfish.

"Whole fish are fairly easy to handle on the grill. Just make sure to oil both the fish and the grill before cooking and have a large spatula (or two) handy for turning the fish."

Z

ZUCCHINI

Once plant breeders finally got the zucchini vine down to size with the very innocent looking "bush-type" plants, home gardeners assumed that the zucchini had been tamed. Not so. While your back is turned, a zucchini will grow as large as your leg. This is decidedly not the size for grilling, nor for much of anything else, unless you live in England, where with such a behemoth, you might be able to win one of their ubiquitous vegetable contests.

No, zucchini is far more tender and tasty when picked at about 4 or 5 inches long. At this size, they can be grilled whole, or cut up and strung on skewers. Zucchini is an essential ingredient in grilled ratatouille (page 332). For more information about grilling zucchini and other summer squash, see Squash, summer, page 223.

"While your back is turned, a zucchini will grow as large as your leg. Or larger."

FLAVORING THE FOOD

FLAVORING THE FOOD

There are a number of ways to flavor grilled food. The time-honored methods covered in this chapter are marinades, sauces, compound butters (and their close cousins, butter sauces) and dry rubs. All will get the job done, and all are open to literally thousands of variations. The one caveat to observe is to keep it simple. Remember, it's the flavor of the *food* that you want to highlight, not the marinade, sauce or what have you.

Marinades are usually broken down into three components: an acid, such as a lemon juice, wine, or vinegar; an oil, such as olive oil or butter; and herbs and spices. The acid portion acts as a tenderizer, although its role as such is often overstated. Acids will tenderize meat to a certain degree, but tough connective tissues, called collagens, are really only broken down by slow cooking or pounding.

Marinades do not have to include all three traditional components to be effective. Some of the simplest marinades can produce delicious results. Soaking a steak in red wine for 15 to 30 minutes before grilling delicately enhances the flavor of the meat. Soaking hamburgers in soy sauce adds distinction to the most inexpensive meat. Lemon butter, Worcestershire sauce and fruit juices are other simple but effective marinades.

The range of flavors that can be created with marinades is limitless. Marinades can be strong, featuring just one herb or spice, such as garlic or rosemary. Or, they can take advantage of traditional herb blends, such as bouquet garni or fine herbs. Marinades can also be mild, just

Compound butters are among the simplest and best ways to add flavor to grilled food.

enough flavor to excite the nose as the fork passes by.

While marinades and sauces are a traditional part of outdoor cooking, they are also at the heart of its creativity. With a simple understanding of herbs and spices and an inventive spirit, you can create delicious new flavor experiences on the backyard grill.

Sauces can be as simple or complex as you care to make them. The number of recipes offered for sauces has been deliberately kept short, but each is open to countless variations, depending on what flavoring ingredients are on hand and, perhaps more importantly, the whim of the cook.

Compound butters are among the simplest and best ways to add flavor to grilled food. As a group, they represent a kind of solidified sauce, meant to be added on top of food hot from the grill. As they melt, their flavors enhance the food rather than overwhelm it. Compound butters are a perfect example of how the more sophisticated good cooking becomes, the more simple it is, as well. Butter sauces, at least as defined on these pages, are just melted compound butters, meant to be poured rather than placed on top of the food.

Dry rubs, are unique to the other means of flavoring grilled food. These mixtures of herbs, spices and other ingredients are the domain of the true, slow-cooking, "Smoky Joe" barbecue chef. To answer the questions of how, when, where, and why with regard to dry rubs is to lay ones self open to scorn and ridicule. Most dry rub recipes are jealously guarded secrets, known only to the chef. Perhaps that's the way they should remain — secret — but the information found on pages 309 to 310 will at least get you started on your way to the barbecue hall of fame.

INGREDIENTS

The following A-to-Z list contains descriptions of the most commonly used marinade, sauce and dry rub ingredients. If you're really ambitious, use it as a shopping list for stocking your pantry.

ANGELICA

Angelica is a licorice-flavored herb, rich in herbal lore and frequently used in confections. The fresh leaves of angelica add a distinctive flavor to any marinade for fish. The simplest way to use angelica is to simply sprinkle chopped fresh leaves directly on the fish as it grills. Finding fresh angelica in any market may be next to impossible, but it is a very easy plant to grow from seed. It produces a large-leafed plant, ornamental enough to grow in the flower border.

ANISE

Anise seeds, licorice-flavored and slightly sweet, are used to flavor a variety of baked goods and the liqueur, anisette. Anise adds a distinctive flavor to any marinade that contains soy sauce. If a licorice flavor appeals to you, add it to Oriental marinades and sauces, along with those other traditional ingredients: ginger, lemon, and hot peppers. To release a maximum flavor of anise seeds, crush or sauté them in oil or butter before using.

BASIL

For many, basil is *the* taste of summer. This pungent, leafy herb has long been treasured in Italian cooking and is, of course, the main ingredient in pesto (see pesto marinade, page 293). Basil's best companions are garlic and tomatoes — a combination of flavors that can't be beat. Also excellent when combined with butter and garlic for use on fish, chicken breasts, or vegetables. Best

"For many, basil is the taste of summer."

fresh, but dried or frozen basil can be substituted in any recipe. Very easy to grow in the garden or in containers.

BAY

Bay leaves are most often seen in their dried form, but can be used fresh, if you're lucky enough to have a bay tree in your garden. The bay leaf favored for culinary use is from the Grecian laurel tree (sometimes called sweet bay tree), botanically known as *Laurus nobilis.* Unless you're in a real pinch, the California bay leaf should not be substituted (see *A Bay by Any Other Name,* page 261).

Bay leaves offer a pungent, aromatic presence, unique in the world of herbs. They are most commonly used in recipes that call for simmering, such as spaghetti, pot roast, or bouillabaisse. Bay leaves also have an important place in Mediterranean marinades, skewer cooking and as an ingredient in the classic herb blend, bouquet garni. Bay is especially good with pork, lamb and fish. Try lacing the leaves between skewered chunks of meat or fish, or laying them directly on top of veal or pork chops while they're on the grill. If a marinade calls for bay leaves, it is always best to heat the marinade before using so it will be infused with bay's special flavor.

CAPERS

Capers are small, unopened flower buds of the caper bush (*Capparis spinosa),* a scrubby plant that grows wild in rocky, dry areas of the Mediterranean. They're usually pickled in a brine, but are occasionally seen in a salted form. The French favor the very small, nonpareil capers, but larger capers are indistinguishable in flavor. Use small capers whole in sauces, or chop larger ones and add with a little lemon juice to compound butters for a pungent, piquant flavor, just right for any grilled fish.

CARAWAY

Caraway seeds are the source of the distinctive flavor in rye bread. The small seeds are strongly flavored and should be used with care. Crushing the seeds releases maximum flavor. To soften seeds, soak in a small amount of boiling water for 15 minutes before using. Frequently used in German recipes (see sauerkraut and potato casserole, page 336) and occasionally in marinades. Caraway is an excellent herb to use in a butter for vegetables.

CELERY

The fresh flavor of celery can be added to sauces or marinades in a variety of forms: Whole fresh stalks can be finely chopped; there's the widely available celery salt (which may be too salty for some people); and whole celery seed, just the thing when an intense celery flavor is desired. Celery in any form combines well with red sauces, fish, and vegetables.

CHERVIL

Chervil looks a little like a delicate, fine-leafed version of parsley. It has an equally delicate flavor, which many people describe as a combination of licorice and celery. Long favored by gourmets, chervil has earned a place in such classic herb blends as fine herbes and bouquet garni. When used in herb butters or marinades, chervil is particularly good with fish, chicken or veal.

CHILI PEPPERS

A complete discussion on the importance of peppers as a cooking spice would fill volumes and touch on cuisines from cultures around the world. Few spices share such

"Long favored by gourmets, chervil has earned a place in such classic herb blends as fine herbs and bouquet garni."

"All peppers are species of the genus Capsicum. But that's about all they have in common."

universal appreciation and few are as valuable to the griller. They are at home in Oriental soy marinades, Southeast Asian recipes, Caribbean cuisine and Middle Eastern dishes, to name just a few.

All peppers are species of the genus *Capsicum*. But that's about all they have in common. Hybridization between species native to many parts of the world have resulted in more than 100 varieties. They range in color from bright yellow to light and dark green to bright red. They can be small and fiery hot, like the serrano chili, to large and mildly sweet, as is the bell pepper. For a rating of the relative "hotness" of various peppers, see page 179.

Peppers are available in a variety of useful forms: fresh, dried, ground, powdered, canned, and in sauces, oils, or pastes. Regardless of form, use the hot peppers sparingly. It's a lot easier to add a little more than it is to take some out. Use added care when cooking with fresh hot peppers. Not only will they make your sauces fiery-hot, but they can burn your skin. Always wear gloves when slicing or cleaning fresh hot peppers, and be careful not to touch your eyes or lips.

Dried, ground and powdered forms of chili pepper, such as chili powder, cayenne and paprika, are especially important when making that esoteric concoction known as "barbecue sauce." Common chili powder contains ground peppers mixed with other herbs and spices, such as cumin, oregano, onion and garlic. Cayenne and paprika are pure ground peppers. Cayenne by itself is very hot; paprika is available in both hot and mild forms. Genuine Hungarian paprika tends to be stronger in flavor.

In addition to paprika's role in barbecue sauces, it has a special affinity to fresh fish. Some people contend that there's a chemical reaction between the two that prevents the fish's skin from becoming tough and hard during the grilling practice (see *Paprika and Fish*, page 163).

CINNAMON

Cinnamon comes from the bark of a tree that grows in India and Ceylon. It has a pungent flavor and aroma, familiar to most people in a variety of dessert recipes. Other cultures, particularly Mediterranean, Caribbean and Middle Eastern, use it to flavor main dishes. Cinnamon is also one of the ingredients found in curry powder.

CITRUS

As a group, citrus represents the most important fruit to the outdoor cook. Lemons and limes are most often used, but other fruits, such as oranges, grapefruit, mandarins and kumquats, offer their own, distinct flavors.

Juice from sour citrus, such as lemons and limes, is a smart alternative to vinegar in marinades, as it combines better with meals that include wine. Freshly squeezed over fresh fish, or combined with butter for an easy but tasty sauce for fish, chicken or vegetables, lemons and limes are a story of versatility. No creative outdoor cook should be without them.

But don't overlook the other types of citrus. Oranges, grapefruit, mandarins and kumquats can play important roles in a variety of sauces and marinades, and marmalades made from these fruits make excellent bastes for chicken and other fowl.

The highest concentration of flavor-rich oils are located in the colorful portion of the peel. To get the most and best flavor from citrus, lightly run the fruit over a grater. (Don't push too hard; the white tissue beneath the colored skin has a bitter flavor.) This grated peel is appropriately called zest. Use small amounts whenever you want a true citrus influence; the citrus flavor from zest is very strong and intensifies with cooking.

When selecting citrus for juice, choose fruit that are comparatively heavy and show no signs of drying out. Before juicing, roll the fruit with the palm of your hand on a hard surface. This ruptures vesicles inside and releases the maximum amount of juice. You can expect about one cup of juice from six medium-size lemons or eight to nine limes. One orange yields about one-quarter cup of juice. Always favor fresh citrus juice in any marinade, sauce or compound butter recipe; bottled, reconstituted citrus juices are just not the same.

"Juice from sour citrus, such as lemons and limes, is a smart alternative to vinegar in marinades, as it combines better with meals that include wine."

CLOVES

These dried, unopened buds of the clover tree *(Caryophyllus aromaticus)* are spicy, oily and aromatic. Used either whole or ground, they're excellent in marinades, fruity sauces and marmalades used as a basting sauce. Cloves are also a common ingredient in curry powders.

Whole cloves are often stuck directly into hams and apples. Whenever you use whole cloves, though, make sure you remove them before serving the food. Biting directly into a whole clove is an unforgettable, and not altogether pleasant, experience.

CORIANDER AND CILANTRO

These are two different flavors that come from the same plant, *Coriandrum sativum.* Coriander, the plant's seeds, are used in a variety of pastries, meat dishes and sausages, and are an integral ingredient in many curries. The leaves of the plant are called cilantro, or Mexican or Chinese parsley. They have a strong, pungent flavor that people either love or hate. (Those who love fresh cilantro can't get enough of it; those who don't usually won't even touch a dish containing it.) Before adding fresh cilantro to any marinade or sauce, it would be prudent to inquire how the diners feel about this distinctive herb.

Fresh cilantro is a classic ingredient in many Mexican, Chinese, Southeast Asian, Caribbean and Mediterranean dishes. It's excellent combined with butter, garlic and ground pepper, then used as a baste for fish, shrimp or prawns.

CUMIN

Cumin comes from the seeds of a plant in the parsley family, native to the Mediterranean. It's most often used in its ground form, although some recipes call for whole seeds. Very distinctive in flavor, cumin is an essential ingredient in curry and chili powders.

CURRY

Curry is not a single spice but a blend of several ground herbs and spices. The exact mixture varies, depending on where it originated or the food it is used on. A curry powder found on the supermarket herb rack might contain coriander, fenugreek, tumeric, celery seed, bay, cumin, pepper, nutmeg, clove, onion, red pepper and ginger. You can adapt a store-bought curry powder to your own tastes simply by adding more of any of those ingredients.

Curries are traditionally linked to spicy Indian and Asian foods, but they are also important to many other cuisines. In outdoor grilling, curries can be rubbed on chicken or beef, or used in marinades for fish or in sauces for vegetables. Curries can be hot and spicy or mild and sedate. Spicy versions can be tamed by dipping the food they are used on in plain yogurt.

DILL

Dried or fresh dill is an excellent accompaniment to grilled fish and almost any vegetable, but particularly new potatoes and carrots. Dill seeds and foliage can be used in marinades, sauces or butters. Try wrapping whole branches around fish steaks or filets before grilling for an attractive and flavorful alternative to a marinade.

FENNEL

Fennel is also an important ingredient in Chinese five-spice powder, a versatile Oriental herb blend. It's also a superb grilling herb. The entire plant — leaves, roots and seeds — can be used for a mild licorice flavor. Fennel is excellent paired up with any grilled fish. Use it in sauces, marinades and herb butters or lightly sprinkle dried leaves over grilled fish. For something different, try wrapping fresh leaves around fish fillets or sprinkle the herb over hot coals for a mild, anise-flavored smoke.

"Dill seeds and foliage can be used in marinades, sauces, or butters."

FRESH FRUIT

Summer means grilling, but it also means an abundance of fresh fruit — a lucky coincidence of which every outdoor cook should take full advantage. Fresh fruits, from peaches to plums to grapes, are an excellent addition to a variety of sauces. Peeled and pitted, they can be pureed or finely chopped and mixed with a little soy or wine for an outstanding basting sauce. The flavor of fresh fruit can be accented with a variety of herbs, particularly ginger and mint. Fruit sauces combine especially well with pork, ham and chicken.

GARLIC

As any garlic-lover will attest, garlic should be used anywhere and everywhere, any time. Garlic butter is excellent with grilled fish or prawns; garlic-soy-chili marinades are Oriental classics; and cut whole cloves can be inserted directly into large beef, lamb or pork roasts or lightly chopped and sprinkled over steaks.

Garlic is also an essential ingredient in many red barbecue sauces. When grilled, it can stand alone as an interesting appetizer (see page 139). If you're not a garlic-lover...well, what can be said?

Fresh garlic cloves provide the best flavor, but don't be afraid to lightly sprinkle a steak or chicken with garlic powder. Garlic powder can also be added to marinades if fresh is not available. If you like garlic during a meal but not afterwards, try chewing on a sprig of fresh parsley or biting into a wedge of lemon. It helps.

GINGER

Ginger is a versatile herb with a unique hot and spicy flavor. Freshly grated or dried and powdered, add it to marinades for game, lamb, pork, chicken, beef or fish. It blends well with almost anything that passes over the grill. Ginger is an important ingredient in recipes from

"As any garlic-lover will attest, garlic should be used anywhere and everywhere, any time."

many cultures, including Japan, Africa, the Mediterranean and Asia. It's a natural in soy, lemon, and garlic marinades, and adds a spicy flavor to fruit sauces.

HORSERADISH

Horseradish has a hot, nose-tingling flavor that's excellent in sauces. The grated root combines particularly well with sour cream and mustard — just the thing for prime rib and ham (see horseradish sauce, page 301). Cocktail sauces for shellfish wouldn't be the same without horseradish. Also try it with mustard and sauerkraut as an accompaniment for sausage.

LIQUID SMOKE

A smoky-flavored liquid used to flavor barbecue sauces. Strongly flavored; best used drop by drop.

MINT

There are many kinds of mint, all of which offer possibilities on the grill. In addition to the common mints, such as spearmint and peppermint, there are orange bergermont mint, apple mint, nutmeg- and caraway-scented mints, and many, many more. The more esoteric types are seldom available in supermarket herb racks, but they're easy to grow in the garden — in fact, they can easily become weeds.

Mints are among the most volatile of the aromatic herbs. As such, their flavor is not easily captured in marinades. Still, just the aroma of mint is often enough to influence tastebuds and provide a pleasant complement to many foods. Mints are natural with pork and lamb, especially chops and roasts. You can achieve the strongest flavors by sprinkling ground leaves over meat

"Mints are among the most volatile of the aromatic herbs. As such, their flavor is not easily captured in marinades."

or by completely wrapping it in fresh branches.

The English are famous for serving "mint sauce" with lamb, which we here in America somehow turned into mint jelly, something that should be avoided like the plague. For a more or less authentic English mint sauce, see page 302. Mints also blend well with fruit-based sauces and some vegetables, such as peas, new potatoes and carrots.

MUSTARDS

All mustards are derived from seeds of the mustard plant, which is either roasted and crushed or powdered. The multitude of prepared mustards come hot or mild, mixed with a variety of herbs, spices, vinegar and wine, or sweetened with honey. Many are excellent right out of the jar as a basting sauce for chicken. All are inseparably wed to hot dogs and hamburgers.

Dried mustard powder is an important ingredient in many barbecue sauces. Combined with water or vinegar and honey, it makes an excellent baste for pork or prawns. With the addition of herbs, spices or wine, the possibilities become endless.

OILS

Some oils, such as corn, safflower, cottonseed, peanut and soybean, are light-textured and virtually flavorless. Others, such as olive, hazelnut, walnut and sesame, have distinctive flavors that are characteristic of their source. Light, flavorless oils are usually inexpensive and commonly used in marinades to help prevent food from drying out when cooked; they also help keep lean food from sticking to the grill.

Oils with pronounced flavors are more expensive but used in smaller quantities. When combined with the right herbs and spices, they contribute their unique personality to a marinade. For example, olive oil is a natural in Mediterranean marinades for shish kabobs

"The multitude of prepared mustards come hot or mild, mixed with a variety of herbs spices, vinegar and wine, or sweetened with honey."

and sesame oils adds a wonderful, nutty flavor to Oriental marinades. Purchase expensive oils in small quantities so you can experiment to see which ones you like best.

Oils will turn rancid in a matter of weeks if not properly stored. Keep them in a cool, dark place, in an air-tight container. If you buy large quantities, divide it up and store in small containers.

ONIONS

There are probably more sauce and marinade recipes that call for at least one member of the onion family than those that do not. Sautéing chopped onions is an important first step in many red barbecue sauces. The garlic-like flavor of shallots is crucial to many simple as well as complex sauces. Chopped chives are a colorful and flavorful addition to both sauces and marinades.

Always use members of the onion family with care. When used to excess, the onion flavor may dominate or mask other, more subtle herbs and spices. Use small amounts in marinades that must sit overnight, unless they are a main ingredient, which is the case with many eastern European marinades.

OREGANO AND MARJORAM

Because these two aromatic herbs are so familiar in flavor, they're often confused. Oregano is stronger and should be used in smaller quantities. Although most people associate oregano and marjoram with Italian red sauces, they also have a significant role in many other cuisines. They're a common ingredient in recipes from many countries along the Mediterranean, in South and Central America and in eastern Europe. Oregano and marjoram combine particularly well with wine marinades, fish and tomatoes.

"The garlic-like flavor of shallots is crucial to many simple as well as complex sauces."

PARSLEY

Parsley is a familiar herb that is as attractive as a garnish as it is a delicious ingredient in marinades. Best used fresh, parsley's peppery flavor is a good complement to other herbs. It combines well with meat, fish or vegetables. Chewing on a sprig helps to sweeten garlic or onion breath.

Parsley is easy to grow in the garden. If possible, plant the flat-leaved Italian parsley; it not only has a stronger parsley flavor, it's next to impossible to find in most markets.

ROSEMARY

Rosemary is a strongly flavored but indispensable herb for the outdoor cook. Use it carefully but faithfully on lamb, pork, beef, game or fowl. Rosemary can be rubbed on or wrapped around food for easy seasoning. Sprinkle it over the coals for a pungent smoke. Blend three tablespoons of dried rosemary with one stick of melted butter to create a superb baste.

"Like other members of the mint family, the various types of sage have a strong flavor."

SAGE

Like other members of the mint family, the various types of sage have a strong flavor. It's often used with meats that have a high fat content, such as duck and goose. It's also an excellent flavoring for pork and all domestic poultry, including turkeys. Sage can be rubbed directly on meat or added to marinades. Try pineapple sage with pork. Clary and garden sage (the most common type) are excellent in stuffings.

Sage is far more versatile than many people realize. If you have a spot for sage in your garden, try planting a favorite variety of this herb.

SAVORY

Summer savory is a mild, sweet herb, used extensively in European countries as a favored flavoring for string beans. Because it loses much of its flavor when dried, summer savory is almost always used fresh. Winter savory has a slightly more bitter taste, but can be successfully used — judiciously — either fresh or dried.

In addition to summer savory's almost magical pairing with string beans, either type is useful in marinades for meats and chicken.

SESAME SEEDS

The nutty flavor of sesame seeds reaches its full potential over hot coals. They are best used on foods that are quickly cooked, such as fish; if they spend too much time on the grill, they tend to burn. Sauté the seeds in butter before using; this will bring out flavor and help them stick to whatever you're cooking. The flavor of sesame is especially good with Oriental soy marinades. To intensify the flavor, add a few drops of sesame oil.

SOY SAUCE

The best soy sauces are made from fermented soybeans, sugar, wheat, salt and malt. All soy sauces originate from the Orient, but vary in thickness, saltiness and, obviously, taste. A trip to an Oriental market will show you the great variety of soy sauces (or shoyo, as the Japanese call them) that are available.

It is an understatement to say that soy sauce is important in Oriental recipes; it is indispensable. However, soy can also be used in a variety of other ways. Use it sparingly instead of salt in any marinade. Or, use it alone as a quick steak or chicken marinade. However you use it, don't underestimate its strength. Soy sauce has a strong flavor; don't be afraid to dilute it with water or lemon juice.

"It is an understatement to say that soy sauce is important in Oriental recipes; it is indispensable."

"One question that's often asked is whether or not it's okay to use inexpensive wine for marinating food."

SPIRITS

Alcoholic beverages find their way into many sauces and marinades. Wine and sherry are used most often, but other spirits are equally valuable. Dark rum is delicious in tropical marinades; stale beer is the basis of many excellent barbecue sauces; and sake, a rice wine, adds character to many Oriental recipes.

Spirits can be used to complement other flavors, such as herbs and spices, or they can be the backbone of a marinade or sauce. Simply soaking a good steak in red wine for 30 minutes prior to grilling enhances its flavor. A few teaspoons of sherry, tarragon, lemon and oil is a simple and delicious "marinade" for fish.

One question that's often asked is whether or not it's okay to use inexpensive wine for marinating food. Once, when I was working in a wine shop, a co-worker fielded just such a question over the telephone. "Of course it's all right," he answered, "you'll just have inexpensive-tasting food." I doubt if that was the answer the caller was looking for, but it contains an element of truth.

Perhaps the best advice is not to use any wine in a marinade that you wouldn't be happy drinking. Using the same wine that will be served with dinner results in a better association of flavors.

SWEETENERS

Sugar, molasses and honey are the primary sweeteners for marinades and sauces, although maple syrup, corn syrup and fruit preserves are occasionally used. Molasses and brown sugar are used for sweet tomato-based barbecue sauces; honey is better in marinades or sauces that feature herbs, spices and fruits.

Any substance that contains sugar has a tendency to burn on the grill. To avoid this, apply sweet sauces during the last 10 to 15 minutes of cooking time.

Tarragon

Tarragon is a versatile herb that lends its sweet, licorice flavor to many sauces and marinades. Best used fresh, it's wonderful with fish, chicken or veal, and a key ingredient in Béarnaise sauce. It also blends well with mustard and lemon sauces. Use only French tarragon; the look-alike Russian tarragon has practically no flavor.

Thyme

The unmistakable flavor of thyme is indispensable to the outdoor cook. In marinades or sauces for pork, fish and chicken, sprinkled over vegetables or combined with other herbs, thyme adds strong or subtle flavor that can turn a simple recipe into a wonderful experience. Thyme combines particularly well with rosemary.

For something different, try the lemon-flavored "lemon thyme" in any marinade or sauce for fish.

Tomato Sauces

Three types of tomato sauces form the basic foundation for red barbecue sauces: unseasoned tomato sauce, catsup and chili sauce. A few variations begin with tomato paste. Considering how subjective barbecue sauces have become, each works equally well; it's all a matter of individual taste.

Catsup and chili sauce contain various herbs and spices, as well as vinegar, with chili sauce being the spiciest. This should be kept in mind when making your own barbecue sauces so you don't over-spice the mixture. If you are experimenting with a new barbecue sauce and it gets too spicy, add plain tomato sauce to dilute the flavor. Any tomato-based sauce can be thickened with tomato paste.

Like sugary sauces, tomato sauces tend to burn and char on the grill. This can be particularly troublesome with foods, such as chicken and ribs, that have long cooking times. To avoid charring, apply the sauce during

"If you are experimenting with a new barbecue sauce and it gets too spicy, add plain tomato sauce to dilute the flavor."

the last 15 minutes of cooking and turn and baste often from then on. If you're one of those who feels that a barbecue sauce develops its true character only if it's on the food from the beginning, coat the food before it goes on the grill, then turn and baste often throughout the cooking time.

Many bottled barbecue sauces can be extremely useful to the outdoor cook. Use them straight out of the bottle or doctor them up with your favorite spices.

VINEGARS

All vinegars are made by fermentation: alcohols or liquids containing sugar are converted into acetic acid. As such, vinegar is the liquid most often used as the acid portion of a marinade. Although malt or cider vinegars are the most common types used, wine vinegar is preferable because it blends so well with many herbs and spices.

The many types of vinegar are greatly varied in flavor. The appropriately named cider vinegar is made from apple cider and is usually light brown in color. White vinegar is made from grain alcohol. It is clear and often used for pickling. English malt vinegar is made from fermented grains and cereals. Rice wine vinegars, naturals for Oriental recipes, are made from fermented sake. Wine vinegar is fermented from red or white wine or sherry; the flavor and color varies accordingly.

Herb vinegars are made by adding one or more herbs to any of the vinegars mentioned above, with wine vinegar being the favorite. The presence of the herb or herbs can be strong or subtle, depending upon the types and amounts used. Experimentation will reveal herb combinations that complement your own palate. To start, combine one cup of fresh herbs with one quart of vinegar in a glass bottle with a tight-fitting cork. Put the herbs in the bottle first, using whole sprigs and branches of fresh herbs (half that amount if the herbs are dry). Warm the vinegar before pouring it into the herb-filled bottles.

Contained in attractive, ornamental bottles, herb vinegars are also a beautiful addition to the kitchen, especially when long angles of sunlight (even that pale

"Contained in attractive, ornamental bottles, herb vinegars are also a beautiful addition to the kitchen…"

winter light) glint off the clear, herb-enhanced liquid, reminding you of the past summer, when the herbs were cut from the garden.

Marinades made with herb vinegars can be as simple as combining equal amounts of water, oil and the herb vinegar of your choice. Additional herbs and other ingredients can be added to accentuate a particular flavor, if desired.

Because vinegars are strongly acidic, they should always be stored in glass containers. Any marinade that includes vinegar should be used or stored in glass or ceramic; metal containers will impart a strong "off" flavor.

"Marinades made with herb vinegars can be as simple as combining equal amounts water, oil, and the herb vinegar of your choice."

MARINADES

What we call a marinade today has its roots in the distant past, long before modern refrigeration. For centuries, brine solutions and pickling techniques were used as preservatives to increase the storage life of fresh meats. Regionally favored herb and spice blends were often added to these preserving solutions to offset their harsh flavor. Gradually, food storage methods improved, but by then, whole populations had become accustomed to particular spice and herb mixtures combined with certain foods. Today, these flavors are all but synonymous with regional cuisines from around the world, and have made their way into a variety of marinades and sauces. Thus we have curry-yogurt marinades and sauces from India, soy-ginger-garlic-pepper mixtures from the Orient, and chili blends from Spain and Mexico. And the list goes on.

While it is true that cooking within a particular ethnic or cultural style requires certain ingredients, the making of a marinade within any specific tradition is still open to customizing. Unlike baking, an exact science demanding careful measurement and attention to detail, marinades the world over are fast and loose. As long as you include a liquid, an oil, and some flavoring, you have the basis for a marinade. In the beginning, you may find yourself using every spice and herb in the rack, just because you can. Over time, you'll find your favorites and, most likely, your marinades will become quite simple.

Unless specifically noted in the recipe, all it takes to make a marinade is to combine the ingredients in a bowl and mix them thoroughly. In a few cases, it will be necessary to heat the ingredients just to the boiling point to bring out the most flavor. If heated, always allow the marinade to cool to room temperature before using. Food added to a hot marinade may partially cook, sealing it off to further flavor penetration. Marinades that contain melted butter will cool to room temperature before they begin to solidify.

"Today, these flavors are all but synonymous with regional cuisines from around the world, and have made their way into a variety of marinades and sauces. Thus we have curry-yogurt marinades and sauces from India, soy-ginger-garlic-pepper mixtures from the Orient, and chili blends from Spain and Mexico."

Equipment
The best containers in which to marinate foods are made of non-corrosive materials, such as glass or glazed earthenware — or, in the case of the Tupperware product, plastic (see page 189). Other materials may contribute "off"

flavors to the marinade and, ultimately, the food. Use a container that's big and deep enough so the food can be positioned in a single layer and easily turned to coat both sides. Foods that are marinated for longer than two or three hours (at room temperature) should be refrigerated. In this case, you will need a container with a cover. Lacking an acceptable container, virtually all marinating can be done in tightly sealed, heavy-duty plastic bags.

Increasing Expectations

Keep the entertainment side of grilling in mind whenever marinating. You can increase your guests' anticipation (not to mention your own) by placing the marinating food in a visible spot and making it look as attractive as possible. Floating citrus slices, sprigs of parsley or other fresh herbs on top of a marinade add color, help catch the eye and whet the appetite.

How Long and How Strong?

Recipes in this book recommend marinating food for periods ranging from 15 minutes to two days. How long it takes depends on how strongly you want the food flavored, the strength of the marinade, and the type of food being marinated. Obviously, for subtle flavor enhancement, marinate for short time periods, especially if the marinade is strong.

Fish should rarely be marinated for more than 30 to 45 minutes, especially if the marinade contains an acid component, such as wine, citrus juice or vinegar. This also holds true with boned, skinless chicken breasts. Marinating too long will cause the fibers of the meat to break down, producing an unappealing, mushy texture. Generally speaking, high-quality foods have excellent flavors of their own that shouldn't be masked by over-marinating.

Don't be fooled by how a marinade tastes straight. A strong marinade may be very unpleasant when sipped from a spoon but excellent when used on meat and cooked over coals. This is often the case with soy marinades.

Some marinades take a long time to absorb the flavor of herbs and spices, especially if you use dried herbs. For recipes that call for a short marinating period, make the marinade several hours in advance so it can develop its full flavor before the food is added.

"Fish should rarely be marinated for more than 30 to 45 minutes, especially if the marinade contains an acid component, such as wine, citrus juice or vinegar."

There is some debate on whether marinades are more effective when covered or left exposed to air. Refrigerated marinades should definitely be covered or they risk picking up stray flavors and odors or, conversely, making everything else in the refrigerator smell and taste like the marinade. Some people feel herbs and spices are more active at room temperature, exposed to fresh air — they're certainly more attractive this way. Others feel that marinades should always be covered to seal in flavors and help prevent discoloration. If temperature in your kitchen is within the normal range (around 70 to 75 degrees F.), foods covered in a marinade should be safe, from a health standpoint, for approximately two hours.

When Sauce Is Marinade and Marinade Is Sauce

The distinction between sauce and marinade can, at times, be confused. In general, sauces are thicker than marinades and are applied over the food after cooking. (The exception to this are barbecue sauces, which some people use as a marinade, and others as a basting sauce while the food cooks.) Marinades are primarily used to flavor food before cooking. They can, however, be used as a basting "sauce" during the grilling process to help keep the food moist.

To make the distinction more confusing, any pleasant-tasting marinade can be transformed into sauce by thickening it. If, after you put the marinated food on the grill, there's a quantity of marinade left over, use it as the basis for a sauce to pour over the grilled food, or place in a bowl for use as "dipping sauce." There are three techniques commonly used to thicken marinades:

1) Add a small amount of cornstarch or flour (a teaspoonful at a time) to the marinade, heat just to the boiling point, stirring constantly. Remove from heat when mixture has achieved the desired consistency.

2) Dissolve a teaspoon of either cornstarch or flour in several tablespoons of lukewarm water. Slowly stir the liquid into hot marinade until it thickens to your liking. Cornstarch will produce a glassy sauce; sauces thickened with flour are less transparent.

3) Thicken the marinade by reducing the liquid. This is done by slowly boiling the marinade until enough liquid has evaporated and thickened. Be advised, however, that thickening by reduction also intensifies flavor and can result in a very powerful sauce.

There are three techniques commonly used to thicken marinades for use as a sauce.

ALL-PURPOSE MARINADE

As the name indicates, this is an excellent all-purpose marinade, especially good for beef (as flank steak) and lamb (as shish-kebob). While the ingredients are vaguely Oriental, the flavor is not. This is also a good marinade for those who do not like the taste (or effects) of garlic. The minced garlic can be replaced with a couple tablespoons of dried minced onions. If you want a pronounced Oriental flavor, replace the powdered ginger with 3 to 4 tablespoons of grated fresh ginger.

¹/₄ cup vegetable or olive oil

¹/₄ cup soy sauce

¹/₂ cup dry sherry

2 cloves garlic, minced

1 small onion, minced

1¹/₂ teaspoons ground ginger

CHINESE-STYLE MARINADE

Sticky, spicy and slightly sweet, this is a particularly tasty marinade for pork spareribs. Any meat marinated or basted with a sauce containing sugar or honey needs to be watched carefully on the grill. If the meat is cooked over coals that are too hot, the sugar in the marinade will caramelize and quickly char. All ribs are at their best when cooked slowly, over a moderate fire, using indirect heat (see page 42); when using this marinade, that advice is doubly important.

1 pint soy sauce

8 ounces hoisin sauce

8 ounces white vinegar

2 tablespoons rice wine vinegar

8 ounces honey

2 ounces chopped garlic

2 tablespoons red pepper flakes

1 pint pineapple juice

6 ounces peanut oil

DIJON MARINADE

This is a flavorful marinade, excellent for all types of poultry. It has enough "ummph" to make its presence known without being overwhelming. I often use it for chicken that I intend to serve cold, as the flavors hold up even after being refrigerated. If injecting flavor into poultry is something you ever do (see *Demon Bulb Baster,* page 207), this is a good marinade to use. This marinade can be modified with the addition of any of your favorite fresh herbs — basil, rosemary, tarragon — you name it.

Whisk all ingredients together. Allow meat to marinate in the mixture for 4 to 6 hours, or overnight, if you want it more intensely flavored.

¹/₂ cup dry white wine (or for a slightly stronger, more complex flavor, substitute dry vermouth

¹/₃ cup olive oil

Juice of one lemon

2 to 3 cloves garlic, minced

3 tablespoons prepared Dijon mustard

Freshly ground black pepper to taste

Fresh Ginger-Garlic Marinade

²/₃ cup sake

Juice of half a lemon

¹/₄ cup vegetable oil

3 or 4 tablespoons fresh ginger, peeled and grated

3 or 4 cloves garlic, minced

This is simplicity defined, and delicious for use with chicken, pork, shrimp or prawns. It will permeate shrimp and prawns still in their shells if you let them soak in the marinade for at least 2 hours. Shelled shrimp and prawns will absorb plenty of flavor in 30 to 45 minutes. Add 2 tablespoons of soy sauce to the leftover marinade, bring it to a boil, allow it to cool, and serve as a dipping sauce. Great for hors d'oeuvres.

Garlic, rosemary & rosé marinade

²/₃ cup rosé wine

¹/₄ cup olive oil

Juice of half a lemon

2 to 3 cloves garlic, minced

2 teaspoons dried rosemary, crushed

Finely ground black pepper to taste

The very distinctive herb rosemary should be used with a light hand. To my taste, it goes best with poultry and lamb, but others would include veal, beef, and pork.

Any dry or semi-dry rosé wine (or blush wines, as they are unblushingly called today) will do. After using what's needed in the marinade, chill the remainder and drink it with your meal.

Feel free to substitute your favorite herbs for the rosemary and thyme.

Greek marinade

³/₄ cup dry white wine

¹/₄ cup olive oil

12 bay leaves

8 strips (about 1 inch or so long) lemon peel, yellow part only

1 small onion, minced

Freshly ground black pepper to taste

The Greeks really know their way around a grill. This marinade is just the thing for lamb that has been cut into cubes or strips, a butterflied leg or even chops. It's also good with chicken or beef. Grill up a few skewers of bell peppers, red onions and cherry tomatoes, make a salad with greens, feta cheese and Greek olives, and you're set!

Combine all ingredients in a small saucepan and bring them to a boil. Allow the mixture to cool to room temperature before using as a marinade. If you're cooking meat on skewers, save the bay leaves from the marinade and add them, here and there, between the pieces of meat.

HERB MARINADE

This is a very simple marinade, excellent for use with mild-flavored meats such as chicken breasts and rabbit. It's also delicious on eggplant or potato wedges. For best results, use this marinade as a basting sauce, as well, liberally dabbing it on whatever you're cooking every 6 minutes or so.

Combine the ingredients in a small saucepan. Bring the mixture just to the boiling point, then allow it to cool to room temperature before using it as a marinade.

3/4 olive oil

1 1/2 teaspoons dried rosemary, crumbled

1 tablespoon dried thyme, crushed

3 or 4 cloves garlic, minced

Freshly ground black pepper to taste

HOT FRESH PLUM MARINADE

This unusual, and unusually good, marinade also works well as a sauce. Any fresh plums will do, but the fat, juicy dark ones (such as 'Elephant Heart') make an exemplary concoction. Skin the plums before cooking or, for additional flavor, leave the skins on, and simply put the sauce into a sieve after cooking, rubbing it through with a wooden spoon.

Combine all ingredients in a medium-sized saucepan and mix well. Cook over low heat, stirring often, until the plums have disintegrated. Bring leftover marinade to a brief boil in a small pan and use it as an outstanding dipping sauce. Add a little water (1 tablespoon at a time) if the sauce becomes too thick.

1 cup fresh ripe plums (6 to 8), pitted and cut into quarters

2 tablespoons Chinese plum sauce

2 tablespoons Chinese hoisin sauce

4 cloves garlic, minced

1/2 teaspoon dry mustard

1 teaspoon red pepper flakes

1 teaspoon fresh ginger, grated

INDIAN YOGURT MARINADE

This is a tasty marinade, especially for chicken and lamb. If you want an intense flavor, skin the chicken before putting it in the marinade. Combine all the ingredients and let stand for 15 minutes or so before adding whatever food you are marinating. The curry flavor intensifies over time.

Delicious garnishes include chopped peanuts, fresh cilantro and perhaps some chutney.

3/4 cup yogurt

1/3 cup vegetable oil

3 or 4 cloves garlic, minced

3 tablespoons curry powder

1 tablespoon ground cumin

1 teaspoon salt

1/8 teaspoon cayenne (more if you like it hot)

LEMON-WHITE WINE MARINADE

This marinade accentuates the flavor of mild foods, without overwhelming them. Use it with veal, chicken, fish and shellfish. Feel free to add a couple tablespoons of your favorite fresh herb. Marinate fish for up to 30 minutes, shellfish for 60 minutes; any longer, and the acidic ingredients in the marinade will "cook" the seafood before you ever get it on the grill. Veal and chicken can be marinated for 4 to 6 hours.

¾ cup dry white wine

⅓ cup olive oil

3 tablespoons chopped onion, shallots, or the white part of green onions

2 cloves of garlic, minced

Juice of 1 lemon

2 tablespoons fresh parsley, finely chopped

LIME-GARLIC MARINADE

This may not sound all that great, but it is one of my favorite marinades. It's an excellent choice for thin strips of pork or beef, giving the meat a tangy, Southern-hemisphere flavor. It can be used on chicken or fish, but don't leave the fish in the marinade for longer than 10 to 15 minutes or the lime juice will "cook" it. Other meats can stay in the marinade for 2 to 3 hours.

I urge you to try this with strips of lean pork (a cut-up a tenderloin or pork chops) and serve with steamed rice (page 337), home-alone beans (page 325) and confetti salsa (page 301), one of my favorite summertime meals. Don't forget a couple of ice-cold ones.

Whatever you do, don't use bottled lime juice, or the type that comes in those little plastic squeeze things. I tried it once in a pinch, and it's definitely not the same as the real thing.

⅔ cup fresh lime juice

6 to 8 cloves garlic, minced

⅓ cup vegetable oil

MARSALA MARINADE

The natural full-bodied, slightly sweet, nutty flavor of marsala makes it an ideal accompaniment to lamb, beef or even wild game. Although I'm not sure why, its flavor reminds me of autumn. If you can't find marsala, a medium-dry sherry can be substituted. Any meat treated with this marinade would be excellent accompanied by those other slightly sweet, earthy root crops — carrots, parsnips or even mashed potatoes.

¾ cup marsala or medium-dry sherry

¼ cup soy sauce

⅓ cup vegetable oil

2 cloves garlic, minced

Freshly ground black pepper to taste

Mexican-style marinade

Fajitas — thin strips of seasoned meat, served with a variety of chopped vegetables and condiments, rolled into steamed fresh flour tortillas — burst onto the culinary scene a few years ago, and seem to be here to stay. They're good! If the only place you've ever had them is a fast-food joint, by all means try making them at home — you'll know then why they were introduced in the first place.

　　This is an all-purpose marinade that works wonders on chicken, lamb or beef. Marinate the meat from 2 to 4 hours.

6 ounces vegetable oil

2 ounces lemon juice

2 ounces pineapple juice

1 tablespoon red wine vinegar

3 ounces water

2 cloves garlic, minced

1½ teaspoons thyme

2 teaspoons chili powder (hot or mild, your choice)

2 teaspoons dried oregano, crushed

1 teaspoon salt

Oriental sweet & hot marinade

This is a great marinade for any meat you plan to cook "low and slow" — over low heat and for a long time, that is. Beef short ribs, country-style pork ribs or even double-cut pork chops are likely candidates.

　　Anything cooked using this full-flavored marinade will only need the simplest of side dishes: steamed rice, perhaps, and a little sautéed Chinese cabbage or bok choy and onions. Hot tea or beer are the beverages of choice.

½ cup soy sauce

½ cup water

¼ cup sesame oil

2 tablespoons brown sugar

½ cup green onion, finely chopped

1 tablespoon garlic, minced

2 tablespoons fresh ginger, grated

1 teaspoon cayenne

Pesto marinade

Pesto, that famous combination of olive oil, Parmesan, pine nuts, basil and garlic, has been over-served on a lot of pasta in recent years. A slight variation on the theme makes a delicious marinade for chicken, lamb, veal, shrimp or even a distinctly flavored fish, such as salmon. One aspect of this variation, by necessity, is the omission of the Parmesan cheese; save it for the pasta. Give this marinade a try, especially if you grow your own basil.

⅓ cup olive oil

½ cup dry white wine (for a more distinctive flavor, try substituting dry vermouth)

3 cloves garlic, minced

½ cup fresh basil, finely shredded and chopped

Freshly ground pepper, to taste

RED WINE MARINADE

3/4 cup dry red wine

1/3 cup olive oil

2 or 3 bay leaves

1 small onion, minced

2 or 3 cloves garlic, minced

Freshly ground black pepper
as much as you care to add

This marinade is well-suited to beef and lamb. Marinate either meat for 6 to 8 hours, or overnight in a refrigerator. Combine all ingredients in a small saucepan and heat just to the boiling point. Allow the mixture to cool to room temperature before using it as a marinade. If there's enough left over, use it to baste the meat while it's on the grill.

SOUTHEAST ASIAN-STYLE MARINADE

1/2 cup sake

1/4 cup soy sauce

1/4 cup vegetable oil

4 tablespoons fresh lemon juice

2 tablespoons fresh ginger, grated

2 to 4 cloves garlic, minced

4 to 7 serrano chilies, minced

True Southeast Asian marinades employ a number of ingredients not normally found in most supermarkets. If you have a taste for Southeast Asian cuisine, which may be among the most complex, delightful and delicious in the world, by all means educate yourself on the unique ingredients they require. (*Practical Thai Cooking,* by Puangkram C. Schmitz and Michael J. Worman, published by Kodansha International is just one of the excellent books available.) In the meantime, the following marinade will give a hint of the pleasures that await you and is very tasty in its own right.

SOUTHWESTERN MARINADE

1/4 cup fresh lime juice

1/4 cup apple juice

1/4 cup vegetable oil

2 cloves garlic, minced

1 teaspoon chili powder
(hot or mild, your choice)

1 teaspoon hot pepper sauce

Freshly ground black pepper
to taste

This is a good all-purpose marinade with a bit of a kick to it. Use it for chicken, beef, pork or lamb. Good for a casual outdoor party; serve any meat flavored with this marinade with steamed flour tortillas, home-alone beans (page 325), and confetti salsa (page 301).

SPICY PEANUT MARINADE

Like Southeast Asian-style marinade, this marinade takes its cue from the wonderfully complex flavors of Thai cooking. If you have trouble imagining what the flavors of peanut butter might be like in a marinade, imagine again. It's great.

This is best used with beef or pork, especially when the meat is cut into thin strips and woven onto skewers (see page 56).

½ cup dry or medium-dry sherry

¼ cup soy sauce

¼ cup vegetable oil

2 to 4 cloves garlic, minced

4 tablespoons peanut butter

2 teaspoons dried red pepper flakes

TERIYAKI MARINADE

Teriyaki marinade may suffer from overexposure, perhaps because of the many bottled preparations now available at supermarkets. In truth, it's an excellent, all-purpose marinade, adding a distinctive flavor to chicken, beef, pork or lamb.

Combine all ingredients in a small saucepan and heat just to the boiling point. Allow to cool to room temperature before marinating the food.

½ cup soy sauce

⅓ cup dry sherry

¼ cup firmly packed brown sugar

¼ cup rice wine vinegar

4 tablespoons vegetable oil

2 cloves garlic, minced

1 tablespoon ground ginger

WILD GAME MARINADE

This marinade can be used for wild game or to make tame game taste a little more "wild." If venison or boar are in short supply, try substituting pork, lamb or Rock Cornish game hens.

Combine all ingredients in a small saucepan and heat just to the boiling point. Allow the mixture to cool to room temperature before using it as a marinade.

¾ cup dry red wine

⅓ cup vegetable oil

1 small onion, minced

1 teaspoon dried thyme

1½ teaspoon juniper berries, crushed

1 teaspoon freshly ground black pepper

SAUCES

To my way of thinking, grilling is a form of cooking that is almost "anti-sauce." Sauces, in the main, are for haute cuisine; grilling, is a rustic, casual way of cooking that does not deserve too much fuss. The inherent flavors of whatever is being grilled are meant to be the stars of the show. Barbecue sauces are, of course, a notable exception. More hostility between various camps has ensued in the name of barbecue sauce than in the history of French cooking.

The only advice I can give on barbecue sauce is found below. The entire barbecue experience is so subjective, there's almost nothing that can be put down in print that isn't going to offend someone, somewhere. But the one great thing about the subject of barbecue is that everyone is right. So enough about barbecue!

Once one leaves the barbecue arena, there are several sauces that work well for grilled food. Two of them are downright difficult to get right; the others two are simplicity defined. If you work at mastering the two difficult ones — Béarnaise and beurre blanc — you'll have gone a long way in ensuring your status as a good, if not great, cook. The recipes that follow have been made countless times under every condition imaginable. In short, they're bulletproof. So even though you may think of yourself of the master of the grill, and wouldn't go near the stove on a bet, try mastering Béarnaise sauce and beurre blanc. They will increase your eating pleasure immeasurably.

Note: Here's a tip that takes the heat off trying either Béarnaise sauce or beurre blanc for the first time. As emulsified sauces, legends have developed around each about how hard they are to "hold" while the entrée cooks. I won't go into the horror stories about separated sauces, etc., etc., but rather, offer one simple solution: Buy a large Thermos — the kind with a large mouth — and keep it handy. Heat the Thermos with hot water while you're making the sauce. Once the sauce has reached the desired consistency, pour the hot water out of the Thermos and pour in the sauce. Cap the Thermos. The sauce will stay perfect for at least two hours. Before serving, give it a couple of quick shakes, then pour it on. If the sauce refuses to cooperate the first time you try to make it, you'll have plenty of time to try again or come up with an alternative.

"Once the sauce has reached the desired consistency, pour the hot water out of the Thermos and pour in the sauce. Cap the Thermos. The sauce will stay perfect for at least two hours."

BUILD YOUR OWN BARBECUE SAUCE

Outdoor cooks disagree on how often, how much, and when barbecue sauce should be applied. Some will only apply sauce just before the food is removed from the grill. This method requires the least amount of sauce, less frequent basting, and preserves the integrity of the sauce. It also avoids charring that is common with tomato-based sauces.

Other outdoor cooks prefer to apply sauce from the very beginning, often soaking the food in sauce before it goes on the grill. This method requires more sauce and frequent basting, but gives the sauce more time to blend with the food and the fire.

An entire book could be written on the countless variations of barbecue sauce, but I'm not sure what purpose it would serve, as everyone seems to have their own personalized deviation. And then there's the burgeoning array of bottled sauces that seem to take up more space on the grocery store shelves each year, some of which are first-rate, as is, right out of the bottle. That said, the list of ingredients at right comprises a master recipe for building your own barbecue sauce. Three variations follow. After that, you're on your own, pardner.

1) Using a large saucepan, sauté onions and garlic in melted butter over medium-high heat. Cook until onions are soft and transparent.

2) Add all other ingredients except tomato sauce and vinegar. Mix well and cook for 5 minutes.

3) Add tomato sauce and vinegar. Lower heat and simmer for 15 minutes.

Use as is, or add the following ingredients to the master recipe for:

Kentucky Smoke Barbecue Sauce
2 tablespoons brown sugar, firmly packed
2 tablespoons lemon juice
1 teaspoon paprika
½ teaspoon liquid smoke

Master Recipe
1 small to medium onion, chopped

¼ cup butter

2 cloves garlic, minced

1 teaspoon paprika

1 tablespoon ground black pepper

2 tablespoons fresh lemon juice

1 teaspoon dry mustard

½ teaspoon hot pepper sauce

½ teaspoon salt

¼ cup cider vinegar

1 16-ounce can tomato sauce

"Outdoor cooks disagree on how often, how much, and when barbecue sauce should be applied."

Or, add the following ingredients to create:

Louisiana Sweet Barbecue Sauce

1 tablespoon brown sugar, firmly packed
¼ cup molasses
2 additional tablespoons cider vinegar
2 tablespoons sweet sherry

For a final variation, add the following ingredients for:

Spicy Rio Grande Sauce

2 garlic cloves, minced
1 7-ounce can diced mild green pepper
2 tablespoons lemon juice
½ teaspoon hot pepper sauce
1 teaspoon cayenne

BÉARNAISE SAUCE

This is the classic tarragon-flavored emulsified butter sauce that goes so well with beef and lamb. It has become a classic, since its invention by an English chef working in France during the reign of Henry IV (in fact, the sauce was invented in honor of the King), simply because it is so good.

There are two ways to go about making Béarnaise, both using the same ingredients: the time-honored method in a double-boiler and a much faster, easier method using an electric blender. Both procedures follow, with the one caveat: The old-fashioned, double-boiler method produces a sauce that's light and delicate in consistency; the blender method version tends to be much thicker. Both taste the same, but I wouldn't be telling the whole story unless that distinction was made. And yes, of course purists prefer the old-fashioned method, but better blender Béarnaise than no Béarnaise at all, I say.

The Blender Method

1) Put the shallots or onions, white wine vinegar, tarragon, and pepper into a small saucepan and bring them

1 tablespoon shallot or onion, finely chopped

3 tablespoons white wine vinegar

1 teaspoon coarsely ground black pepper

1 teaspoon dry tarragon, or 2 to 3 sprigs fresh tarragon, finely chopped

3 egg yolks

1 cup (½ pound) butter, melted and still hot

to a boil. Reduce rapidly over high heat until only 1 or 2 teaspoons of liquid remain. Watch carefully, swirling the mixture around almost constantly. This process will only take a few minutes and will, by the way, make your entire kitchen smell like vinegar. The aroma doesn't last long, however.

2) Remove the shallot and vinegar mixture from the stove and allow it to cool.

3) Put the egg yolks and the cooled shallot and vinegar mixture in a blender. Process until well-blended, about 1 minute or so.

4) Melt the butter and put into a container from which it is easy to pour, like an old-fashioned glass measuring cup, the kind with a handle and a small pourer.

5) Turn the blender on high and add the hot butter, drip-by-drip at first, gradually increasing it to a steady stream as the mixture begins to thicken.

6) *Voilà tout!* Serve immediately or pour (more like spoon) the sauce into a preheated Thermos bottle for later use (see *Note* on page 296).

Time-honored Method
1) Put the shallots or onions, white wine vinegar, tarragon and pepper into a small saucepan and bring them to a boil. Reduce rapidly over high heat until only 1 or 2 teaspoons of liquid remain. Watch carefully, stirring or swirling the mixture almost constantly.

2) Remove the shallot and vinegar mixture from the stove and allow it to cool.

3) Add the egg yolks to the saucepan with the cooled shallot and vinegar reduction. Using a wire whisk, beat for 1 minute or so. Remove the pan from the heat.

4) Cut two sticks of butter into approximately 10 pats.

5) Place the pan with the egg yolk, shallot and vinegar mixture over a larger pan of simmering water. The

Béarnaise sauce has become a classic since its invention by an English chef working in France during the reign of Henry IV.

easiest way to accomplish this is by transferring the mixture to the top part of a double-boiler, but the mechanics of this operation are up to you.

6) Slowly increase the heat under the double-boiler (or what have you) while whisking the mixture. When the mixture begins to thicken a bit, start adding the butter, one pat at a time, whisking all the while. (*Note:* If you enjoy such things, have a glass of wine *prior* to this process; there won't be any time during it.) Don't add the next pat of butter until the previous one has completely disappeared.

7) By the time the last pat of butter has been incorporated, you should have a sauce that's approximately the consistency of mayonnaise. Serve immediately or pour the sauce into a pre-heated Thermos bottle for later use (see page 296).

BEURRE BLANC

Beurre blanc, or by its very literal translation, "white butter" sauce, is one of the best things to come off the top of the stove. It's simply the best over a perfectly grilled piece of fish, and can be so easily flavored with any herb or other ingredient that knowing how to make this classic is one bit of expertise that you should add to your culinary arsenal.

3 or 4 shallots or ¹/₄ cup onion, finely chopped

¹/₄ cup white wine vinegar

¹/₄ cup white wine (or for a more complex flavor, the same amount of dry vermouth)

2 cups (2 sticks) butter, cut into about 10 pats

1) Put the shallots or onions, white wine vinegar, and white wine into a small saucepan and bring to a boil. Reduce rapidly over high heat until only 2 tablespoons of liquid remain. Watch carefully, stirring or swirling the mixture more or less constantly.

2) Reduce the heat to medium and begin adding the butter, one pat at a time, to the shallot and vinegar mixture, whisking constantly. Allow each pat of butter to dissolve before adding the next.

3) By the time the last pat of butter has been added, the sauce should be thick and creamy. Use immediately or

pour into preheated Thermos bottle (see *Note* on page 296) to hold for later use.

Note: This recipe produces a basic beurre blanc. It can be easily flavored by adding 2 to 3 tablespoons of your favorite herb, finely chopped, to the shallot and vinegar mixture, or by substituting an equal amount of lemon or lime juice for the white wine vinegar.

CONFETTI SALSA

This spicy, full-flavored mixture of fresh vegetables is at its best during the height of the summer, but it is so good it can even be made with those less-than-perfect winter tomatoes. Surprisingly, your choice of bottled salsa will determine the spiciness of the sauce.

Confetti salsa is excellent on top of cowboy beans (page 321), home-alone beans (page 325), or any grilled meat.

Mix all the ingredients together in a large bowl. Allow the salsa to sit at room temperature for an hour or so before using to let flavors mingle. It will last for 3 to 4 days in a refrigerator.

Note: If you don't care for the flavor of cilantro, substitute fresh parsley and 1 tablespoon of oregano.

1 large or 2 medium vine-ripe tomatoes, diced

1 green bell pepper, diced

1 red sweet bell pepper, diced

1 yellow sweet bell pepper or 18 yellow pear tomatoes, diced

¾ cup red onion, chopped

½ cup fresh cilantro, chopped

Juice of one large lime

1 tablespoon vegetable oil

Salt and freshly ground black pepper, to taste

2 tablespoons red wine vinegar

⅓ cup of your favorite bottled salsa

HORSERADISH SAUCE

There are those who prefer their horseradish as fresh and as hot as it can be. Others would rather its kick was diluted a bit. This recipe is for the latter.

Combine all ingredients and let the sauce sit for 1 hour or so before using. Just the thing for a charcoal-roasted, standing rib roast.

⅓ cup horseradish

⅓ cup sour cream

1 teaspoon sugar

Dash of salt

1 tablespoon white wine vinegar

1 teaspoon dry mustard (optional)

MIGNONETTE SAUCE

½ cup champagne or white wine vinegar

½ cup dry white wine

1 tablespoon minced shallots

Cracked white or black pepper to taste (don't hold back)

Alice Waters of Chez Panisse fame popularized this dipping sauce for raw oysters. I like it with any grilled shellfish — oysters, clams or mussels. Waters uses champagne vinegar in her recipe; a good-quality white wine vinegar is an acceptable substitute. (*Note:* Food authority E. S. Dallas, in *Kettner's Book of the Table*, advises that mignonette is "white whole pepper, not ground." Dallas' definition notwithstanding, I recommend cracking it to increase its potency.)

To make mignonette sauce, simply combine the ingredients and serve in a small bowl as a dipping sauce.

OLD-STYLE MINT SAUCE

2 tablespoons fresh mint, finely chopped

1 tablespoon brown sugar

½ cup vinegar (any will do, but white wine or champagne vinegar is best)

This is a very old English recipe for a tart-sweet mint sauce, customarily served with lamb. Somehow, we Americans started substituting mint jelly in place of the mint sauce, a dubious substitution if there ever was one. The amounts of any or all of the three ingredients can be modified to suit your taste.

Put the ingredients in a small jar and cover with a lid. Shake the mixture well and let it stand at room temperature for at least an hour before using. This mint sauce will keep indefinitely in a refrigerator.

WHITE SAUCE

2 tablespoons butter

2 tablespoons all-purpose flour

1 cup milk

Salt and pepper (ground white pepper is preferred) to taste

A simple white sauce (known to the French as Béchamel) is so easy to make and can be transformed into so many different variations, it should be in every cook's arsenal. Classic variations include Velouté (substitute chicken stock for the milk to produce a poultry sauce); Mornay sauce (prepare as indicated below, but add ½ cup grated Parmesan cheese and a pinch of grated nutmeg — excellent on all types of vegetables, pasta and fish); and cheddar cheese sauce (stir ½ cup grated cheddar cheese into the finished white sauce while it's still hot).

Melt the butter in a heavy-bottomed 1½-quart saucepan over medium heat. Add the flour, one tablespoon at a time, stirring constantly with a wire whisk. (A wooden spoon will do in a pinch.) This mixture is known as a roux. It should immediately start to bubble up and thicken.

Stir constantly until the roux turns a light golden color. Once that has been achieved, (it will take approximately 4 to 5 minutes), immediately remove the saucepan from the heat. (If the roux is allowed to darken any further, it will affect the flavor of the sauce.) Gradually add the milk, stirring constantly. Return the pan to the heat and allow the mixture to come to a boil, whisking all the while. (It won't take long.) Add salt and pepper to taste.

Makes 1 cup of sauce.

Somehow, we Americans started substituting mint jelly for the English mint sauce — a dubious substitution if there ever was one.

COMPOUND BUTTERS
& BUTTER SAUCES

Using a compound butter is perhaps the easiest and most convenient method of seasoning grilled food. It may also be one of the most reliable. Butter brings out the best flavor of herbs and places them at your fingertips. Easily stored in a freezer, a slice or scoop can be brought out at any time to enhance the flavor of meat, fowl, fish, fruits or vegetables.

Compound butters can be flavored with a single herb or a combination of several, and any other flavoring you might desire. They can be weak or strong, depending upon your personal taste.

As a general rule for compound butters, use 2 to 4 tablespoons of fresh herb (or more, depending on the intensity of the herb), 3 teaspoons dried, or 1 teaspoon seed for each stick or ¼ pound of butter.

Allow the butter to come to room temperature. Add the dry or chopped fresh herb of your choice and any other flavorings to the butter and beat the butter with a fork or wire whisk to thoroughly mix. Allow to stand at room temperature for an hour or so (or in a refrigerator for at least 3 hours) for the flavors to mingle. If you're feeling fancy, the softened, flavored butter can be packed into molds, formed into balls, curls, or pats, or shaped with your hands into logs and then chilled.

To use, simply place a tablespoon or more directly on top of almost any meat or vegetable hot off the grill. Very simple and very delicious.

Herb butters are best stored frozen; otherwise, they begin to deteriorate within 24 to 36 hours.

The following recipes indicate a few possibilities of combining herbs and other ingredients with butter. The concept is so simple and open to so many variations, feel free to experiment.

Note: Any of the following compound butters can be transformed into "butter sauces" by simply melting them before pouring over the grilled food. Some people prefer it that way. The choice is up to you.

"Butter brings out the best flavor of herbs and places them at your fingertips."

Basil butter

Simple and delicious for all types of poultry, fish or vegetables, especially in midsummer, when basil is in all its glory.

Mix softened butter, basil, and garlic together well. Allow to stand for 1 hour at room temperature or 3 hours refrigerated. Use as is, or —

Sauté the basil and garlic in butter. Serve hot over any of the above suggestions.

1/4 cup butter

1/2 cup fresh basil, finely chopped

1 clove garlic, minced or pressed

Cilantro lime butter

Excellent on fish, shrimp, prawns or even pork chops.

Combine butter, garlic, cilantro, lime juice and freshly ground pepper. Mix well with a fork and use as a compound butter, or sauté the garlic in the butter and allow to cool slightly. Add the cilantro and lime juice. Mix well and use as a sauce.

1/4 cup butter

1 garlic clove, minced or pressed

1 tablespoon fresh cilantro, finely chopped

1 tablespoon fresh lime juice

Freshly ground pepper, to taste

Fine herbes butter

A good all-purpose compound butter, excellent with meat, fish and vegetables.

Combine all ingredients in a small bowl. Mix well with a fork. Serve at room temperature or melt and use as a sauce.

1/4 pound butter, softened

1 tablespoon fresh chives, chopped

1 tablespoon fresh tarragon, chopped

1 teaspoon dried leaf chervil

Garlic butter

Basic garlic butter varies, depending on how much you like garlic. A good way to start is with two or three cloves, minced or crushed, in three tablespoons of melted butter. Sauté over low heat for 1 to 2 minutes. If you like it strong, add more garlic cloves; if you like it weak, add less. It will intensify in flavor the longer you let it sit before using.

3 tablespoons butter, softened

2 to 3 garlic cloves, minced or pressed

Pour melted garlic butter directly over a variety of grilled foods or use to make garlic bread. It also combines well with other herbs and flavors, including lemon juice, fresh parsley, cilantro, basil, rosemary and tarragon.

LEMON BUTTER

1 tablespoon fresh lemon juice

¼ cup butter

1 tablespoon fresh parsley, chopped

Salt and pepper to taste

Excellent on grilled chicken breasts or any grilled fish.

Melt butter in a small saucepan. Add parsley. Remove from heat and let partially cool. Add lemon juice, salt and pepper to taste. Use warm as a sauce, or allow to cool completely before serving as a compound butter on top of hot grilled food.

NICOISE BUTTER

¼ pound butter

Juice of one lemon

2 garlic cloves, finely minced or pressed

4 (or more) anchovies

2 tablespoons fresh parsley, finely chopped

1 teaspoon freshly ground pepper

This intensely flavored butter is outstanding on swordfish, shark, or grilled shrimp.

Melt butter in a small saucepan. Add remaining ingredients, using a fork or spoon to mash the anchovy into unrecognizable bits. (Even people who say they hate anchovies will like this sauce, as long as they can't see them.) Use warm as a sauce, or allow to cool completely before serving as a compound butter on top of fish or shellfish hot off the grill.

TARRAGON BUTTER

½ cup butter, softened

2 medium shallots, finely chopped

2 tablespoons fresh parsley, finely chopped

2 teaspoons vinegar

1 tablespoons fresh tarragon, chopped

Excellent on grilled beef steaks and almost any type of poultry. Place butter in a small bowl. Mix all other ingredients in a blender or food processor. Combine herb mixture with butter and mix thoroughly with a fork. Shape into a log and refrigerate for 1 hour. Place a small slice of the tarragon butter on each steak. Alternately, after combining all the ingredients, melt and use as a sauce.

DRY RUBS

Dry rubs are comprised of a variety of dry seasonings, meant to be rubbed into the meat prior to grilling. Because they will not burn (as marinades that contain sugar, fruit or tomato), dry rubs are the favored method for flavoring any food that requires a long cooking time on the grill, such as brisket of beef and pork spareribs.

Dry rubs are the special pets of that specialized form of cooking over the coals known as *barbecue*. It's not unusual for years of experimentation to go into the creation of the "perfect" dry rub. Indeed, there are many annual competitions held across the country that award big prizes for the best barbecue chicken, ribs or what-have-you, with the secret to success almost always in the rub. More often than not, dry rubs have a Southwestern flair to them, with at least a hint of chili powder, cumin or paprika.

You can create a wonderfully herby crust on grilled food by using a dry marinade or paste. This can be as simple as dusting with powdered herbs, such as ground black pepper, paprika, cayenne or garlic powder, one layer over another (interestingly, this is the method preferred by two of the winningest members of barbecue contests, the Schroeger brothers). Or it can involve a mortar and pestle, an electric spice grinder or some other method of grinding the various dry ingredients into a uniform mixture. Some aficionados add a tablespoon of oil to a mixture of herbs and flavorings and vigorously rub the "paste" into the food. This works particularly well on large roasts, game and chicken.

"Grind all ingredients in an electric spice grinder or by hand with a mortar and pestle (this being the favored way, especially if the mortar is one of those heavy ceramic ones, with the grooves inside)."

Ingredients

There's something about creating a dry rub that brings out the alchemist in even the most level-headed of cooks. Faced with a long list of potential ingredients and infinite variations, most adults are immediately transported back to being a kid with their first chemistry set. If you recall how some of those experiments turned out … well, the same thing can happen with dry rubs. There's no real sense, however, in trying to hold anyone back; the perfect dry rub always seems to be just a half-teaspoon of paprika away.

To indicate the scope of the dry rub universe, the following list contains the most common dry rub ingredients, used in one combination or another:

allspice
basil
bay leaves, ground
black pepper
brown sugar
cardamom
cayenne
celery salt
chili powder
Chinese five-spice mixture
cinnamon
cloves, ground
coriander seed
cumin, ground
dark brown sugar
dry mustard
fennel seed, crushed
garlic salt
garlic powder
ginger, ground
granulated garlic
lemon peel, grated
lemon pepper
lemon powder
lemon salt
monosodium glutamate
nutmeg
onion powder
onion salt
oregano
paprika (hot or mild)
rosemary
salt
sugar
thyme
white pepper

If this list appears to contain everything from the herb and spice section of your local market, it just about does. While there are no hard-and-fast rules regarding the

"…the perfect dry rub always seems to be just a half-teaspoon of paprika away."

makeup of a dry rub, the following recipes will at least give you an idea of the proportions for a few successful combinations. After that, you're on your own.

BARBECUE-STYLE DRY RUB

If you've spent much time around barbecue restaurants, barbecue competitions, or even an accomplished backyard barbecuer, you know that using a dry rub prior to slow cooking, or barbecuing, any meat is the preferred way of flavoring the food. The ubiquitous barbecue sauce is for adding after the meat comes off the grill.

The dry rub presented here is a more-or-less traditional combination of flavors. By all means, feel free to adjust amounts, or add or subtract ingredients. To prepare the rub, simply mix all ingredients together. Store leftover in an airtight jar or in a freezer.

Rub the mixture into the meat (chicken, ribs or brisket), wrap tightly with plastic wrap and store in a refrigerator for 6 to 8 hours or overnight.

1 tablespoon black pepper, ground

2 teaspoons cayenne

2 tablespoons chili powder

2 tablespoons cumin

2 tablespoons dark brown sugar

1 tablespoon oregano, ground

4 tablespoons paprika

2 tablespoons salt

1 tablespoon sugar

1 tablespoon white pepper, ground

DR. EMBREY'S DRY RUB

Like most exemplary dry rubs, this recipe is the result of many years of experimentation. In fact, this is how Mr. Embrey became Dr. Embrey: After spending so much time in Kitchen Chemistry 101, Slippery Rock University felt compelled to recognize his efforts with an honorary degree. Not long after, Dr. Embrey won the Grand Championship at the prestigious American Royal Barbecue Cook-Off in Kansas City with this rub. It's inclusion in this book marks one of the first times anyone in the history of barbecue has willingly relinquished an award-winning dry rub recipe. Savor it.

Grind all ingredients in an electric spice grinder or by hand with a mortar and pestle (this being the favored way, especially if the mortar is one of those heavy ceramic ones, with the grooves inside). Mix the ground ingredients together well. Store in a glass or ceramic container with a tight-fitting lid. The rub will keep its potency for a month or so at room temperature; it will last indefinitely in a freezer.

3 tablespoons celery salt

6 tablespoons chili powder

1 tablespoon Chinese five-spice mixture

1 tablespoon dry mustard, (Coleman's preferred)

20 tablespoons dark brown sugar

3 tablespoons garlic powder

6 tablespoon lemon pepper (Durkee's preferred)

1 tablespoon Morton's Nature's Seasoning

2 tablespoons MSG

4 tablespoons paprika, mild

To use, rub the meat or poultry with the spice mixture — a little or a lot, depending on how strongly flavored you want the final outcome. If you're using poultry with the skin intact, consider pushing a little of the rub under the skin. Let the bird sit for a couple of hours at room temperature or 6 to 8 hours in a refrigerator before grilling.

❧

DRY RUB FOR LAMB OR PORK

1 teaspoon black pepper
¹/₂ teaspoon cayenne
2 teaspoons garlic powder
1 teaspoon oregano
1 tablespoon paprika, mild
2 teaspoons rosemary
¹/₂ teaspoon salt
¹/₂ teaspoon thyme
1 teaspoon white pepper

This dry rub is outstanding on lamb or pork, but with its lack of chili powder, is not in the barbecue style. For best results, coat the lamb or pork with a little olive oil, apply the rub, then tightly wrap the meat in plastic wrap and place it in a refrigerator overnight. If time is running short, apply the rub and simply allow the meat to sit at room temperature for 1 hour before grilling.

Crush thyme, oregano, and rosemary in a spice grinder or mortar or pestle. Combine with other ingredients and mix well. Makes enough for one or two cuts of meat, depending on size. To make more, multiply ingredients proportionately. Store leftover rub in airtight jar or keep in a freezer.

❧

NON-TRADITIONAL DRY RUB

4 tablespoons salt
6 tablespoons brown sugar
1 tablespoon dry lemon powder
2 tablespoons MSG
2¹/₂ tablespoons black pepper
1 tablespoon paprika, mild

When you're in the mood for ribs or brisket, but not necessarily in the "Smoky Joe," slow-cooked barbecue style, give this rub a try. If you use this recipe on ribs, pull the membrane off the back of the ribs before applying the rub. With either ribs or brisket, coat the meat with vegetable oil before adding the rub. Massage it in a little and tightly wrap the meat in plastic wrap. Store the meat in a refrigerator for 6 to 8 hours or, for maximum flavoring, overnight.

Grind all ingredients in an electric spice grinder or by hand with a mortar and pestle. Mix the ground ingredients together well. Store in a glass or ceramic container with a tight-fitting lid. The rub will keep its potency for a month or so at room temperature; it will last indefinitely in a freezer.

After applying the dry rub to any meat, allow to sit at room temperature for an hour or, better yet, wrap the food in plastic wrap, and store in the refrigerator for 6 to 8 hours or overnight.

CLASSIC SIDE DISHES

CLASSIC SIDE DISHES

What qualifies as a classic side dish to grilled food? Something as simple as possible. Grilling is cooking in its most elementary form. Complicated side dishes just don't belong on the same plate as grilled chops or a salmon steak.

The dishes described in this chapter are, not surprisingly, overwhelmingly of the carbohydrate type — rice, pasta, beans, potatoes and the like. Most can be prepared ahead of time, kept covered in the refrigerator, and slipped into the oven about the same time as you light the grill. This is an important consideration, especially if you're the chief cook and bottle-washer: Dividing your attention between the grill and the oven, not to mention the sink, requires skillful juggling. If fate has been kind and you have a partner who is willing and able to take over the kitchen responsibilities, count your blessings!

It seems to be a fact of life that most people who come by grilling naturally feel out of their element when standing in front of the stove. To that end, I have deliberately kept the list of side dishes short. Knowing how to make a half-dozen of these side dishes well — whether it's steamed rice, parslied new potatoes or pasta with fresh tomatoes — will probably be enough to see you through an entire lifetime of grilling.

The recipes in most cookbooks overlook that one important ingredient — confidence. And the easiest way to gain confidence, even if you'd rather be outdoors tending the grill, is simply to repeat a recipe over and over until success becomes second nature. The recipes that follow are of the "war-horse" variety: sturdy and reliable enough to withstand a long run; delicious enough to warrant repeat performance.

"BAKED" BASMATI RICE

1 cup basmati rice

1 teaspoon salt

Approximately 3 tablespoons of vegetable oil

A few threads saffron, pulverized between your thumb and forefinger

I'm crazy for this dish, but it may have something to do with a lifelong love of any food that's soft in the middle and crunchy at the edges. If you've never had basmati rice before, you're in for a real treat, whether you like crunchy crusts or not. With extra-long grains, a flowery, buttery aroma while being cooked and superior flavor and texture, basmati is well worth its extra cost. As delicious as it is simply boiled, following the directions that come with the rice, it is even better when prepared as follows:

1) Place the rice in a strainer and rinse it in cold water.

2) Put the rinsed rice in a saucepan, add salt and cover with 1 inch of water.

3) Bring rice to a boil over medium-high heat. Immediately lower the heat and allow rice to simmer, uncovered, until soft — about 15 to 20 minutes. Individual grains of rice, when bitten into, should not be chalky.

4) Strain the rice and rinse with cold water.

5) Coat the bottom and sides of a heavy skillet (a well-seasoned cast iron or heavy non-stick skillet work well) with oil and heat over medium heat. Once the skillet is warm, add the rice and sprinkle with saffron. Cover skillet with a clean towel; put a lid or a large plate over the towel. Reduce heat to low.

6) Cook the towel-covered rice for 20 to 25 minutes.

7) Remove the lid and the towel. Using a flexible spatula or knife, loosen the rice from the edges of the skillet. Invert a plate (an inch or so larger in diameter than the skillet) over the skillet and, holding the plate in place, turn the skillet upside down. Voilà! A lightly browned, big, wonderfully delicious rice cake. Serve immediately.

Serves 4.

Note: A hybrid between the Asian basmati and domestic long grain rice, called Texmati (having been developed in Texas) is now widely available. If you can't find basmati, Texmati can be substituted with excellent results.

BAKED POTATOES

There are few things better than a big, hot baked potato. Although they can be cooked directly in hot coals or wrapped in foil and cooked on the grill, both methods have their drawbacks for the true baked potato lover. Cooking directly in the coals eliminates the possibility of eating the potato skins, which many consider the best part. And wrapping potatoes in foil keeps too much moisture in the potato, keeping them from developing that fluffy, flaky interior — the hallmark of a well-baked potato.

The best way to bake a potato is the easiest. Preheat your oven to 375 degrees F. Scrub (with water and a scrub brush) as many brown-skinned baking potatoes (no other kind will do) as there are diners, and poke a few holes in each one with a fork or the tip of a sharp knife. The holes allow steam to escape and prevent the potatoes from exploding in your oven. If you forget to poke holes in the potatoes, and one or more happens to blow up in your oven, I guarantee it's a mistake you'll only make once — talk about a mess!

Put the potatoes in the oven and bake for at least one hour. If the hour is up before the rest of the meal is ready to serve, do not reduce the temperature in the oven. Doing so will cause the potatoes to start collapsing on themselves, ruining the flaky interior and steaming the crunchiness right out of the skins. Far better to just let the potatoes keep baking at 350 degrees F. until the meal is ready. Although it has been done, it's almost impossible to overcook a baked potato.

Serve with plenty of butter, sour cream, chives (or chopped green onions) and freshly ground black pepper. Eat the whole thing. Even the skins. Your mother would be proud of you.

As many baking potatoes as you care to cook

A working oven

*1 10-ounce package fresh or
frozen black-eyed peas*

1 small onion, minced

½ cup chicken stock

1 teaspoon chili powder

Salt and pepper to taste

Chopped fresh parsley

BLACK-EYED PEAS

Black-eyed peas have a distinctive, earthy taste. "Earthy" may not sound particularly appealing, but I think it's apt. However black-eyed peas are described, there *is* something about the characteristic flavor of black-eyed peas that complements most grilled foods. This fact is borne out by the unlikely pairing of a grilled fillet of salmon and black-eyed peas, as offered at an equally unlikely eatery — namely, the Grill Room at the Ritz Hotel in Kansas City. Layer upon layer of anomaly aside, salmon and black-eyed peas go together beautifully.

Black-eyed peas are available dried, frozen and "fresh". (Actually they're reconstituted dried black-eyeds.) Reconstituted or frozen black-eyed peas can be prepared quite simply: Sauté the onion in butter over medium heat until soft but not brown. Add the fresh or frozen black-eyed peas, chicken stock and chili powder. Continue to cook over medium heat until peas are just tender, about 15 minutes. Add salt and pepper to taste. Garnish with chopped fresh parsley.

Serves 4 as a side dish.

BLACK-EYED PEAS FOR A CROWD

If you're cooking for a crowd (like on New Year's Day, when the humble black-eyed pea takes on magical properties of good luck for the coming year) or watching your budget — or both — opt for dried black-eyed peas. A pound of dried black-eyed peas will serve 6 to 8 people as a side dish and cost less than a dollar.

This recipe produces a heartier dish than the preceding recipe for black-eyed peas.

1) Rinse the black-eyed peas, pour them into a 3-quart saucepan and cover with 2 inches of water. Bring to a rapid boil for 2 minutes. Remove from heat and let stand for 1 hour. Drain.

2) Sauté the onions in vegetable oil (in a large pot) until they're soft but not brown. Add bay leaf, peppercorns, chili powder, cumin, optional ham hock and drained peas.

3) Add enough chicken stock to cover the black-eyed peas by 1 inch.

4) Cover the pot, cocking the lid slightly to allow some of the moisture to escape. Bring to a boil, then lower heat to a simmer. Cook for 1 to 1½ hours or until the black-eyed peas are tender. If you've added the ham hock, cut the meat off the bone and add it back to the beans. Add salt to taste.

5) Serve with chopped parsley or fresh cilantro and whatever hot sauce suits your fancy.

Serves a lot.

1 pound dried black-eyed peas

2 medium onions, finely chopped

3 tablespoons vegetable oil

1 large bay leaf

6 whole peppercorns

2 to 3 tablespoons chili powder

1 tablespoon ground cumin

3 cups chicken stock

1 smoked ham hock (cut into 1-inch pieces), optional

For garnish: Chopped fresh parsley or cilantro

BOILED NEW POTATOES

New potatoes
Butter
Chopped fresh dill

Talk about a classic dish! Boiled new potatoes, tender and steaming, served with nothing more than a little butter and chopped dill, can be found in just about every old-fashioned grill restaurant in this country and in Europe. The little ones (about the size of a pullet egg) are considered first choice; the larger new potatoes may not be quite as attractive on a plate, but they're still great eating. If you'd like to try your hand at growing your own new potatoes, see page 203 for more information.

Wash and scrub the new potatoes under cold water, but do not peel. Put them in a pot and cover with 2 inches of water. Add 1 teaspoon of salt per quart of water and bring it to a boil. Cook the potatoes until it's possible to easily insert a sharp knife to the center. The length of time it takes will depend on the size of the potatoes: 3-inch diameter potatoes will take 20 to 25 minutes. Drain and toss with as much butter and chopped fresh dill as you like. Serve hot.

COLD RICE AND PEA SALAD

4 cups cooked rice(preferably warm)
½ cup mayonnaise
3 tablespoons Dijon mustard
¼ cup olive oil
2 tablespoons red or white wine vinegar
1 tablespoon curry powder (optional)
1 package frozen peas, cooked (petitie or baby peas are best)
½ cup finely chopped green onion
Salt and pepper to taste

Cold rice salads used to be quite popular. As these things go, they went, replaced, I think, with pasta salads. Although a cold rice salad can be made with leftover *cold* rice, it is better to combine all ingredients while the rice is still hot and refrigerate the salad.

Mix mayonnaise, mustard, olive oil, vinegar and optional curry powder. Combine this mixture with hot or cold rice. Taste and correct seasoning with salt and pepper. If the rice seems a little dry, make a little more "sauce" and add it in. Gently mix the peas and green onions into the rice. Chill and serve straight from the bowl. Or, if you're feeling fancy, lightly oil a bowl, press the rice salad into it, chill for 2 or more hours, and then turn the salad upside down onto a bed of lettuce. Sure to impress even the hard-to-impress.

Serves 4 to 6.

COLESLAW

The cumin in this coleslaw was inspired by a recipe from Julia Child. It was a great recipe that somehow became lost in a succession of moves from one house to another. The recipe may have been lost, but cumin in coleslaw has lived on. For some reason, this dish pairs up nicely with the black-eyed peas on pages 318 and 319, especially if you happen to be cooking up some hot links on the grill and a loaf of cornbread in the oven. Omit the cumin if you don't like its flavor.

Combine first eight ingredients (lowfat substitutes work fine) in a large bowl and mix well. Taste and adjust accordingly. Add in parsley, green onion, bell pepper and grated apple. (Quarter and core the apple but don't peel it before grating. This will help prevent the skin of your fingers from becoming part of the salad.) Add the shredded cabbage and mix thoroughly. Chill for at least 1 hour before serving.

Serves 6 to 8.

1 teaspoon ground cumin

1 teaspoon salt

1 tablespoon Dijon mustard

Juice of half a lemon

3 tablespoons vinegar (any variety)

1/3 cup sour cream

1/3 cup plain yogurt

1/2 cup mayonnaise

1/4 cup parsley, chopped

1 tart green apple (like 'Granny Smith'), grated

1 bunch green onions, chopped

2 bell peppers, diced

3 cups green cabbage, finely chopped

3 cups purple cabbage, finely chopped

❦

COWBOY BEANS

This is a great side dish for grilled sausages, brisket or a thick steak cut into thin slices. Team up with some warm cornbread and a big bowl of coleslaw and you've got the makings of a great party. If only whole ham hocks are available, ask the butcher to run it through a band saw, cutting it into 1-inch slices; this makes it easier to remove the meat from the bones after it's been cooked.

1) Rinse the beans. Pour them into a large pot and cover with 2 inches of water. Bring to a boil, then simmer for 2 minutes. Remove the beans from the heat, cover and let them stand for 1 hour. Drain.

2) Sauté onions and garlic in bacon grease or oil (in the large pot) until soft but not browned.

3) Add the beans to the onions and garlic, then add the remaining ingredients (do not drain the tomatoes). Stir the mixture and bring it to a boil. Reduce heat to a

1 pound dry pinto beans

3 tablespoons bacon grease or vegetable oil

2 onions, finely chopped

3 cloves garlic, minced or pressed

1 12-ounce bottle of beer

1 14 1/2-ounce can of chicken stock

1 pound smoked ham hocks, cut into 1-inch pieces

1 28-ounce can diced tomatoes

2 to 3 tablespoons chili powder

1 tablespoon ground cumin

1 teaspoon oregano

2 bay leaves

8 whole black peppercorns

simmer. Cover the pot and cook for 1 to 2 hours, until beans are soft but not mushy. Add additional beer or chicken stock, if necessary.

4) When beans are soft, remove ham hocks. Cut meat from the bones into bite-sized pieces. Return meat to the pot; discard bones.

5) Although condiments take these beans out of the cowboy category, serve with sour cream, your favorite salsa and chopped fresh cilantro, if desired.

CREAMED SPINACH

This is an old-fashioned dish, still popular in old-fashioned grill restaurants in San Francisco, where an old-fashioned clientele still knows what's good for them. Absolutely first-rate served with hot-off-the-grill salmon, swordfish or halibut.

Note: The best way to drain cooked spinach is to place it between two dinner plates and, holding them sideways over the sink, squeeze the heck out of the plates. This works like a charm.

2 packages frozen chopped spinach

2 tablespoons butter or margarine

2 tablespoons all-purpose flour

1 cup half-and-half (light cream)

1/2 teaspoon dry mustard

1/2 teaspoon salt

1/8 teaspoon nutmeg

1) Cook the frozen spinach according to package directions. Drain well, using the method described above. Set spinach aside.

2) Melt butter in a heavy-bottomed saucepan over medium heat. Add flour, 1 tablespoon at a time, stirring constantly with a wooden spoon or wire whisk. Cook for 2 to 3 minutes, but do not allow the mixture to brown.

3) Add the half-and-half to the butter and flour. Continue to stir over medium heat until the sauce boils and thickens. Raise the heat slightly, if necessary. Add salt, dry mustard and nutmeg. Mix well.

4) Add spinach to cream sauce. Mix well and serve hot.

Serves 4 to 6.

GALETTE OF POTATOES

The French name for this dish, *Galette de Pommes de Terre*, is impressive and perhaps a little intimidating. This is, indeed, a dish that will impress whomever you serve it to, but by all means don't be intimidated by it. A galette of potatoes is rustic, farmhouse cooking at its best and there's no need to fret over it.

1) Wash and peel the potatoes, then slice them into ³⁄₁₆-inch slices, as evenly as possible. Put them in a bowl of cold water until you're ready for the next step (or the potatoes will turn brown).

2) Heat the butter and oil in a large heavy skillet, one with a lid. Add the garlic and cook for 30 seconds. Drain and dry the potato slices on paper towels. Add the potato slices to the pan, arranging them in overlapping, concentric circles. Sprinkle each layer with a little of the tarragon, if desired. When all the potatoes have been arranged in the pan, press them down firmly with a lid or plate that fits inside the pan. The object is to get them to hold together a bit.

3) Cover the pan and cook over medium heat for 5 minutes. Remove the lid and continue cooking for 15 minutes or so, but adjust heat if you think the potatoes on the bottom are going from brown to burned.

4) Place a plate (one that's larger than the skillet by at least a couple of inches) over the skillet, hold it in place, and turn the potatoes upside down. Add 1 tablespoon of butter to the skillet. Ease the potatoes back into the skillet to brown the other side of the "cake." Cook for 15 minutes over medium heat.

Note: Flipping the potatoes takes a bit of finesse; the skillet is heavy and hot. It helps to loosen the potatoes with a spatula or knife before flipping.

5) Flip the galette onto its serving plate (using the same method as in step 4), sprinkle with chopped parsley and serve immediately.

Serves 4.

4 large baking potatoes (with brown or white skins)

3 tablespoons olive or vegetable oil

3 tablespoons butter

3 or 4 cloves garlic, minced

4 tablespoons chopped fresh tarragon (optional)

Salt and pepper to taste

Chopped fresh parsley

GARLIC MASHED POTATOES

The addition of garlic to mashed potatoes causes some people to go into paroxysms of delight. The procedure can be as simple as pressing as many cloves of fresh garlic into the potatoes as you mash them (see mashed potatoes, page 324). If that's too easy, gently sauté whole, peeled garlic cloves in butter until they fall apart, then press them through a sieve. Add the sieved garlic to the potatoes as you are mashing them. Sautéing the garlic results in a more kind and gentle version of this dish, but still plenty distinctive. If you want to remain on speaking terms with everyone throughout the evening, make sure that they, too, eat their potatoes.

HOMINY "SOUFFLÉ"

This is nothing like the fragile soufflés to which you may be accustomed. This is a sturdy dish, one that's just right for serving with ham or pork.

4 tablespoons butter

¼ cup all-purpose flour

1 cup hot milk (heat, but don't boil)

Pinch of cayenne (or 4 shakes Tabasco Sauce)

1 cup cheddar cheese, grated (aged, sharp cheddar is best)

4 eggs, well beaten

1 15½-ounce can hominy (white, yellow, or golden), drained

1 to 2 tablespoons butter or margarine for baking dish

1 4-ounce can diced green chilies (optional)

1) Preheat oven to 375 degrees F.

2) Melt 4 tablespoons butter in a heavy-bottomed saucepan over medium-high heat. Using a wooden spoon or wire whisk, stir in the flour and blend until smooth — about 2 or 3 minutes.

3) Slowly add the hot milk to the butter and flour mixture, stirring constantly. Continue to stir for 2 to 3 minutes until the mixture is thick and smooth. Add cayenne or Tabasco, cheese, hominy and optional chili peppers. Stir until the cheese has melted.

4) Remove the mixture from the heat and allow it to cool for 5 minutes or so. While it's cooling, beat the eggs.

5) Take about ¼ cup of the cooled hominy mixture and add it to the beaten eggs. After stirring, return the hominy and eggs to the saucepan; mix well.

6) Grease an ovenproof bowl or baking dish with butter

or margarine and dust it with cornmeal. Pour the hominy mixture into the baking dish and bake for 40 to 45 minutes, until the "soufflé" has set. Serve hot from the oven.

Serves 4.

HOME-ALONE BEANS

When you're home alone, the object of preparing dinner should be to make something so good that you won't start whining about being alone. A tasty bowl of beans is usually the last thing the single diner thinks about preparing, simply because most recipes for beans produce enough for a battalion or two. This recipe, such that it is, makes just enough for those occasions when you find yourself home alone. Eat them too often, and you may be home alone a lot. Excellent with any leftover grilled meat, or as a fast side dish.

Note: If canned Ro-Tel Diced Tomatoes and Green Chilies are not available where you live, think about moving or write to Ro-Tel directly and tell them to get on the stick.

1) Pour the beans into a sieve or colander. Rinse under cold water.

2) Put rinsed beans, Ro-Tel Diced Tomatoes and Green Chilies, chili powder and cumin into a saucepan.

3) Bring beans to a boil. Reduce to a simmer and allow the beans to cook for 30 minutes or so. Stir every once in a while.

Absolutely delicious served with steamed rice (page 337), a big dollop of confetti salsa (page 301) and any leftover skewered tidbits from grill.

Serves 1 as a main course; 2 as a side dish.

1 16-ounce can of your favorite type of beans (pinto, black, white, you name it)

1 10-ounce can Ro-Tel Diced Tomatoes and Green Chilies

1 tablespoon chili powder

1 to 2 teaspoons ground cumin

ITALIAN WHITE BEAN SALAD

1 16-ounce package dried small white or navy beans

2 bay leaves

1 large onion, stuck with two whole cloves

3 cloves garlic, skinned and flattened

8 whole black peppercorns

4 medium, ripe tomatoes, diced

1 cup of fresh parsley, chopped

Vinaigrette dressing (see page 71)

Salt and pepper to taste

Whole lettuce leaves (preferably butter or romaine)

Sliced tomatoes

This is an excellent dish for a summer buffet. Serve with cold grilled chicken, thin slices off a thick beef steak or pork loin. Although it may sound a little strange, in Italy these beans are often paired up with canned tuna (use an expensive tuna, packed in oil, for this variation) and served as a main course. Simply chill both the beans and the tuna. At serving time, spread the tuna in big chunks over the beans. Don't knock it 'til you've tried it — it's delicious.

1) Rinse the beans in cold water. Place the beans, onion stuck with cloves, bay leaves, garlic and peppercorns in a 3-quart saucepan and cover with 2 inches of water.

2) Bring to a rapid boil for 2 minutes. Remove the mixture from the heat and let it stand for 1 hour.

3) Return the beans to the heat and bring them to a boil. Reduce heat and let beans simmer for 1 to 1½ hours, until they are tender but not mushy.

4) Drain beans. While they're still hot, place them in a bowl with chopped tomatoes and parsley. Add vinaigrette and mix well. Cover and chill in refrigerator. Just before serving, mix again. Add additional vinaigrette if needed and salt and pepper to taste.

5) Line a bowl with whole lettuce leaves. Place bean salad on top of leaves and surround with thick slices of vine-ripened tomatoes. Benissimo!

Serves 8 as a side dish.

MARINATED CUCUMBERS

Marinated cucumbers go well with almost any grilled fish. They're good as a side dish or as a substitute for a green salad. Best if they're made the night before you intend to serve them. The seedless, hothouse type is preferred, but the garden variety will do just fine.

1) In a saucepan, combine water, vinegar, salt and sugar. Bring to a boil, stir for 2 minutes and remove from heat.

2) Peel cucumbers. While they are still whole, score the entire length of the cucumbers with the tines of a fork. Although it's not necessary, it gives the individual cucumber slices a decorative pattern at the edges. Slice thinly, about ⅛-inch thick, and place the cucumbers in a bowl.

3) While still hot, pour the vinegar and water solution over the cucumber slices. Add the parsley or dill and stir. Cover and chill in a refrigerator.

Serves 4 to 6.

2 cucumbers, peeled and sliced

⅔ cup white vinegar

⅔ cup water

1 teaspoon salt

½ teaspoon sugar

¼ cup chopped fresh parsley or dill

MASHED POTATOES

True comfort food and the perfect thing to serve with any roast meat or poultry. The secret to mashed potatoes is to use good, mealy potatoes (large brown-skinned ones, not the smaller new potatoes) and to cook them thoroughly before mashing. Count on one large potato per person; more if there are a large number of kids around the table.

1) Choose a pot that will hold as many potatoes as you plan to cook with a little room left over. Fill the pot about half full with water. Peel the potatoes, removing out any dark spots. Cut them into halves or quarters and immediately plop them into the pan of water. (Peeled potatoes will darken quickly when exposed to air.)

2) When the potatoes have been added to the pot, there

6 large brown- or white-skinned baking potatoes

¾ cup milk

4 to 6 tablespoons butter or margarine

Salt and pepper to taste

should be about 1 inch of water covering the top layer. Bring the water and potatoes to a boil. Lower the heat slightly, and cook until the potatoes are very tender. This could take from 15 to 30 minutes. You'll know that the potatoes have reached the desired state of tenderness when they pierce easily with the tip of a sharp knife or fork, practically breaking apart. Drain the potatoes completely and return them to the pan.

3) While the potatoes are boiling, combine milk and butter in a small pan and heat, but don't boil. Add about half the hot milk and butter mixture to the drained potatoes and start mashing the daylights out of them. An old-fashioned, hand-held potato masher works great for this, especially if you're in a vengeful mood. Most electric appliances and mixers over-whip the potatoes, producing less-than-desirable results. Keep mashing, adding more of the hot milk and butter mixture, until they've reached the consistency you desire.

4) Season with salt and pepper to taste. If you don't want any black specks in your mashed potatoes, use finely ground white pepper. Serve the mashed potatoes hot from the pan, or put on a hot platter, cover with foil and place in a warm oven until you're ready to serve them.

Serves 4 to 6.

PASTA

Any pasta served as a side dish to grilled food should be kept as simple as possible. As a rule, I tend to stay away from cream sauces, simply because they create a pasta too rich to qualify as a side dish — at least in this era of endless calorie-counting.

If you cross off cream and butter from the list of ingredients, dried pasta is the type of pasta you want to buy. Fresh pasta, as tantalizing as it may appear, is traditionally used only with cream and butter sauces. Dried pasta, on the other hand, is usually moistened with olive oil, a broth or a sauce made from cooked or raw tomatoes. Additional ingredients — all types of vegetables, garlic, chopped fresh herbs and, of course, freshly grated Parmesan — can be added, according to a recipe or the whim of the cook. Unless you're really starved for protein, omit meat (whether it's shellfish, sausage or poultry) from any pasta served as a side dish.

Although I know it offends purists, instead of matching the right shape of pasta to the right type of sauce, I simply use whatever pasta happens to be handy, be it spaghetti, vermicelli, ziti, penne or elbow macaroni. In Italy, where they take these matters seriously, such a cavalier attitude might result in a kitchen arrest. So far, however, these mix-and-match efforts haven't offended any of the clientele that regularly gathers around my kitchen table, but I could be in trouble once they graduate from grammar school...

Here's a few tips for whipping up a fast pasta side dish. No matter how much pasta you're cooking, cook it in a lot of water — more than what you may think is necessary. Follow the directions given on the pasta package; different types have surprisingly different cooking times. While the pasta is cooking, pour a couple of tablespoons of good-quality olive oil into a large, oven-proof bowl and slip it into a 250-degree F. oven. Chop up whatever it is that you're going to toss with the cooked pasta. Following are a few favorites:

a) A lot of chopped fresh parsley or basil, garlic, freshly ground black pepper and a little olive oil. Top with freshly grated Parmesan. Couldn't be any simpler, or more delicious. Great with grilled poultry of any type.

b) Fresh, chopped, vine-ripened tomatoes, garlic and chopped fresh basil. Top with freshly grated Parmesan, or not, as you wish. Good with thin slices of grilled beef.

c) Thin slices of lightly sautéed zucchini, chopped parsley, a little fresh lemon juice and olive oil. Excellent with grilled fish.

d) Chopped fresh spinach, sliced black olives and a little hot chicken broth. Add the spinach and olives to the hot pasta. Pour just enough hot chicken stock to wilt the spinach and moisten the pasta. Toss. Top with freshly grated Parmesan cheese. Good with almost anything.

e) Chopped shallots, chopped fresh vine-ripened tomatoes, salt and pepper, and a pinch (or two or three) of freshly grated orange rind. Sauté the chopped shallots in a little olive until soft, then add the chopped tomatoes. Simmer until the tomatoes are soft and have lost some of their moisture. Salt and pepper to taste. Add grated orange rind, pinch by pinch, until just a hint of its presence can be detected. Mix with cooked pasta and top with chopped fresh parsley. So good, you may forget about the entrée!

In Italy, pasta is rarely served any other way than hot off the stove. In fact, it's more or less standard procedure to wait until everyone is sitting around the table before putting the pasta into the pot. Here again, I've relaxed the procedure and often serve any of the above simple pastas at room temperature, especially if the entrée is also at room temperature. This is a relaxed way of cooking, just right for the dog days of summer.

POLENTA WITH PARMESAN

7 cups water

1 tablespoon salt

2 cups coarsely ground polenta cornmeal

1 stick butter, cut into cubes

¹/₂ cup Parmesan cheese, grated

There's no middle ground when it comes to polenta — people either love it or they can't stand it. Basically an Italian version of cornmeal mush, polenta is just the thing when nothing but an industrial-strength load of carbohydrates will do. Which is not to say polenta can't be elegant. As far as I'm concerned, when polenta is paired with grilled quail, the combination goes off the culinary charts into some rarefied realm.

Like its Italian cousin, risotto, polenta needs the proper ingredients to be the real thing. In this case, regular cornmeal won't do; it's too fine. It's the coarser cornmeal ground for polenta that you want. And while you're at it, don't skimp on the Parmesan. Look for Regianno, if you can find it, or some other imported Parmesan of exceptional quality and flavor.

1) Bring salted water to a boil in a large pot — one with a handle you can grip comfortably. (You're going to be gripping it for about 20 minutes, so you might as well be comfortable.)

2) Reduce heat to the point where water is at a low boil. Add the cornmeal, one handful at a time, letting it slowly escape through your fingers. Keep stirring, stirring, stirring, adding the cornmeal one handful after another, until it is used up.

3) Stir until polenta starts to pull away from the sides of the pot. Add butter and parmesan cheese. Stir until blended. Pour onto a hot platter and serve it forth.

Note: In some Italian groceries, you'll find "Instant Polenta," which cooks up in a matter of minutes. It's more expensive than regular polenta, but certainly a lot easier to make and every bit as good.

Serves 4.

POMMES FRITES

French-fried potatoes, or *pommes frites,* as the French call them, are delicious with almost any grilled fare — especially steaks, chops and fish. Double-frying is the secret to achieving the best results.

Approximately 1 large baking potato per person, peeled

4 cups vegetable oil

Salt to tasate

1) Wash and scrub the potatoes in cold water, but do not peel.

2) Use a sharp knife to cut the potatoes into uniform, ⅜-inch square sticks, 3 to 4 inches long, or use a food processor.

3) In a deep, heavy pan, heat at least 4 cups of oil (peanut oil is excellent) to 300 degrees F. Add potatoes, in approximately three even batches, and cook for 4 to 5 minutes each. Use a long-handled fork to keep the potatoes from sticking together as they cook. The goal is to partially cook or soften the potatoes; not brown them.

4) After 4 or 5 minutes, remove the potatoes with a slotted spoon and place them on a cookie sheet that's lined with several thicknesses of paper toweling. At this point the potatoes can be held at room temperature

for 3 or 4 hours, or overnight, loosely covered in a refrigerator.

5) At serving time, reheat the oil — this time to 375 degrees F. Divide the partially cooked fries into three even batches and fry each for approximately 3 minutes or until they turn a light golden-brown. Remove the potatoes from the oil with a slotted spoon, drain them on paper toweling, and pour them into a basket. Sprinkle with salt to taste.

Serves 4.

❧

RATATOUILLE

One of the true pleasures of summer, this melange of vegetables from Provence can be cooked on top of the stove, in the oven or on the grill. The following procedure calls for grilling the vegetables on skewers, a process that gives the ratatouille a rustic, authentic flavor. The amounts given for the various vegetables are approximate; feel free to adjust up or down, depending on your mood or what's available from your garden.

Note: Eggplant is known for its ability to soak up vast quantities of olive oil when sautéed; grilled eggplant, however, requires only a brushing of oil to turn out tender and perfect.

1 large eggplant, peeled and cut into 1-inch cubes

1 medium onion, cut into quarters

3 zucchini (or any other summer squash) cut into ½-inch rounds

2 bell peppers, cut into strips about 1-inch-wide

12 paste or "plum" tomatoes (or 18 cherry tomatoes)

½ cup good-quality olive oil

3 to 4 cloves garlic, minced

½ teaspoon oregano

1 or 2 tablespoons fresh basil, chopped

Salt and freshly ground pepper to taste

1) Place eggplant, onion, bell pepper and tomatoes each on their own skewers. Brush liberally with olive oil.

2) Grill the skewered vegetables directly over moderate to hot coals. Turn frequently to avoid charring. A refined, if unorthodox, method for grilling different vegetables simultaneously involves layering them: Put the most dense — peppers, onions and squash — directly on the grill with the softer vegetables — tomatoes and eggplant — layered on top. When it comes time to turn each skewer, this method requires a little "backing and forthing," but the results will be perfect. Remove the vegetables from the grill as they begin to soften, but while they still have some "tooth" to them.

3) As each type of vegetable is done, slide the pieces off

the skewers into a large bowl. Halve or quarter the tomatoes before mixing them with the other vegetables. Season with olive oil, lemon juice, garlic, oregano, basil, salt and freshly ground pepper to taste. Toss lightly.

4) Serve immediately, or cover and refrigerate. This dish actually tastes better the day after it has been assembled, so you might want to plan ahead. Serve cold or at room temperature.

Serves 6 to 8.

RISOTTO

If the only place you've ever had risotto is in a restaurant, do yourself a favor — try making it at home. To my mind, risotto is one of those homey, comfort foods not meant to be prepared in public (at least not in America). Be advised, however: Risotto is so good, it can become addictive.

What makes risotto, *risotto* — creamy, tender and delicious — is the rice itself. Risotto, despite what some people may claim, must be made with a unique, almost round, short-grain rice from Italy. The only rice exported to this country for making risotto is Arborio; in Italy they have a choice of Arborio, Canaroli, Nano or Vialone. The secret of these plump little grains of rice from northern Italy is that they contain sufficient starch to absorb large quantities of liquid, which in turn results in risotto's characteristic creaminess.

The traditional process for making risotto is somewhat long, laborious and tricky. It requires attention and patience — hallmarks not usually associated with American home cooks. The American need for speed can be ameliorated by pouring yourself a glass of wine, finding someone to talk to, and by thinking of all the upper body exercise you're getting as you stir, stir, stir. As far as being tricky, it's trying to find that one heavy pot and that particular setting on the stove that causes most people problems. Once found, you'll be well on your way to producing consistently successful results.

The following instructions for a simple, basic risotto

2 tablespoons butter

1 small onion, peeled and minced

1 cup Arborio rice, rinsed

⅓ cup dry white wine

4 to 5 cups hot chicken broth

Salt and pepper to taste

½ cup heavy cream (optional)

2 tablespoons butter (optional)

3 to 4 tablespoons Parmesan cheese (optional)

are from Select Origins (Box N, Southhampton, NY 11968), an importer of Arborio rice. If you have problems finding Arborio rice in your area, drop them a line and they'll fix you up. Once you master this recipe, you will be able to improvise by adding any number of ingredients — from artichokes to chicken livers — although the simpler the better, as far as I'm concerned.

1) Melt butter in a heavy 3-quart enamel saucepan. Add onion and sauté over low heat for 3 to 4 minutes until they're very soft but not browned.

2) Add rice and blend with onion mixture. Add wine and cook over moderately high heat until wine is completely evaporated.

3) Start adding the broth ½ cup at a time, stirring. Keep heat moderately high so the rice absorbs the liquid but does not dry out too quickly. Continue adding the broth ½ cup at a time as the liquid is absorbed.

4) After about 20 minutes, start adding broth ¼ cup at a time. If rice is still partly chewy, partially cover the saucepan and let the rice cook a little more slowly, letting it absorb the liquid. Keep an eye on it. The result must be a creamy mass with a kernel that is soft but still chewy.

5) When the rice is done, taste and season carefully with salt and pepper. Add the optional cream and butter. Stir well. Cook another 2 to 3 minutes, or until cream is well-absorbed.

6) Add the optional Parmesan and stir to blend. Transfer the rice to a hot serving dish and garnish with a sprinkling of chopped parsley.

Serves 4 to 6.

Note: You may not need the entire amount of broth indicated; it all depends on the degree of heat at which you're cooking the risotto. Risotto that is partially covered halfway through the cooking time will absorb much less stock (sometimes no more than 2 to 3 cups). Although at its best when served immediately, risotto can be kept warm in the top of a double-boiler, over hot but not boiling water, for about 1 hour.

This is the way we've made risotto in our house for many years. Because it made us slow down and wallow around in some kind of anticipatory delight, we came to enjoy the process as much as the results — the equivalent of culinary foreplay. I suspect this because when a fantastically simple and speedy alternative came along, it met with a lot of resistance around here. In the interest of research, we finally gave it a try, and, well, it works beautifully. What's lost in the anticipatory department is gained in frequency: The following method for preparing risotto in a pressure cooker (reprinted with permission from Lorna Sass's wonderful book, *Cooking Under Pressure)*, is so easy we now use it every time.

Risotto with Gruyere and Parmesan

Heat the butter and oil in the [pressure cooker]. Sauté the onion until soft but not brown, about 2 minutes. Stir in the rice, making sure to coat it thoroughly with fat. Stir in 3½ cups of the stock. (Watch for sputtering oil.)

Lock the lid in place, over high heat, and bring to high pressure. Adjust the heat to maintain high pressure and cook for 6 minutes. Reduce pressure with a quick-release method [consult manufacturer's instructions]. Remove the lid, tilting it away from you to allow any excess steam to escape.

Taste the rice, and if it's not sufficiently cooked, add a bit more stock as you stir. Cook over medium heat until the additional liquid has been absorbed and the rice is desired consistency, another minute or two. When the rice is ready, stir in the Gruyere and Parmesan, and add salt to taste. Serve immediately.

Serves 4 to 6.

❦

2 tablespoons butter

1 tablespoon olive oil

⅓ cup finely minced onions

1½ cups Arborio rice

3½ to 4 cups vegetable or chicken stock or bouillon

1 cup grated Gruyere cheese (4 ounces)

¼ cup grated Parmesan cheese

Salt to taste, if desired

SAUERKRAUT AND POTATO CASSEROLE

4 slices bacon

3 or 4 good-sized potatoes, peeled and cut into ¼-inch-thick pieces

1 27-ounce can sauerkraut, drained and rinsed

1 large apple, grated

¾ cup beer or chicken stock (or half of each)

1 tablespoon caraway seeds or juniper berries, crushed

Freshly ground pepper to taste

4 tablespoons butter

This is a hearty side dish, best served when it's cold and blowing outside. Great with any type of grilled pork, ham or sausages. Rinse the sauerkraut after draining if a less salty dish is desired.

1) Preheat the oven to 350 degrees F.

2) Cook slices of bacon. Set strips aside and use the rendered grease to coat a baking dish or casserole.

3) Combine the potato slices, sauerkraut, grated apple, beer or chicken stock, pepper and caraway seeds or juniper berries. Lightly toss.

4) Pour the mixture into the baking dish. Dot it with 4 tablespoons of butter and cover the dish with foil. Bake for 60 minutes, or until the potatoes are soft.

Serves 4 to 6.

SAUTÉED PEAS WITH LETTUCE

1 10-ounce package frozen green peas

2 tablespoons butter or margarine

2 cups shredded iceberg lettuce

4 tablespoons parlsey, finely chopped

½ teaspoon sugar

A few grains of nutmeg (less than ⅛ teaspoon)

Salt, to taste

The first time I saw a recipe for green peas sautéed with lettuce I thought someone had made a mistake: Lettuce is for salads, not for cooking. Just to make sure, I gave it a try. Ever since, peas have never been cooked any other way around here. Even people who supposedly hate peas like these. Just don't overcook the peas; they should still be bright green when served. If you can find them, buy the little baby peas, or *petit pois,* as the French say.

1) Melt the butter in a frying pan over medium-high heat. Add the lettuce while the butter is still bubbling and sauté for a minute or two. Add frozen peas, parsley, sugar, nutmeg and a dash of salt.

2) Reduce heat to medium, cover and cook for 6 to 8 minutes, just until the peas are tender and hot.

Serves 4.

STEAMED RICE

The pleasing blandness of steamed rice is the perfect accompaniment to spicy Asian, Caribbean and Mexican grilled food. It is also one of the few things that actually helps alleviate the pain should you accidentally overdose on exceedingly hot peppers. (Water does not.)

Long-grain rice is what most Americans visualize when they think of steamed rice — dry, fluffy and tender. Short-grain rice, which is chewier and stickier, is favored by most cooks from Asia and the Southern hemisphere. The choice is up to you.

For the record, there is nothing easier to cook than a pot of steamed rice. When in doubt, follow the directions given on the package. Most packagers and cookbooks claim that 1 cup of uncooked rice will provide enough steamed rice for six people. For those cutting back on meat, rice can go a long way in filling the gap. In these situations, count on one cup of uncooked rice feeding three or four people.

Bring water, salt and optional butter to a boil in a heavy-bottomed saucepan (2-quart capacity or larger) — one with a snug-fitting lid. Add the rice, stir, and allow to return to a boil. Cover the pan and reduce the heat to low. Allow the rice to cook, covered, for 15 minutes. Remove from heat. Leave the lid on and allow the rice to steam for an additional 5 minutes before serving. Fluff rice before serving using a two-pronged fork; using anything else, including a regular fork or a spoon, will probably result in sticky, mashed rice.

1 cup uncooked rice

2 cups water

1 teaspoon salt (optional)

1 tablespoon butter or margarine (optional)

STEAMED PARSLIED RICE

Use the directions given above for Steamed Rice, adding ¼ cup finely chopped parsley when fluffing the rice.

1 cup wild rice

3 cups chicken stock (or water)

1/2 cup chopped onion

2 to 3 cups sliced mushrooms

1/4 cup butter

1 teaspoon salt (omit if using chicken stock)

1/2 teaspoon pepper

2 tablespoons butter (for greasing the casserole dish)

WILD RICE CASSEROLE

The unique flavor of wild rice is well-suited as an accompaniment to hearty grilled fare such as roasts and any type of game. People who know wild rice well almost always cook it in chicken stock rather than water; use whichever you prefer.

1) Preheat oven to 350 degrees F.

2) Butter the bottom and sides of a 1½-quart ovenproof casserole.

3) Melt butter in a skillet. Sauté onion and mushrooms over medium-high heat until soft. Pour sautéed mushrooms and onions into buttered casserole, and add the remaining ingredients. Cover (with a piece of aluminum foil, if necessary) and bake for 1 hour. Casserole is ready for serving when all the liquid has been absorbed and the rice is tender.

Serves 4.

RECIPE INDEX

INDEX

Note: Encyclopedia entries appear in boldface type.

A

B

C

K

L

M

N

New potatoes, grilled, 196; boiled, 320; *also see* Old Country New Potatoes, 203

Nicoise butter, 306

Non-traditional dry rub, 310-311

O

Octopus, **173-174**

Oils, 278-279

Old-style mint sauce, 302

Onion, **174**, 279

Ono, **175**; *also see* Wahoo, 253-254

Open grills, 22-24; *also see* Uncovered Grill Techniques, 40-41

Oregano, 279

Oriental sweet and hot marinade, 293

Outdoor Cooks as Characters, 254-255

Oysters, **175-176**; *also see* Oyster Lore, 175

P

Pacific snapper, **220**; *also see* Rockfish, 207-208

Paillards; *see* Chicken, breast (boneless and skinless), 102-104 and Pounding Paillards, 103

"Pandora's Turkey", **242-245**

Paprika, *see* Chili peppers, 271-272; *also see* Paprika and Fish, 163

Parsley, 280

Parsnips, **177**

Partridge, **178**

Pasta, 328-330

Pastrami, **179**

Peas, *see recipes for* Black-eyed peas, 318; black-eyed peas for a crowd, 319; Cold rice and pea salad, 320 and Sautéed peas with lettuce, 336

Peppers, **179**; *also see* Bell peppers, 91-92; Rating Hot Peppers, 178-179 and Chili peppers, 271-272

Peppers, bell, **91-92**

Pesto marinade, 293

Petrale, **179**; *also see* Sole, 221-222

Pheasant, *see* Wild pheasant, **256**; *also see* Spit Cooking, 46-55

Pig, whole roast, **180**; *also see* Spit Cooking, 46-55

Pigeon, **180-181**

Pike, **181-182**

Pineapple, **182-183**

Plantains, **183**

Plum marinade, *see* Hot fresh plum marinade, 291

Polenta, **183-184**

Polenta with Parmesan, 330-331

Polish sausage, 212-213

Pollock, **184-185**

Pommes frites, 331

Pompano, Florida, **185-186**; *also see* The Ten Best Grilling Fish, 133

Porgy, **186-187**

Pork, 187-196; *also see* Spit Cooking, 46-55; The "T" Word, 187; Brine for Pork Loin, 191; Pig Facts, 193; Jamaican Jerk, 195 and Dry rub for lamb or pork, 310-311

Pork, chops, **187-188**

Pork, fresh ham, **188-190**

Pork, ground, **190**

Pork, leg roast, **190**; *also see* Pork, fresh ham, 188-190

Pork, leg steak, **191**; *also see* Pork, chops, 187-188

Pork, loin roast, (bone-in), **191-192**; *also see* Spit Cooking, 46-55

Pork, loin roast (boneless), **192**

Pork, ribs, **192-195**; *also see* Spit Cooking, 46-55

Pork, ribs, country-style, **120**; *also see* Pork, ribs, 192-195

Pork, tenderloin, **195-196**

Pork, trichinosis, *see* The "T" Word, 187

Potatoes, **197**; *also see recipes for* Grilled New Potatoes, 196; Grilled Potato Wedges, 196; Grilled Potato Skins, 197; Grilled & Filled Potato Skins, 197; Old Country New Potatoes, 203; Baked potatoes, 317; Boiled new potatoes, 320; Galette of potatoes, 323; Garlic mashed potatoes, 324;

Q

R

S

T

U

V

W

Y

Z